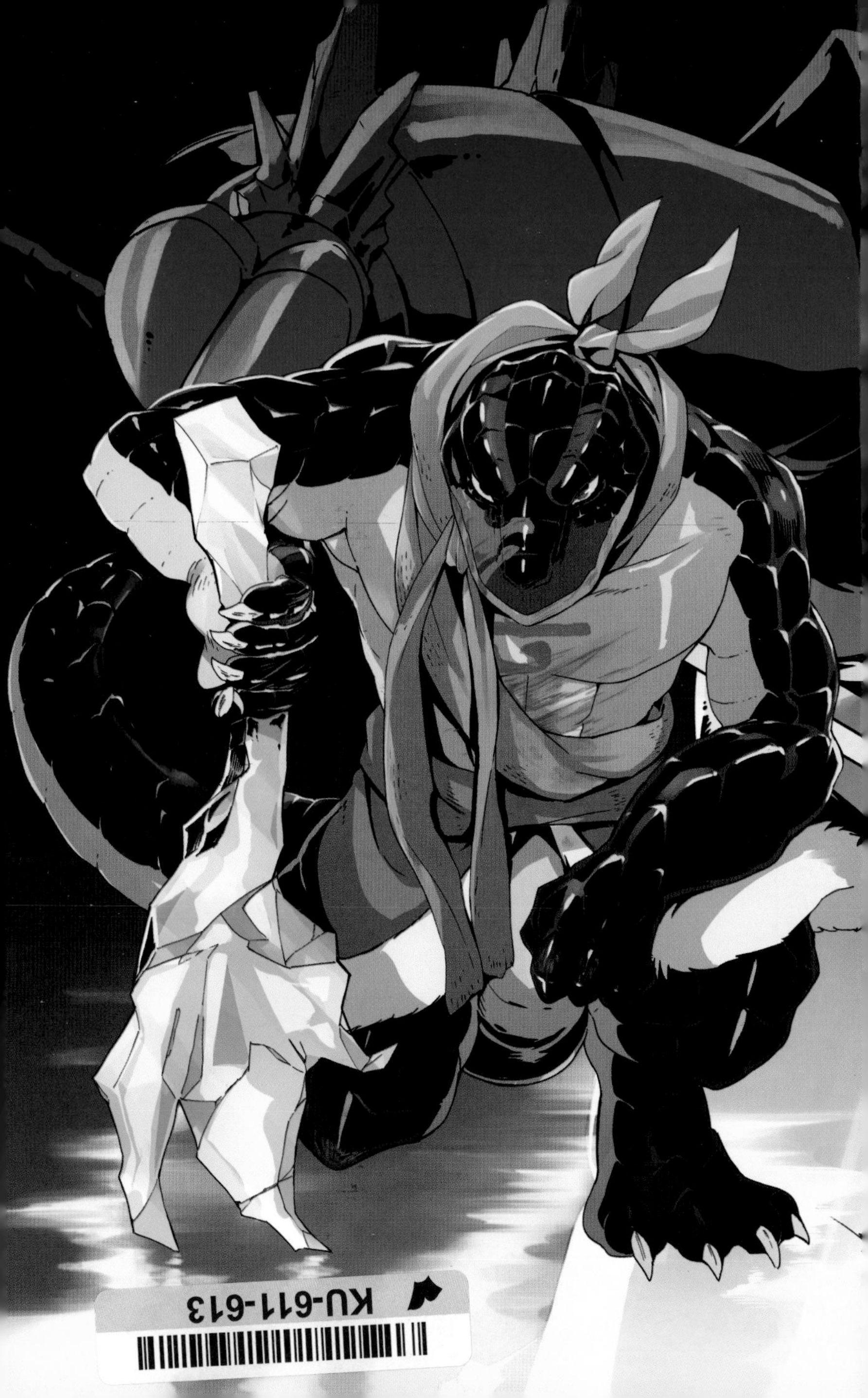

OVERLORD

Original Story:
Kugane Maruyama

7

Art:
Hugin Miyama

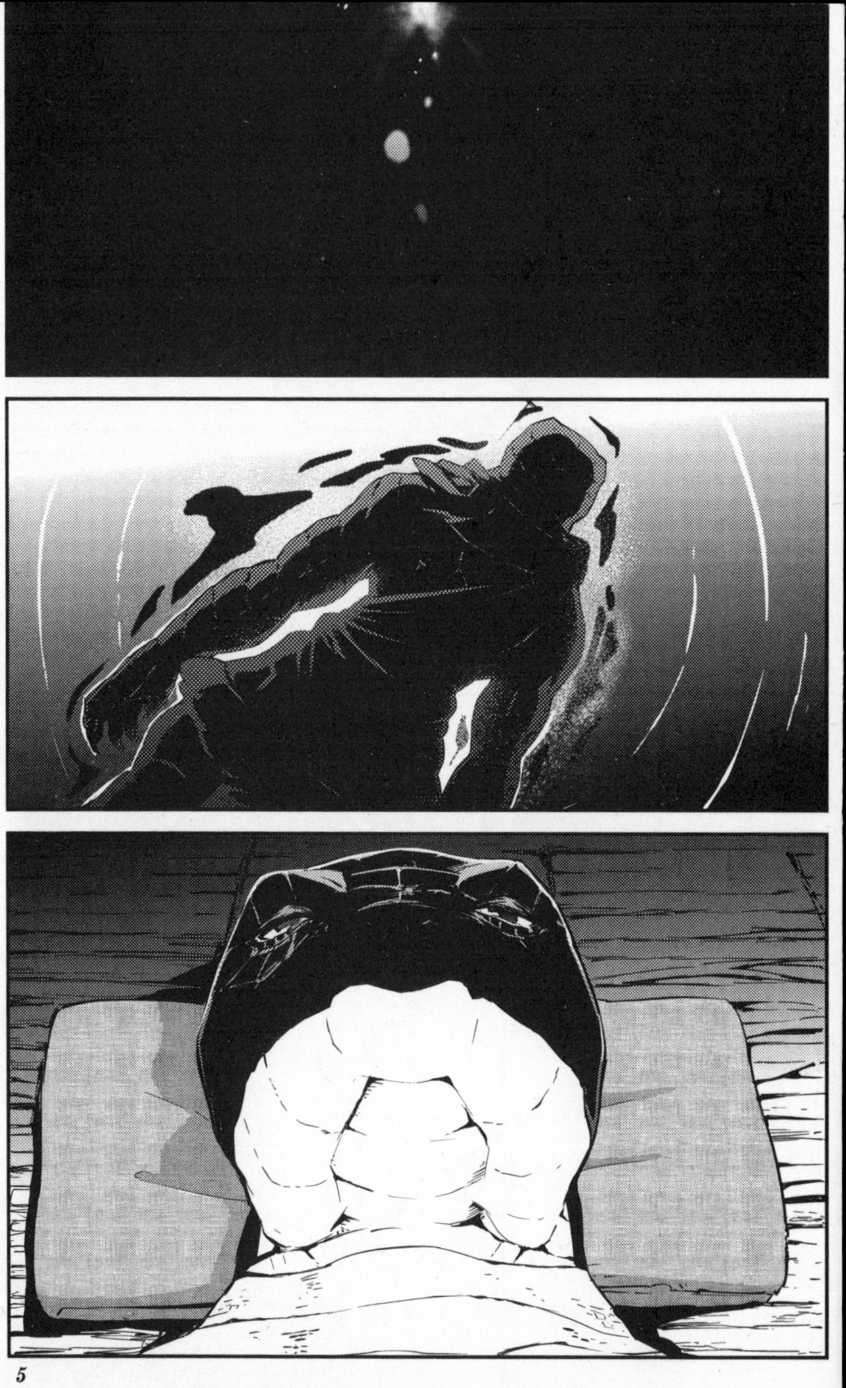

I'M ALIVE...

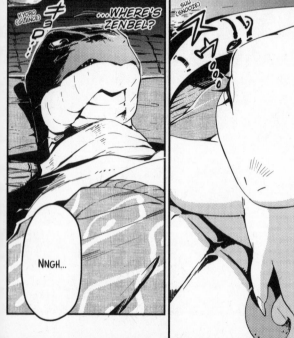

KYORO
(GLANCE)

...WHERE'S ZENBEL?

NNGH...

SUU
(SNOOZE)

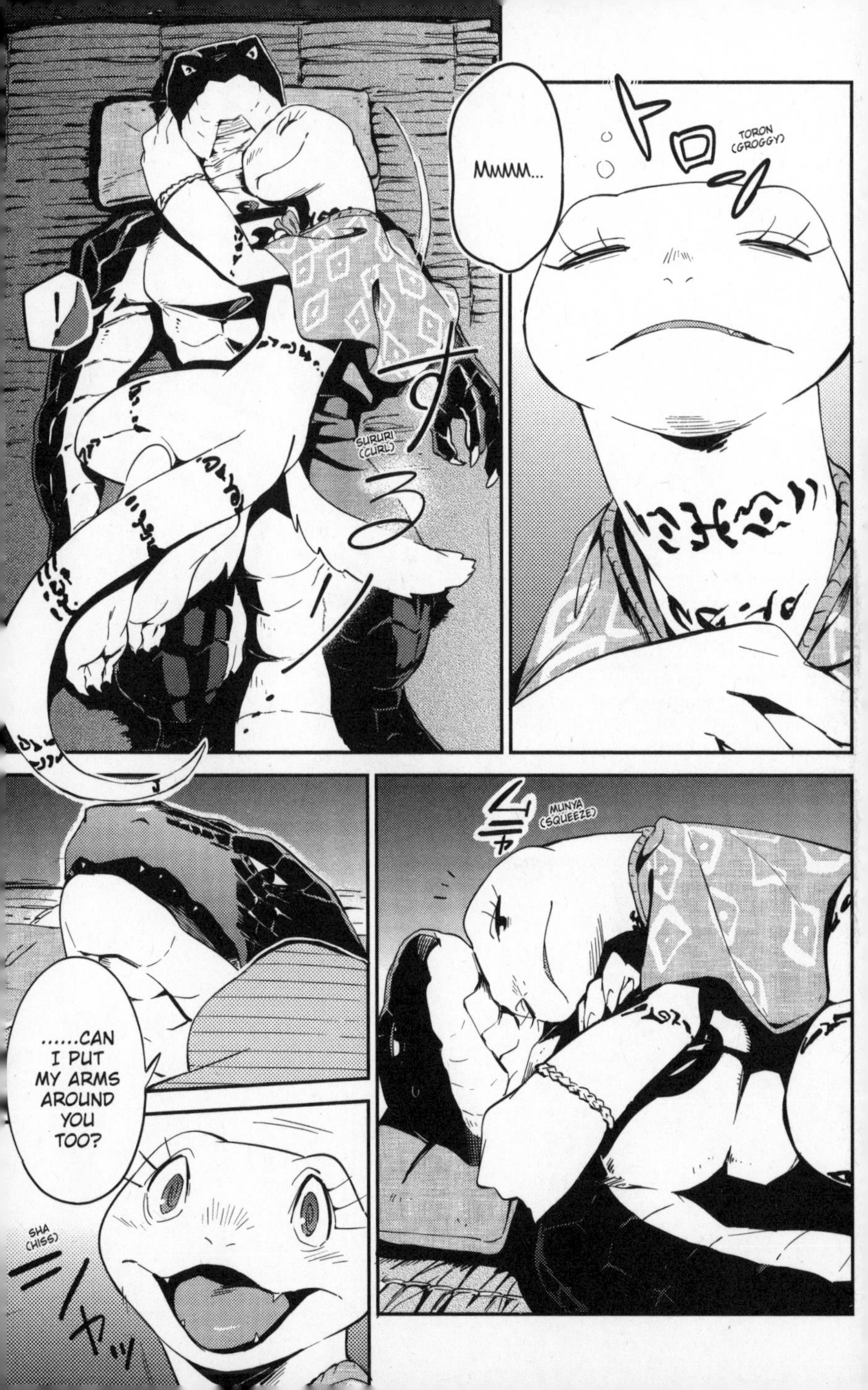
TORON (GROGGY)
MMMM...
SURURI (CURL)
MUNYA (SQUEEZE)
......CAN I PUT MY ARMS AROUND YOU TOO?
SHA (HISS)

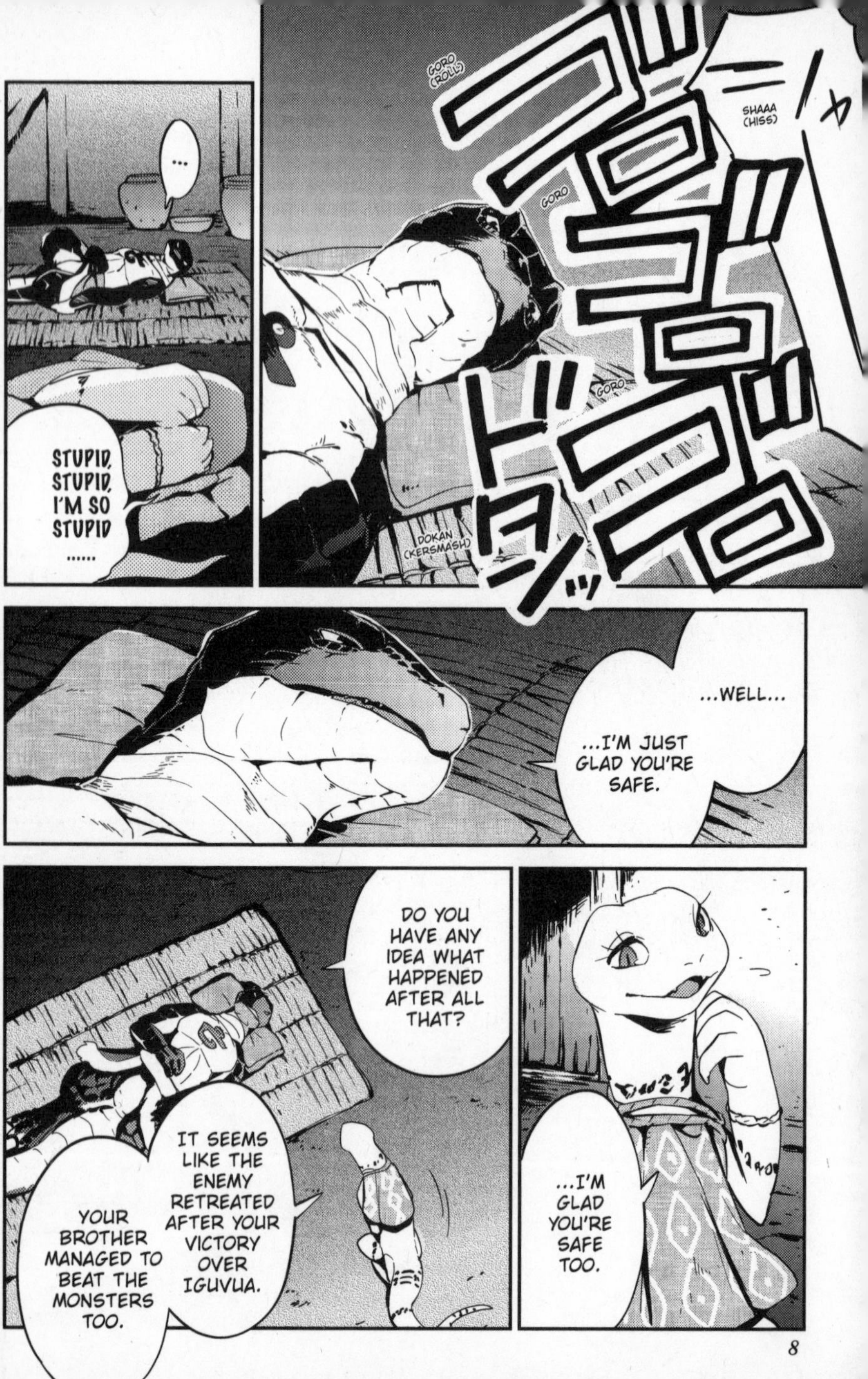
SHAAA (HISS)
GORO (ROLL)
GORO
GORO
DOKAN (KERSMASH)
...
STUPID, STUPID, I'M SO STUPID ......
...WELL...
...I'M JUST GLAD YOU'RE SAFE.
...I'M GLAD YOU'RE SAFE TOO.
DO YOU HAVE ANY IDEA WHAT HAPPENED AFTER ALL THAT?
IT SEEMS LIKE THE ENEMY RETREATED AFTER YOUR VICTORY OVER IGUVUA.
YOUR BROTHER MANAGED TO BEAT THE MONSTERS TOO.

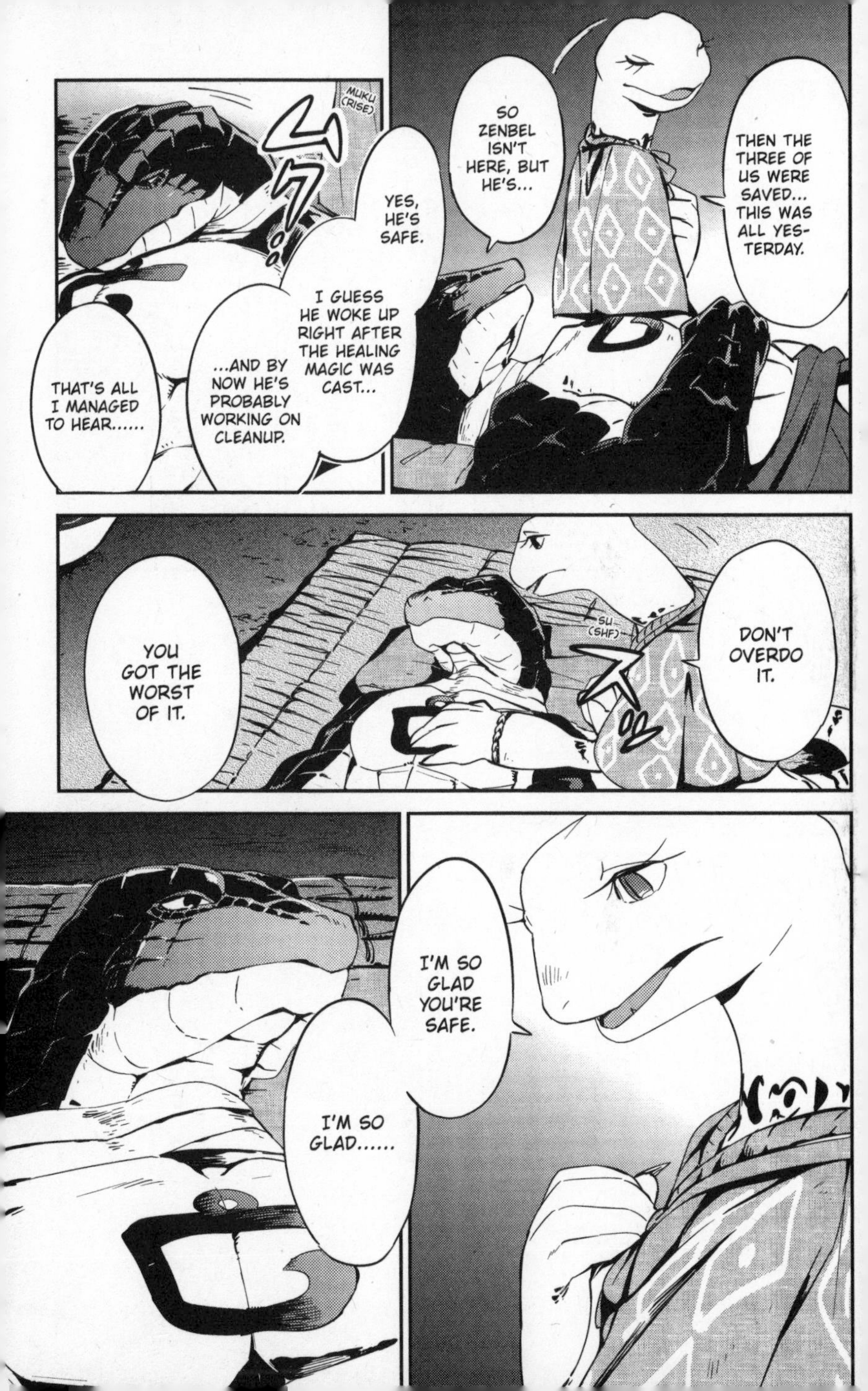
THEN THE THREE OF US WERE SAVED... THIS WAS ALL YESTERDAY.
SO ZENBEL ISN'T HERE, BUT HE'S...
MUKU (RISE)
YES, HE'S SAFE.
I GUESS HE WOKE UP RIGHT AFTER THE HEALING MAGIC WAS CAST...
...AND BY NOW HE'S PROBABLY WORKING ON CLEANUP.
THAT'S ALL I MANAGED TO HEAR......
DON'T OVERDO IT.
SU (SHF)
YOU GOT THE WORST OF IT.
I'M SO GLAD YOU'RE SAFE.
I'M SO GLAD......

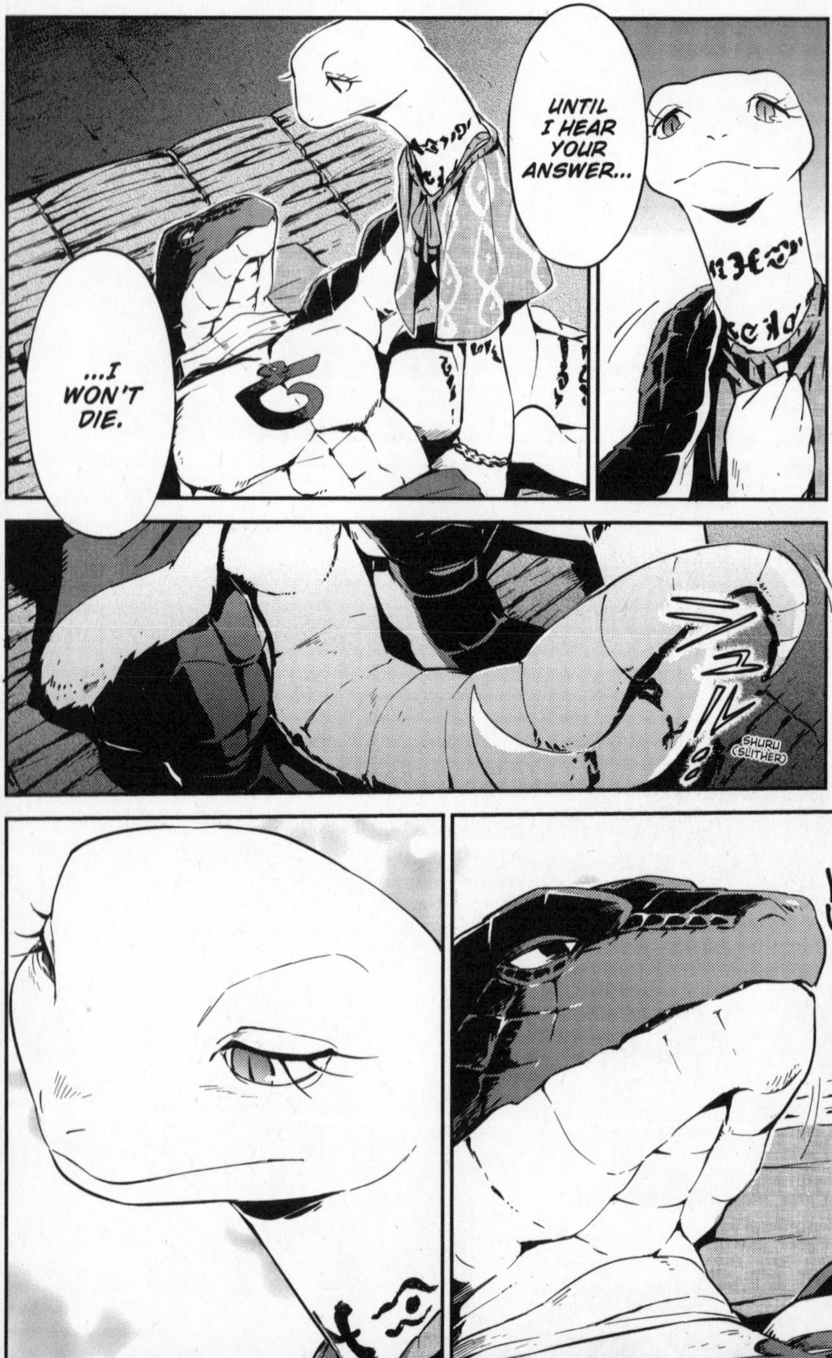
UNTIL I HEAR YOUR ANSWER...
...I WON'T DIE.
SHURU (SLITHER)
KURURU...

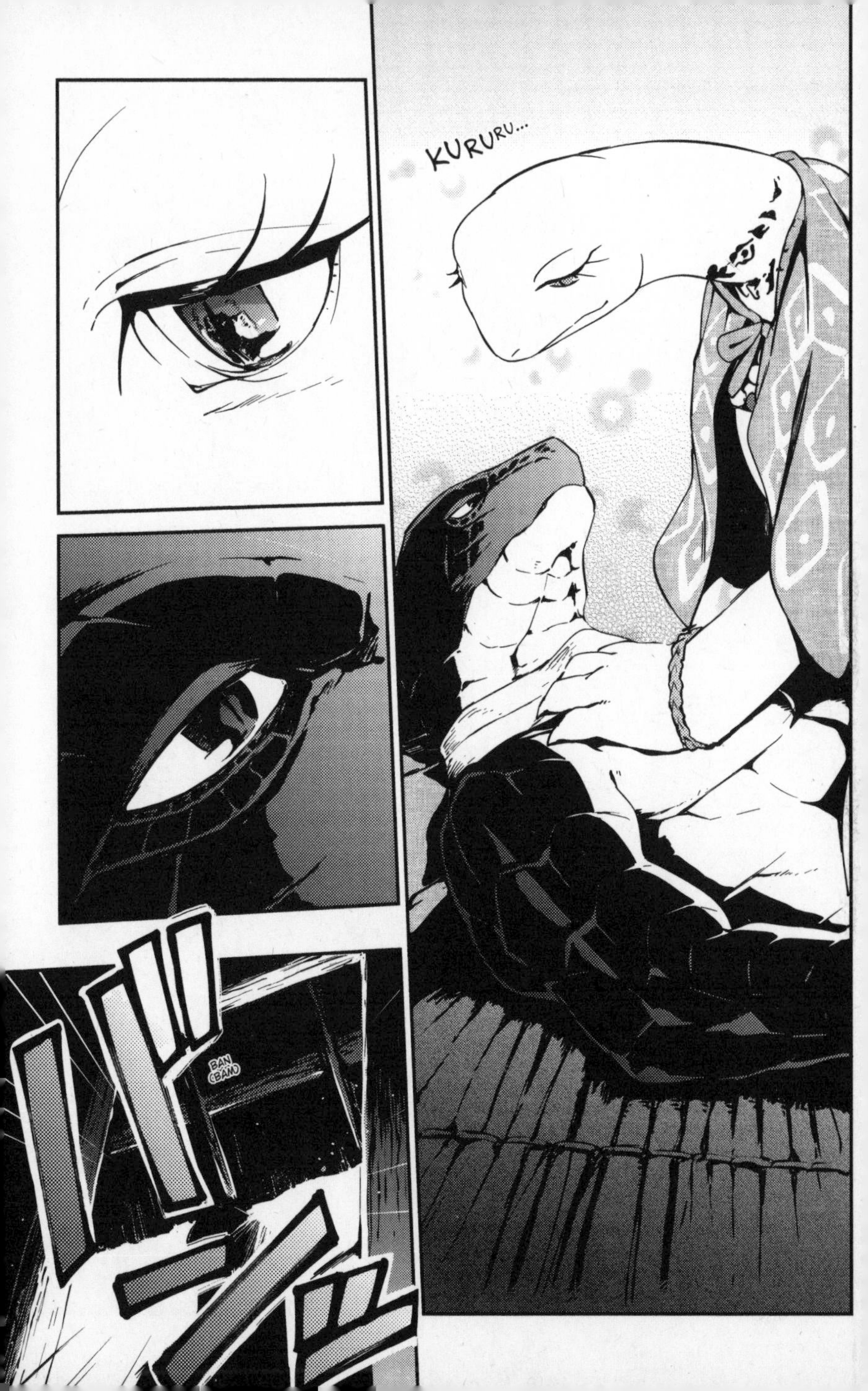
KURURU...
BAN BAN

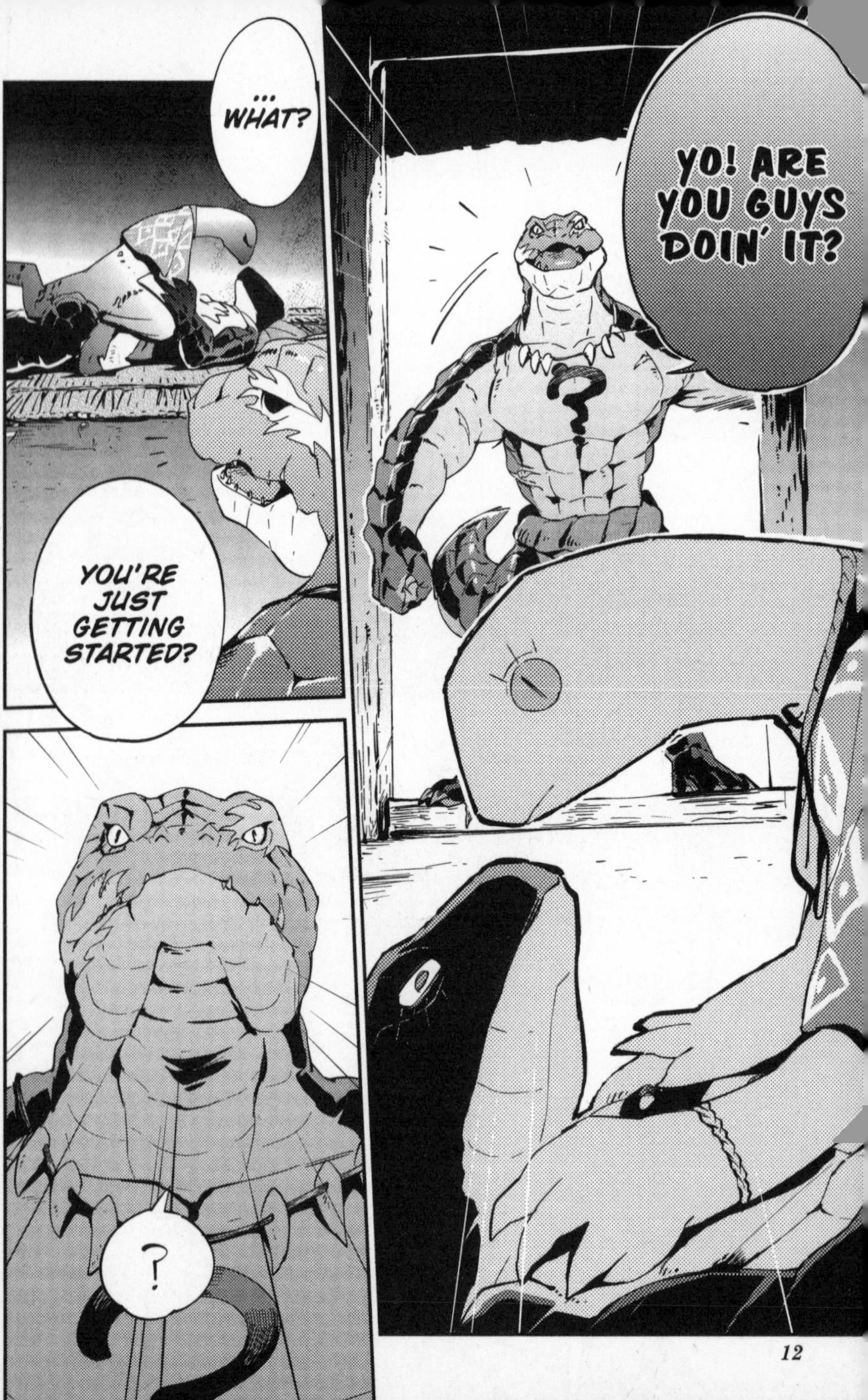
YO! ARE YOU GUYS DOIN' IT?
...WHAT?
YOU'RE JUST GETTING STARTED?
?

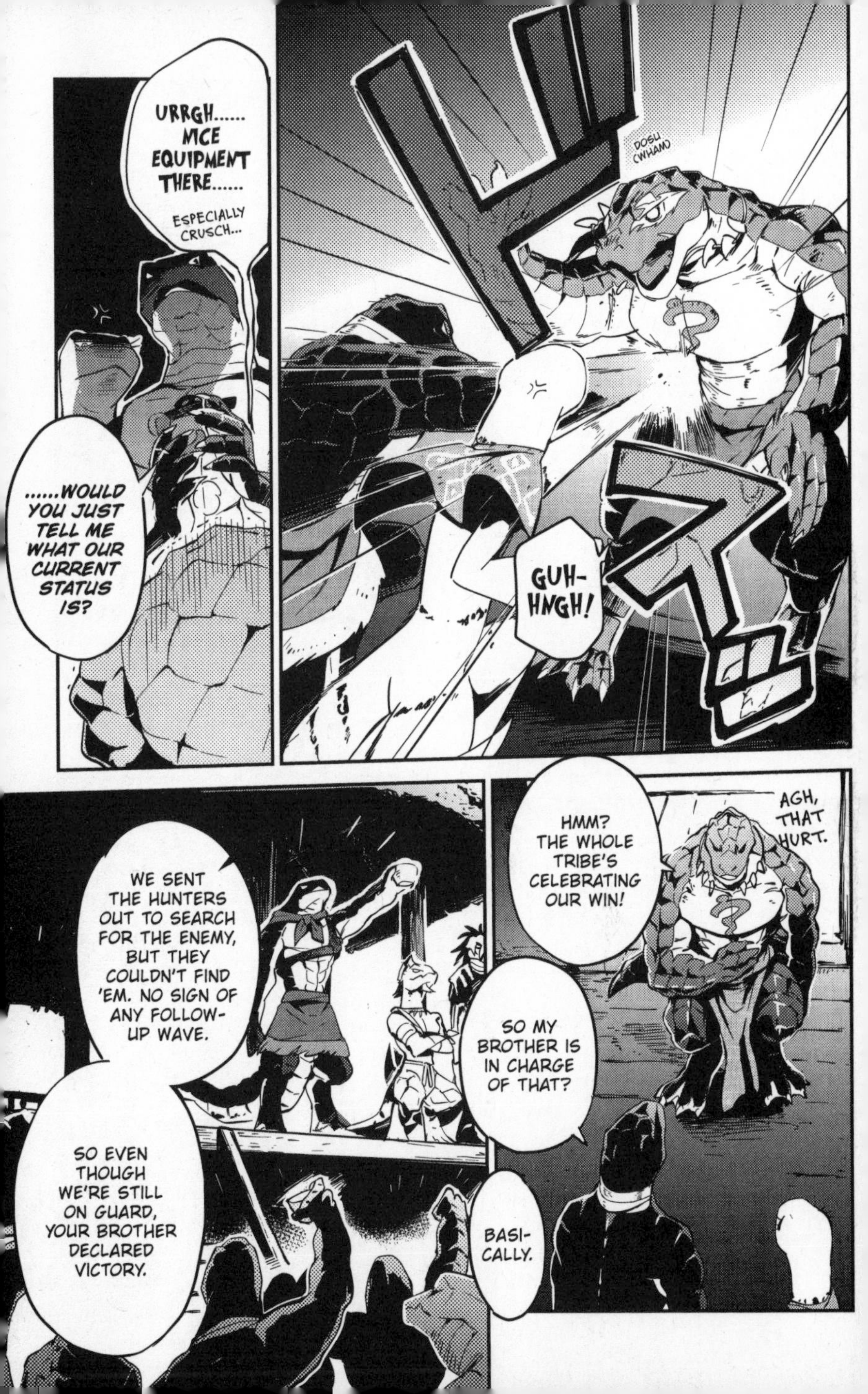
DOSU (WHAM)
GUH-HNGH!
URRGH...... NICE EQUIPMENT THERE......
ESPECIALLY CRUSCH...
......WOULD YOU JUST TELL ME WHAT OUR CURRENT STATUS IS?
AGH, THAT HURT.
HMM? THE WHOLE TRIBE'S CELEBRATING OUR WIN!
WE SENT THE HUNTERS OUT TO SEARCH FOR THE ENEMY, BUT THEY COULDN'T FIND 'EM. NO SIGN OF ANY FOLLOW-UP WAVE.
SO EVEN THOUGH WE'RE STILL ON GUARD, YOUR BROTHER DECLARED VICTORY.
SO MY BROTHER IS IN CHARGE OF THAT?
BASI-CALLY.

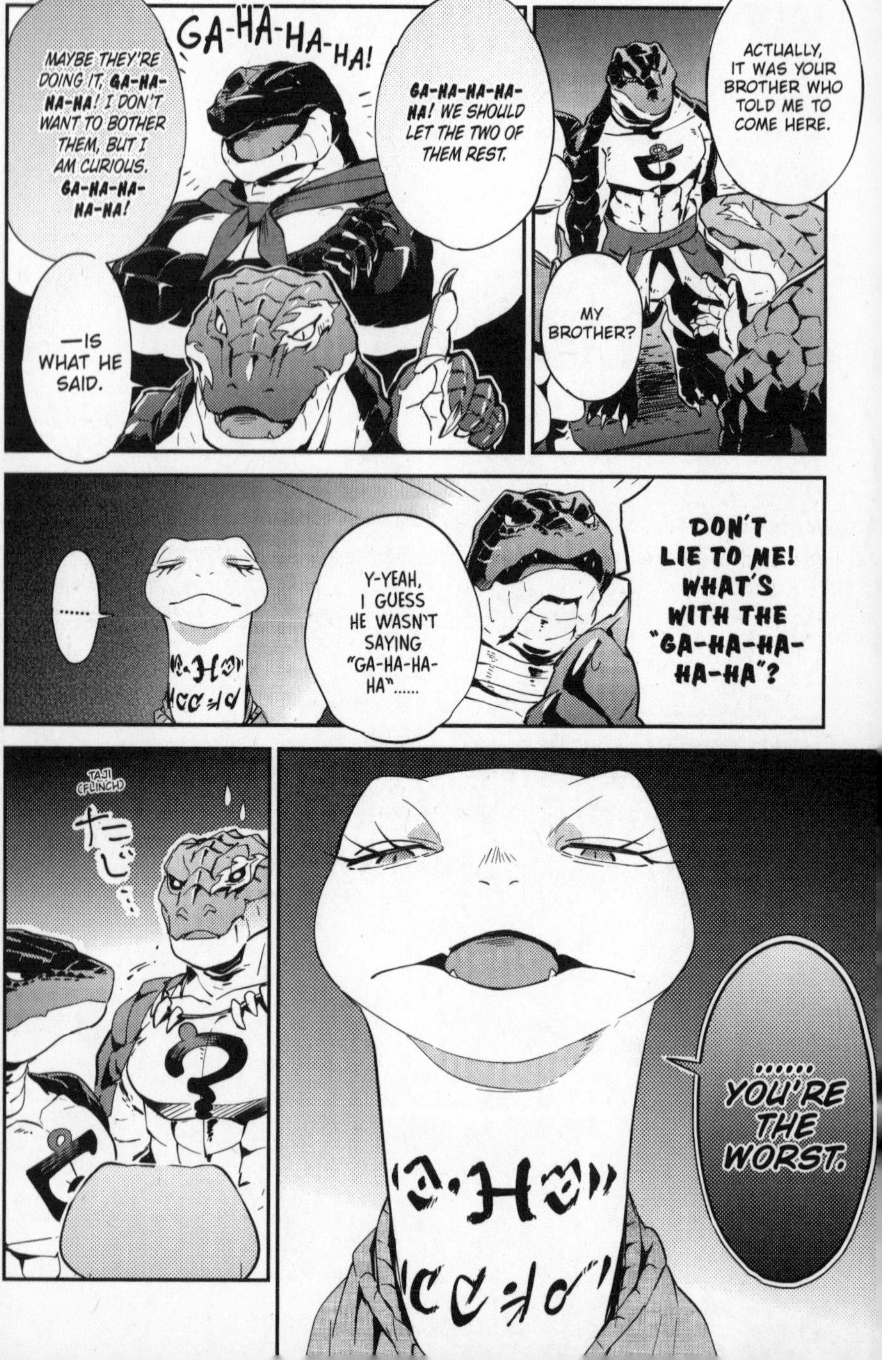
ACTUALLY, IT WAS YOUR BROTHER WHO TOLD ME TO COME HERE.
MY BROTHER?
GA-HA-HA-HA!
GA-HA-HA-HA-HA! WE SHOULD LET THE TWO OF THEM REST.
MAYBE THEY'RE DOING IT, GA-HA-HA-HA! I DON'T WANT TO BOTHER THEM, BUT I AM CURIOUS. GA-HA-HA-HA-HA!
—IS WHAT HE SAID.
DON'T LIE TO ME! WHAT'S WITH THE "GA-HA-HA-HA-HA"?
Y-YEAH, I GUESS HE WASN'T SAYING "GA-HA-HA-HA"......
......
......YOU'RE THE WORST.
TAJI (FLINCH)

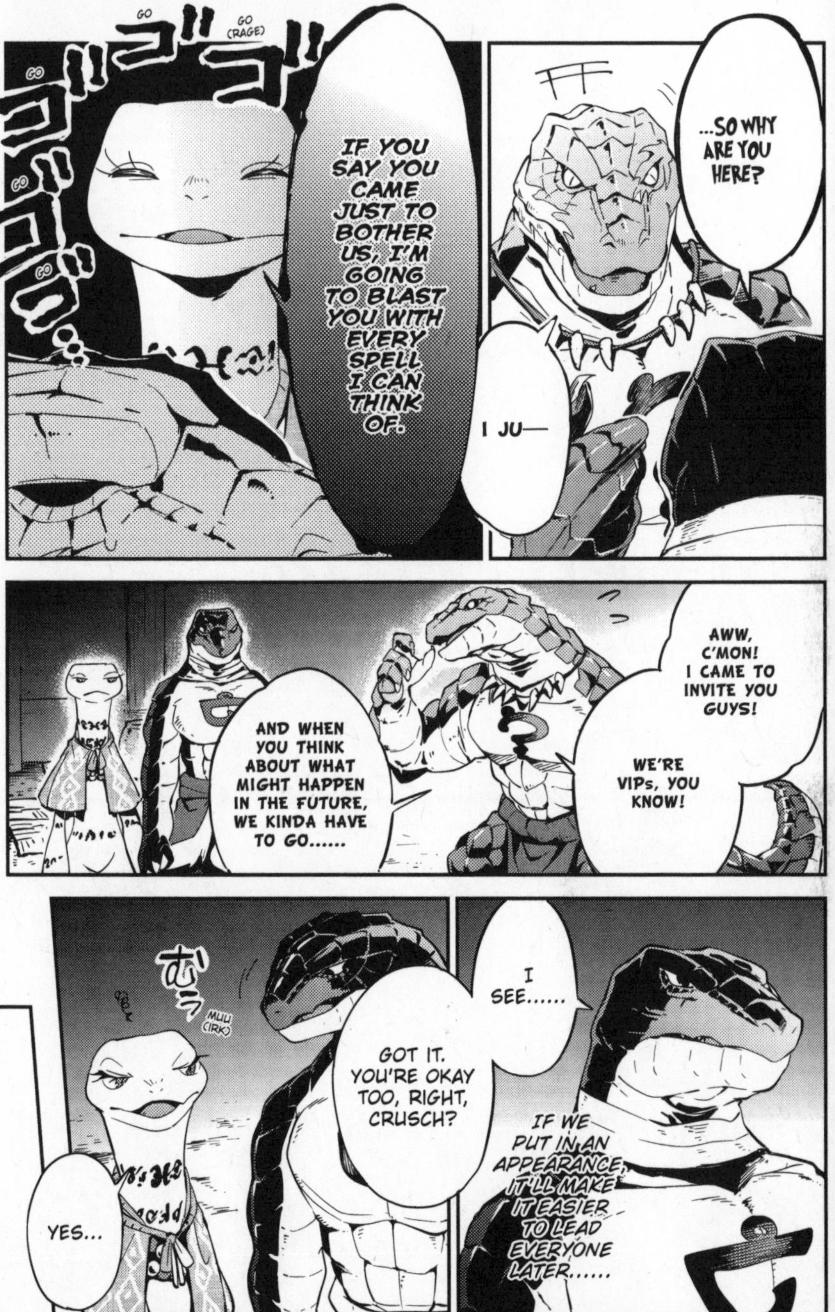
...SO WHY ARE YOU HERE?
I JU—
GO
GO (RAGE)
GO
GO
GO
IF YOU SAY YOU CAME JUST TO BOTHER US, I'M GOING TO BLAST YOU WITH EVERY SPELL I CAN THINK OF.
AWW, C'MON! I CAME TO INVITE YOU GUYS!
WE'RE VIPs, YOU KNOW!
AND WHEN YOU THINK ABOUT WHAT MIGHT HAPPEN IN THE FUTURE, WE KINDA HAVE TO GO......
I SEE......
IF WE PUT IN AN APPEARANCE, IT'LL MAKE IT EASIER TO LEAD EVERYONE LATER......
GOT IT. YOU'RE OKAY TOO, RIGHT, CRUSCH?
MUU (IRK)
YES...

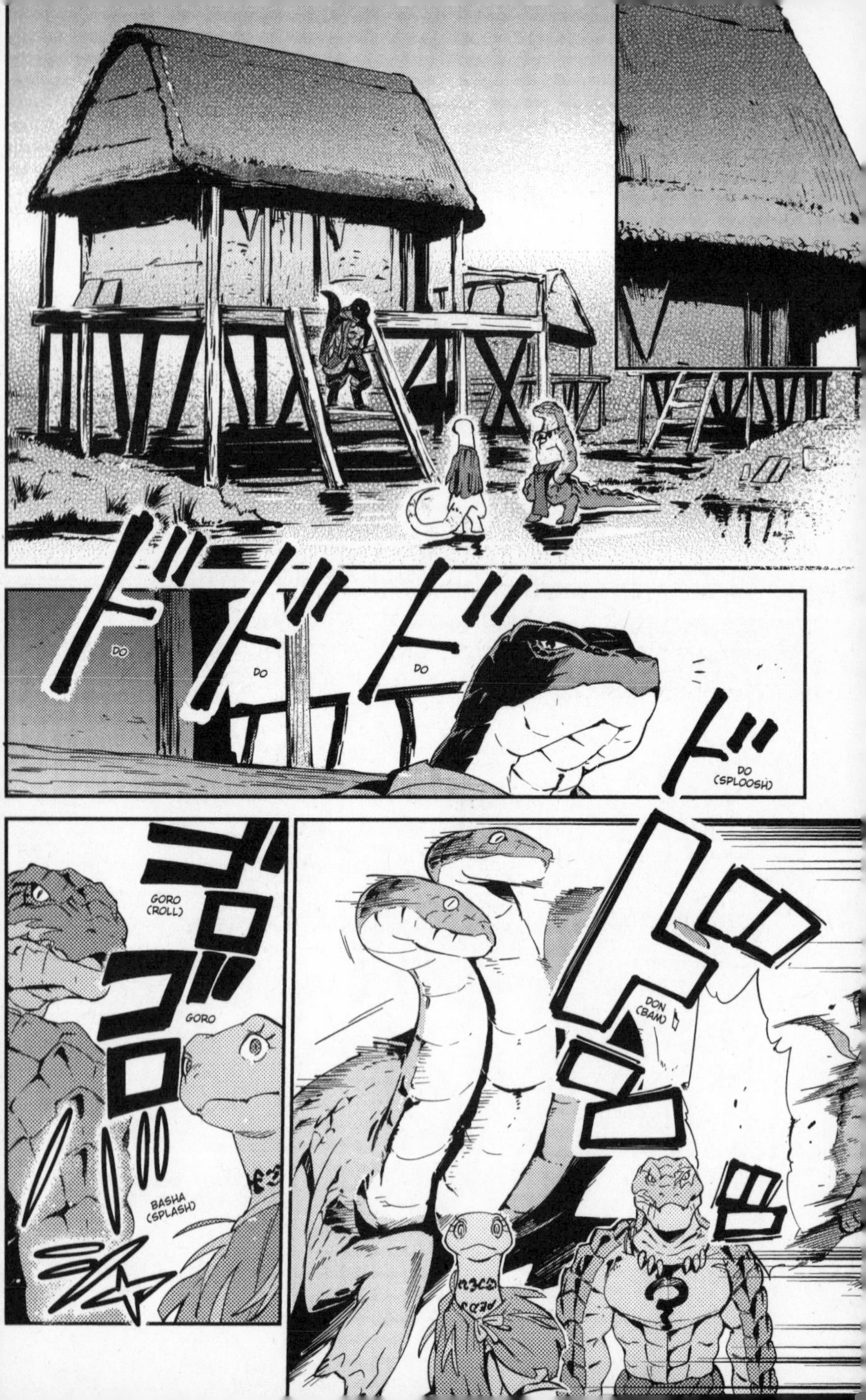
DO
DO
DO
DO
(SPLOOSH)
DON
(BAM)
GORO
(ROLL)
GORO
BASHA
(SPLASH)

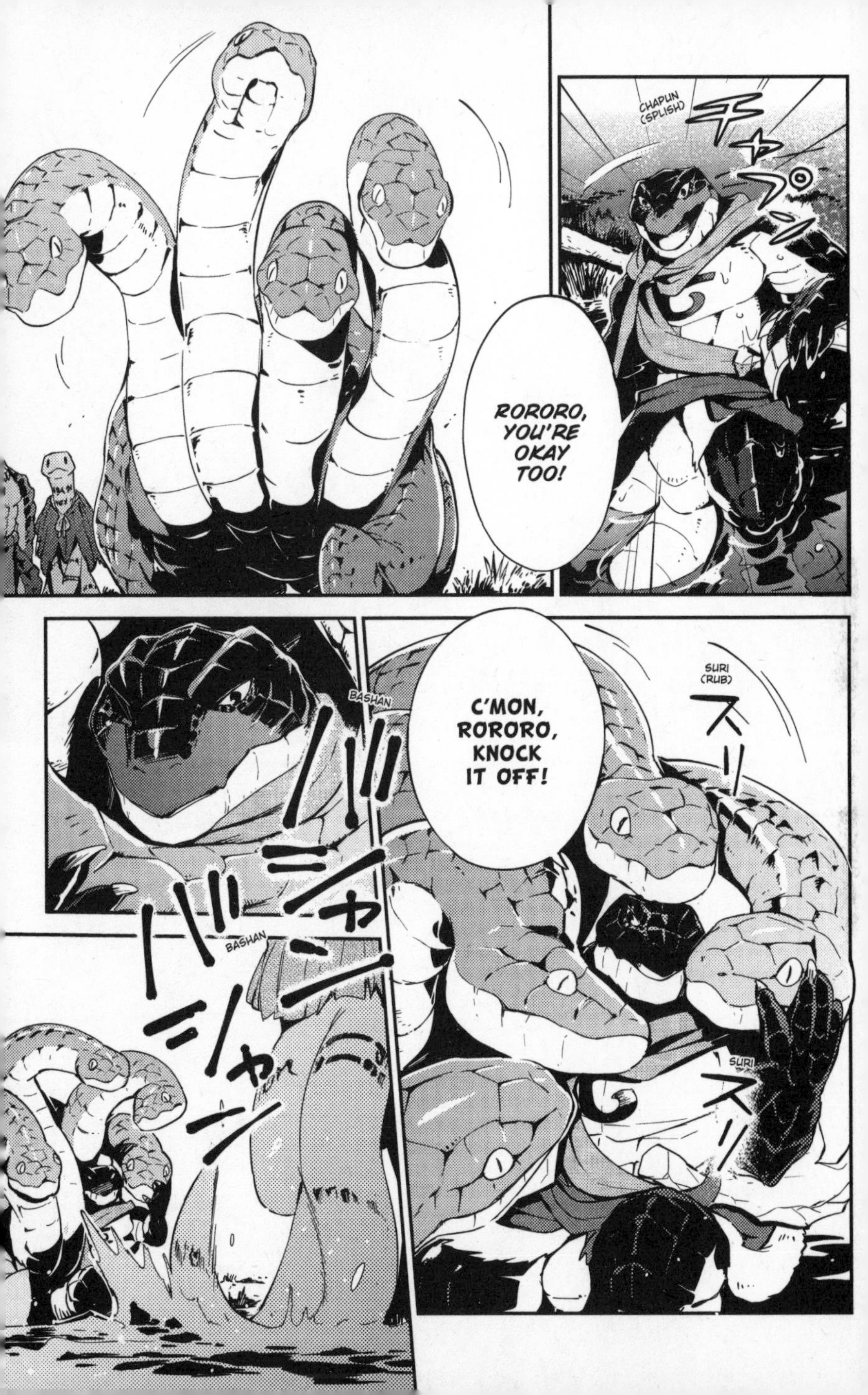
CHAPUN (SPLISH)
RORORO, YOU'RE OKAY TOO!
C'MON, RORORO, KNOCK IT OFF!
SURI (RUB)
SURI
BASHAN
BASHAN

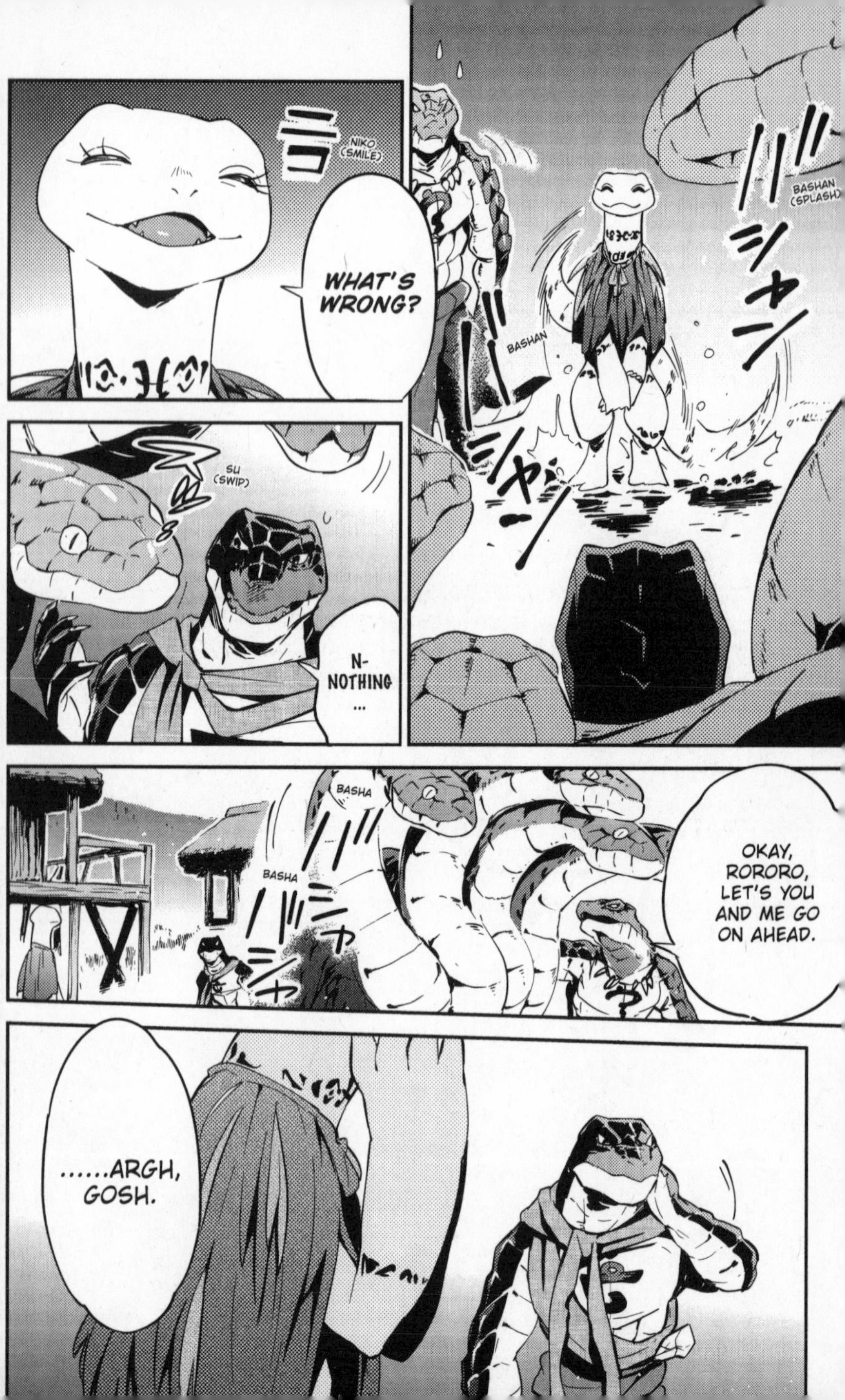
BASHAN (SPLASH)
BASHAN
NIKO (SMILE)
WHAT'S WRONG?
SU (SWIP)
N-NOTHING...
OKAY, RORORO, LET'S YOU AND ME GO ON AHEAD.
BASHA
BASHA
......ARGH, GOSH.

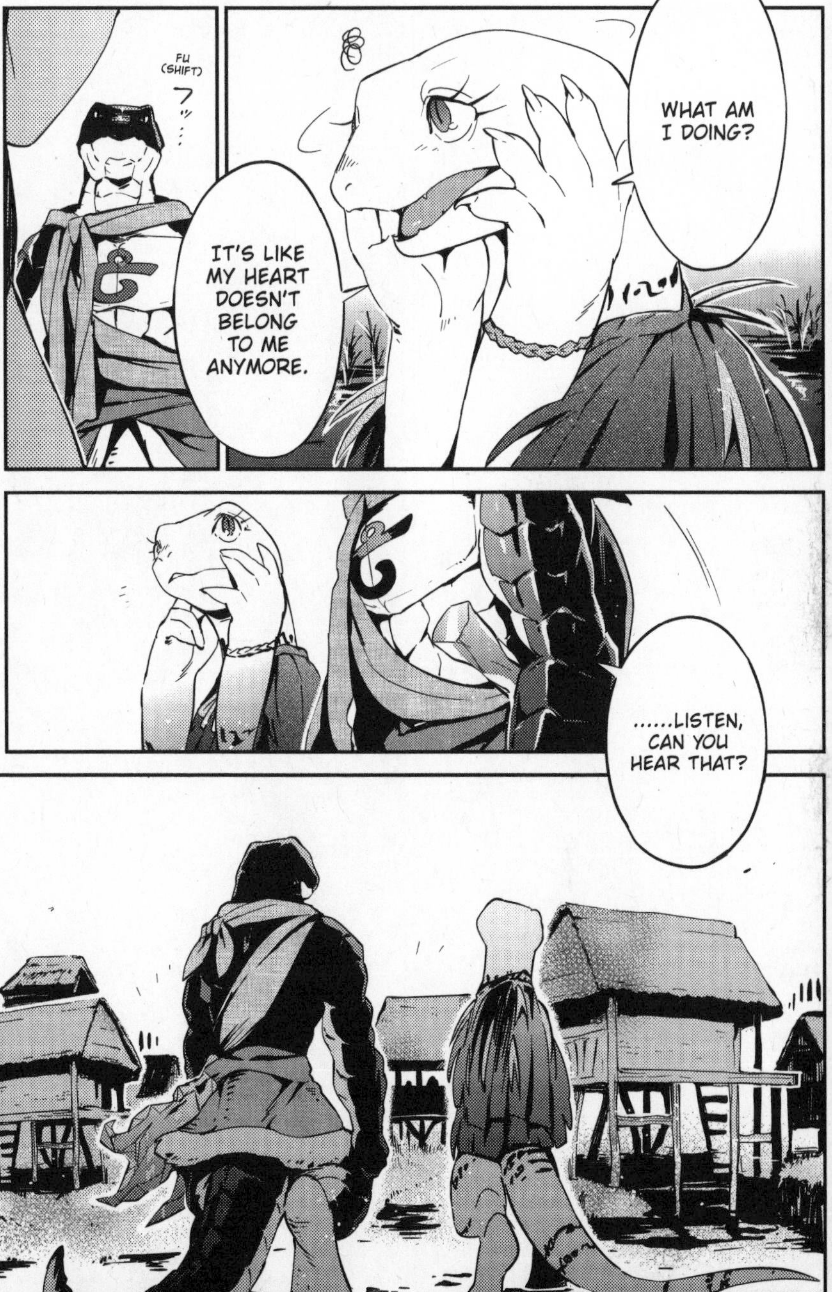
WHAT AM I DOING?
IT'S LIKE MY HEART DOESN'T BELONG TO ME ANYMORE.
FU (SHIFT)
......LISTEN, CAN YOU HEAR THAT?

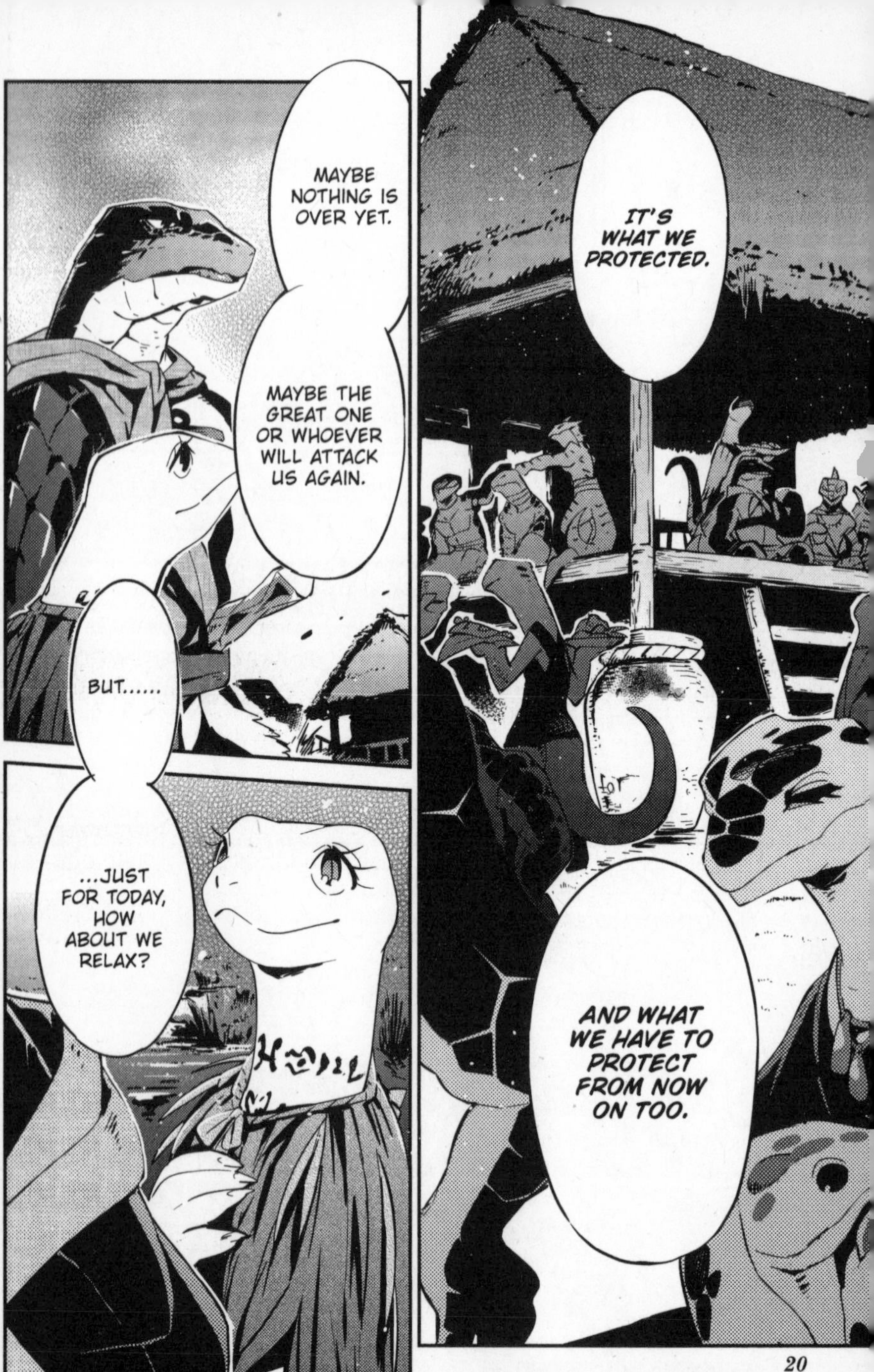
IT'S WHAT WE PROTECTED.
AND WHAT WE HAVE TO PROTECT FROM NOW ON TOO.
MAYBE NOTHING IS OVER YET.
MAYBE THE GREAT ONE OR WHOEVER WILL ATTACK US AGAIN.
BUT......
...JUST FOR TODAY, HOW ABOUT WE RELAX?

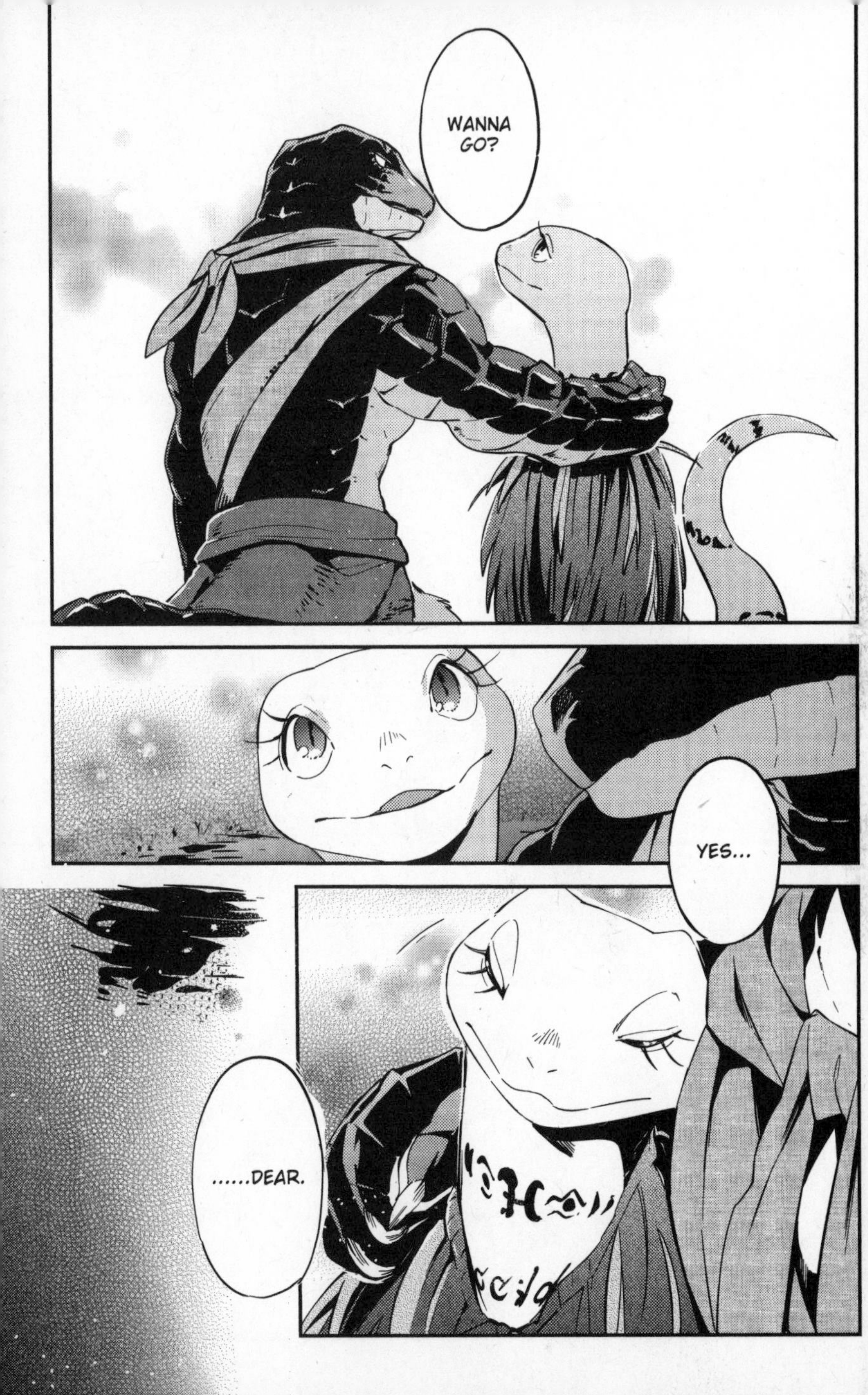
WANNA GO?
YES...
......DEAR.

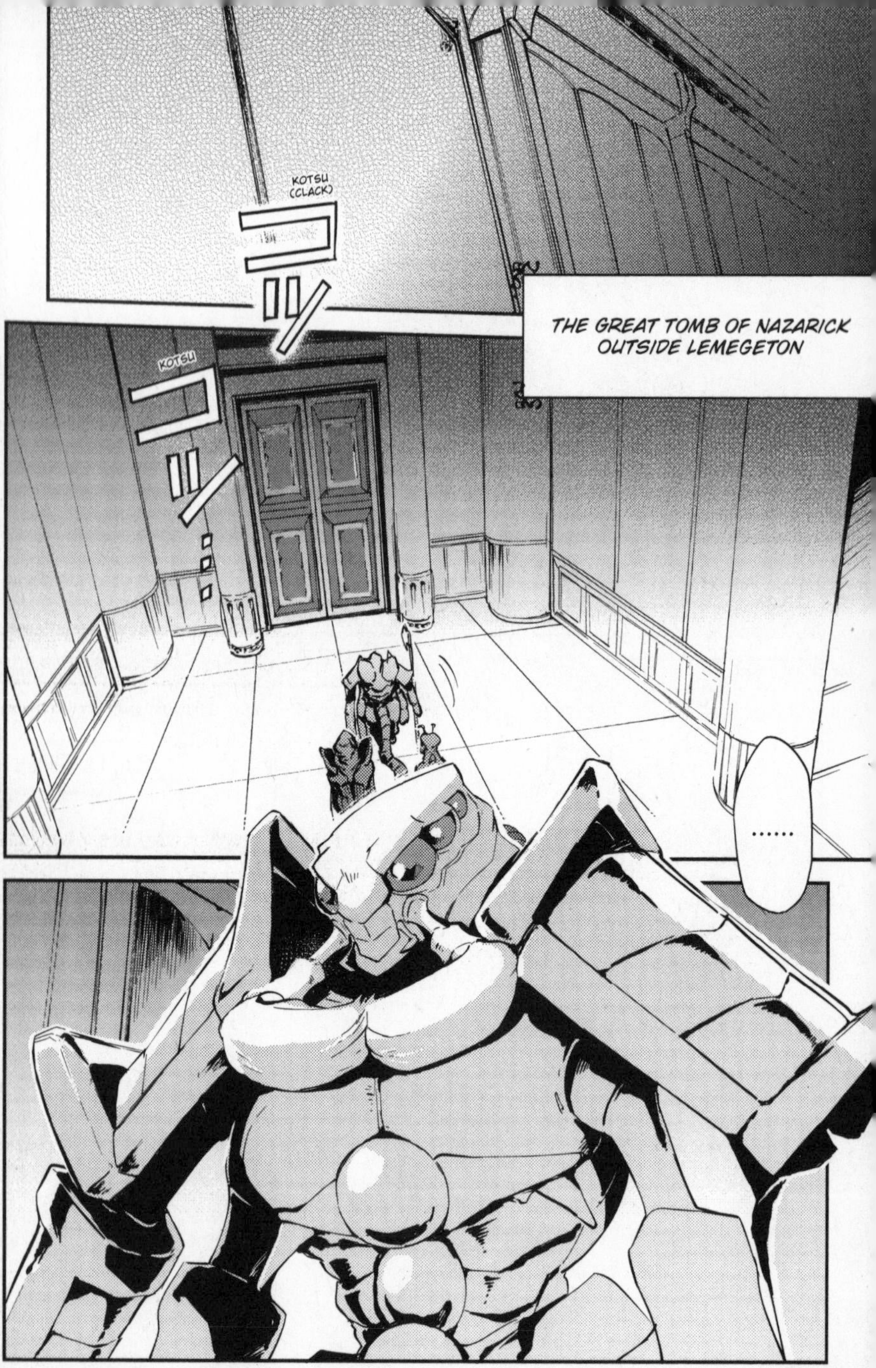
KOTSU (CLACK)
THE GREAT TOMB OF NAZARICK
OUTSIDE LEMEGETON
KOTSU
......

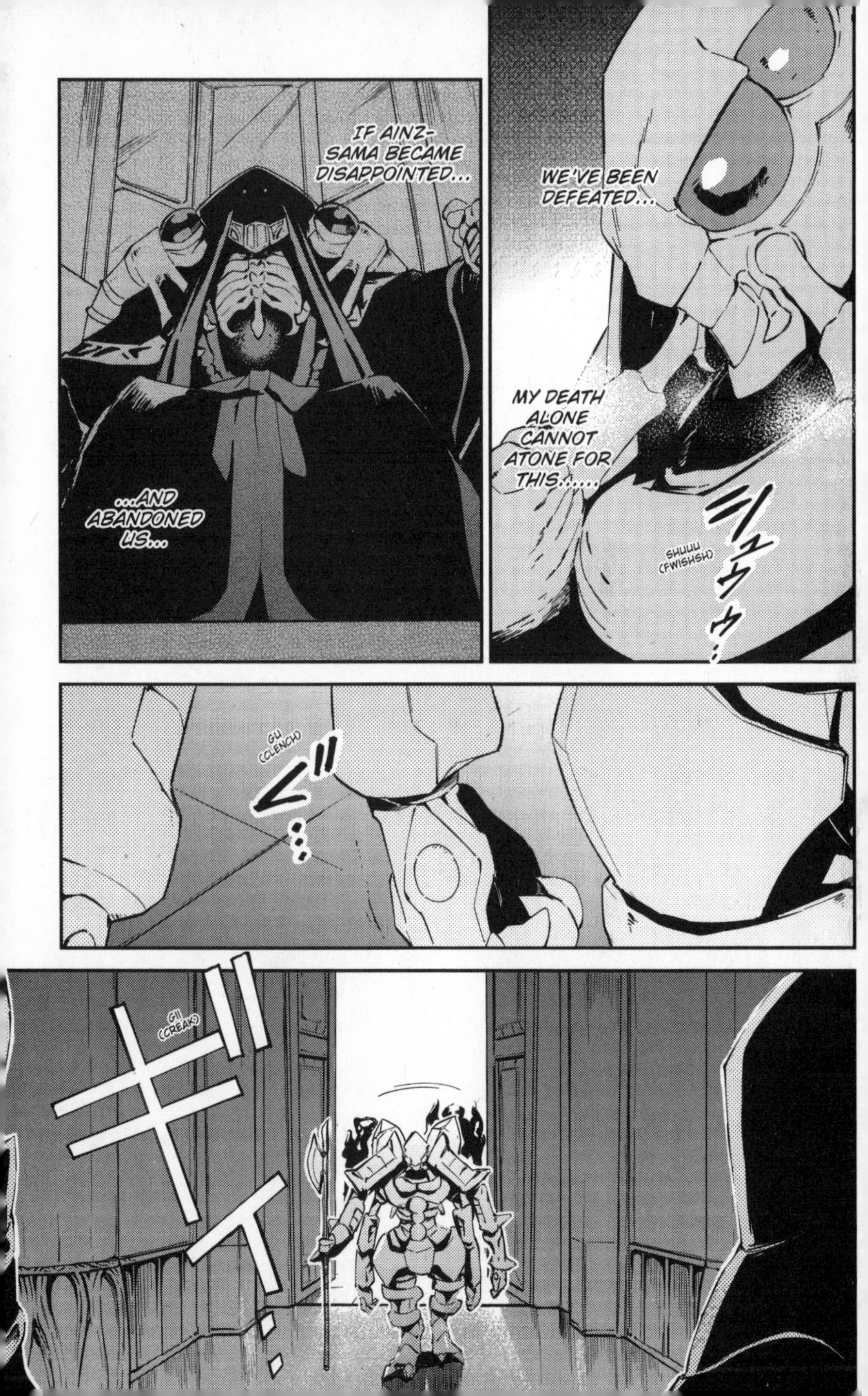
WE'VE BEEN DEFEATED...
MY DEATH ALONE CANNOT ATONE FOR THIS......
SHUUU (FWISHSH)
IF AINZ-SAMA BECAME DISAPPOINTED...
...AND ABANDONED US...
GU (CLENCH)
GII (CREAK)

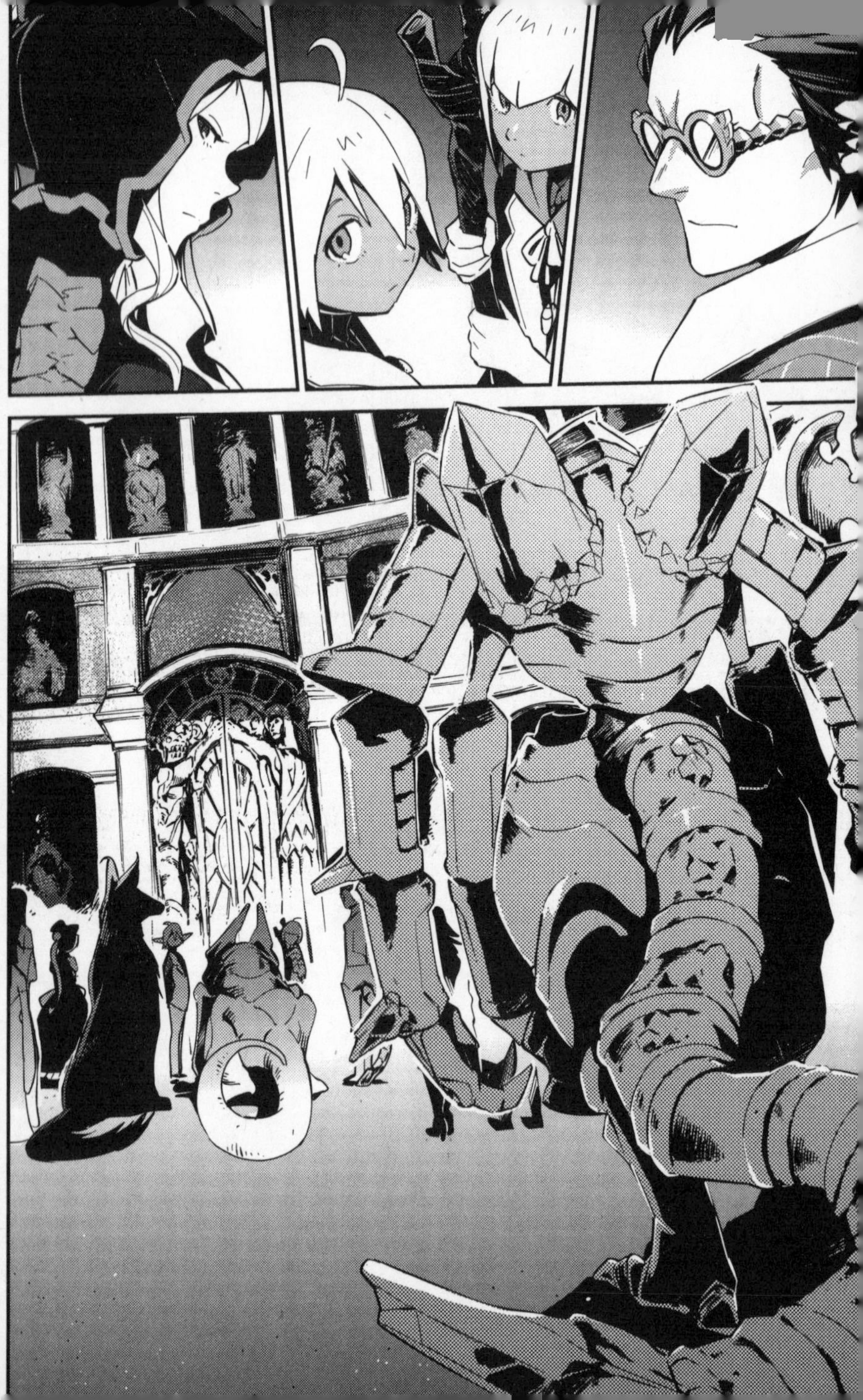

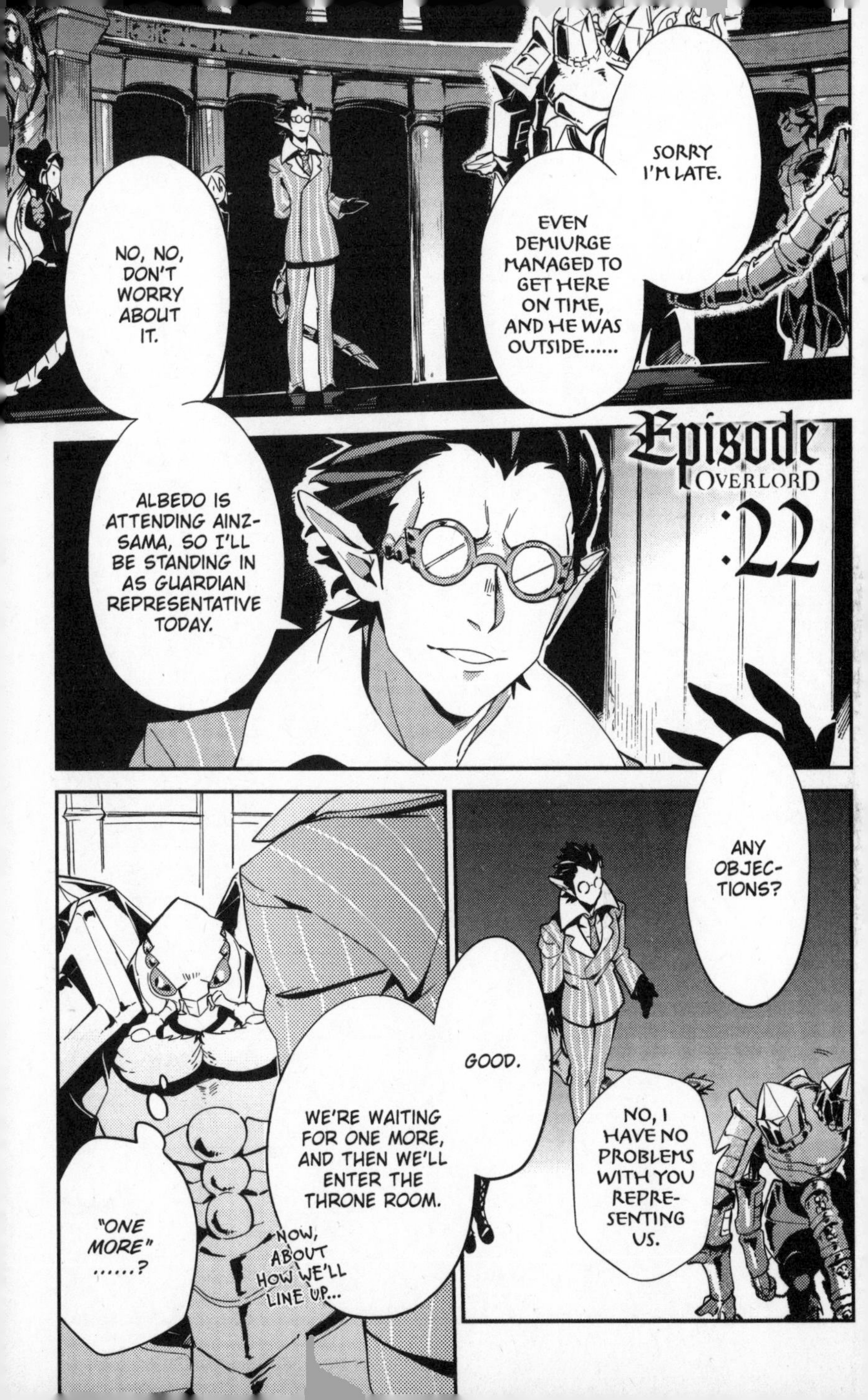
SORRY I'M LATE.
EVEN DEMIURGE MANAGED TO GET HERE ON TIME, AND HE WAS OUTSIDE......
NO, NO, DON'T WORRY ABOUT IT.
Episode OVERLORD :22
ALBEDO IS ATTENDING AINZ-SAMA, SO I'LL BE STANDING IN AS GUARDIAN REPRESENTATIVE TODAY.
ANY OBJECTIONS?
NO, I HAVE NO PROBLEMS WITH YOU REPRESENTING US.
GOOD.
WE'RE WAITING FOR ONE MORE, AND THEN WE'LL ENTER THE THRONE ROOM.
NOW, ABOUT HOW WE'LL LINE UP...
"ONE MORE" ......?

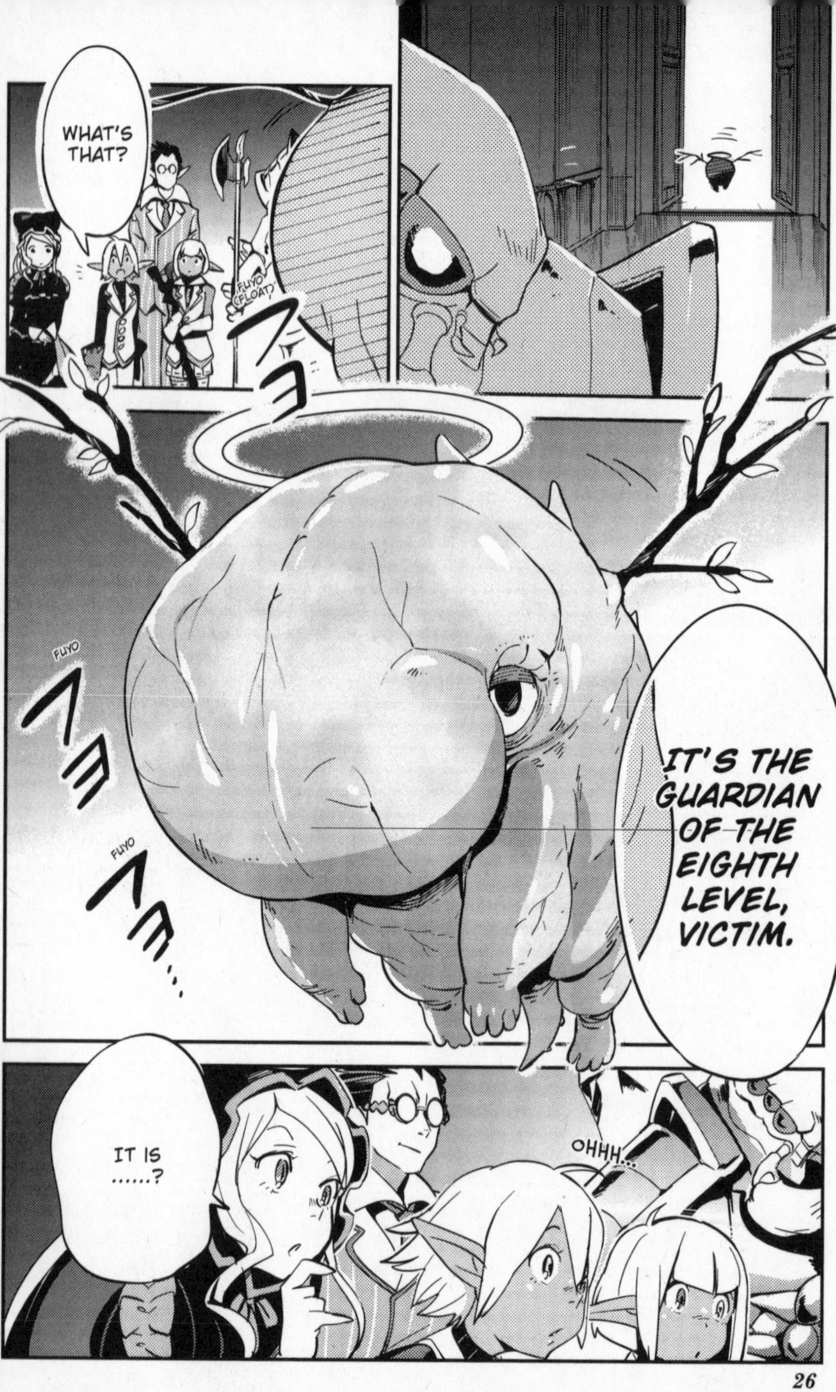
FUYO (FLOAT)
WHAT'S THAT?
IT'S THE GUARDIAN OF THE EIGHTH LEVEL, VICTIM.
FUYO
FUYO
OHHH...
IT IS ......?

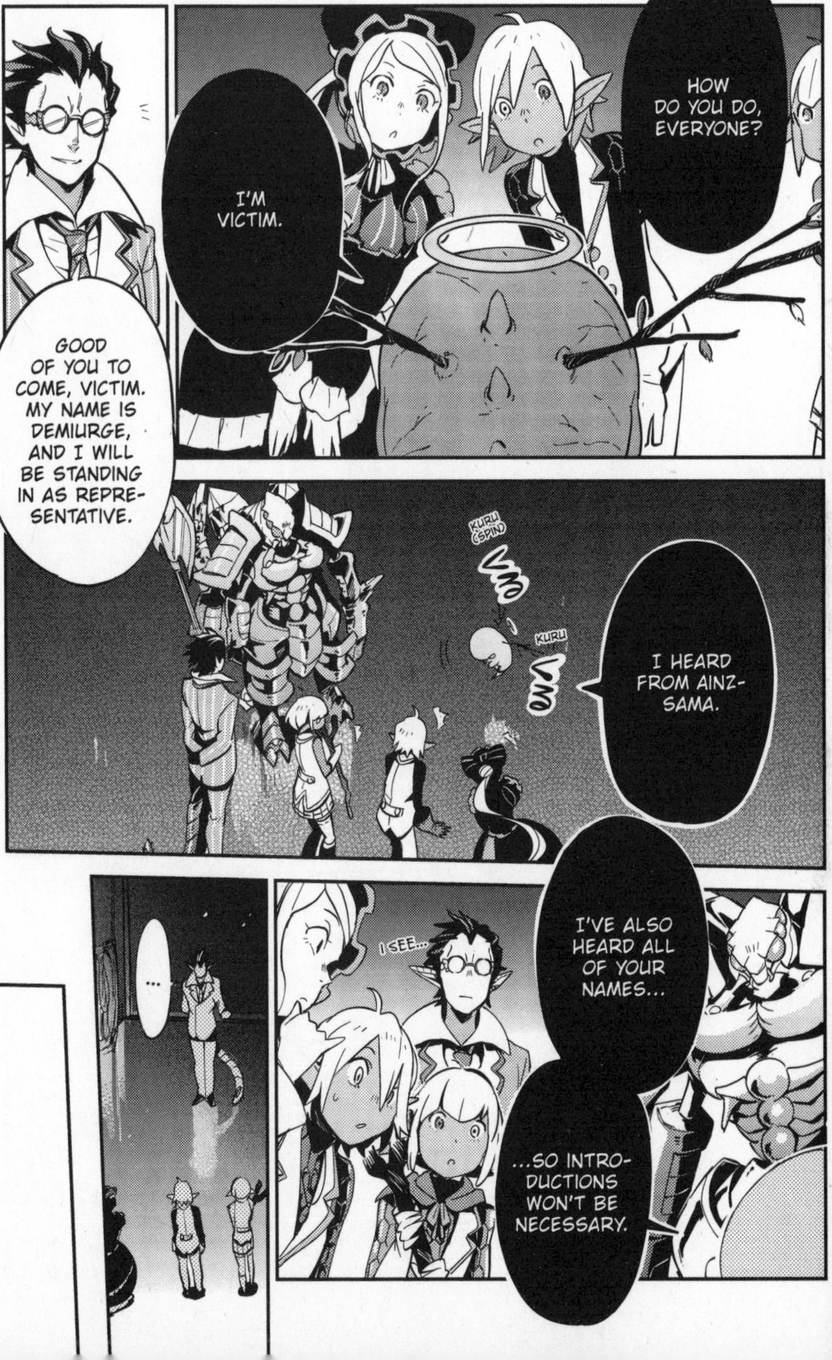
HOW DO YOU DO, EVERYONE?
I'M VICTIM.
GOOD OF YOU TO COME, VICTIM. MY NAME IS DEMIURGE, AND I WILL BE STANDING IN AS REPRESENTATIVE.
KURU (SPIN)
KURU
I HEARD FROM AINZ-SAMA.
I'VE ALSO HEARD ALL OF YOUR NAMES...
I SEE...
...SO INTRODUCTIONS WON'T BE NECESSARY.
...

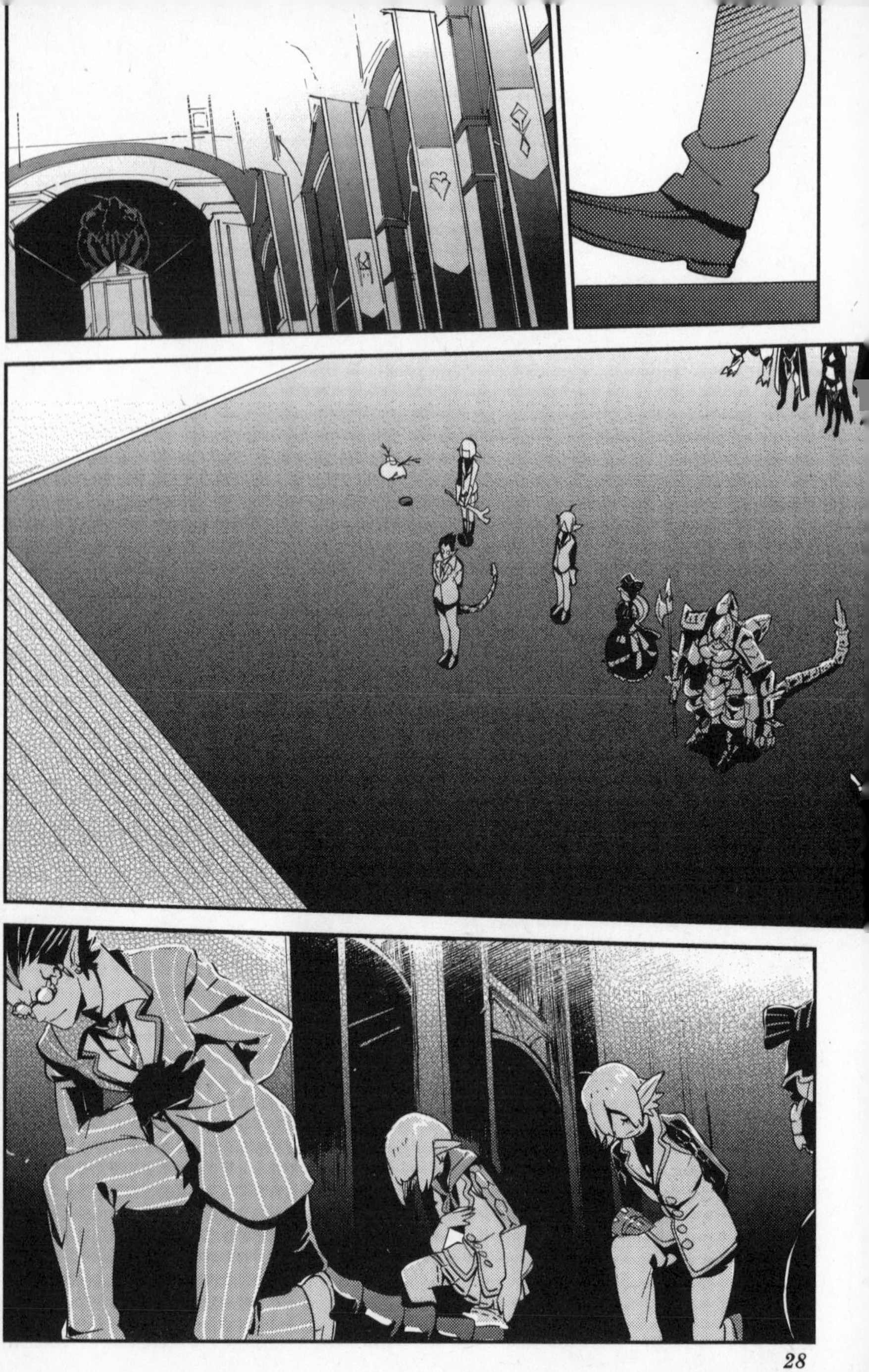

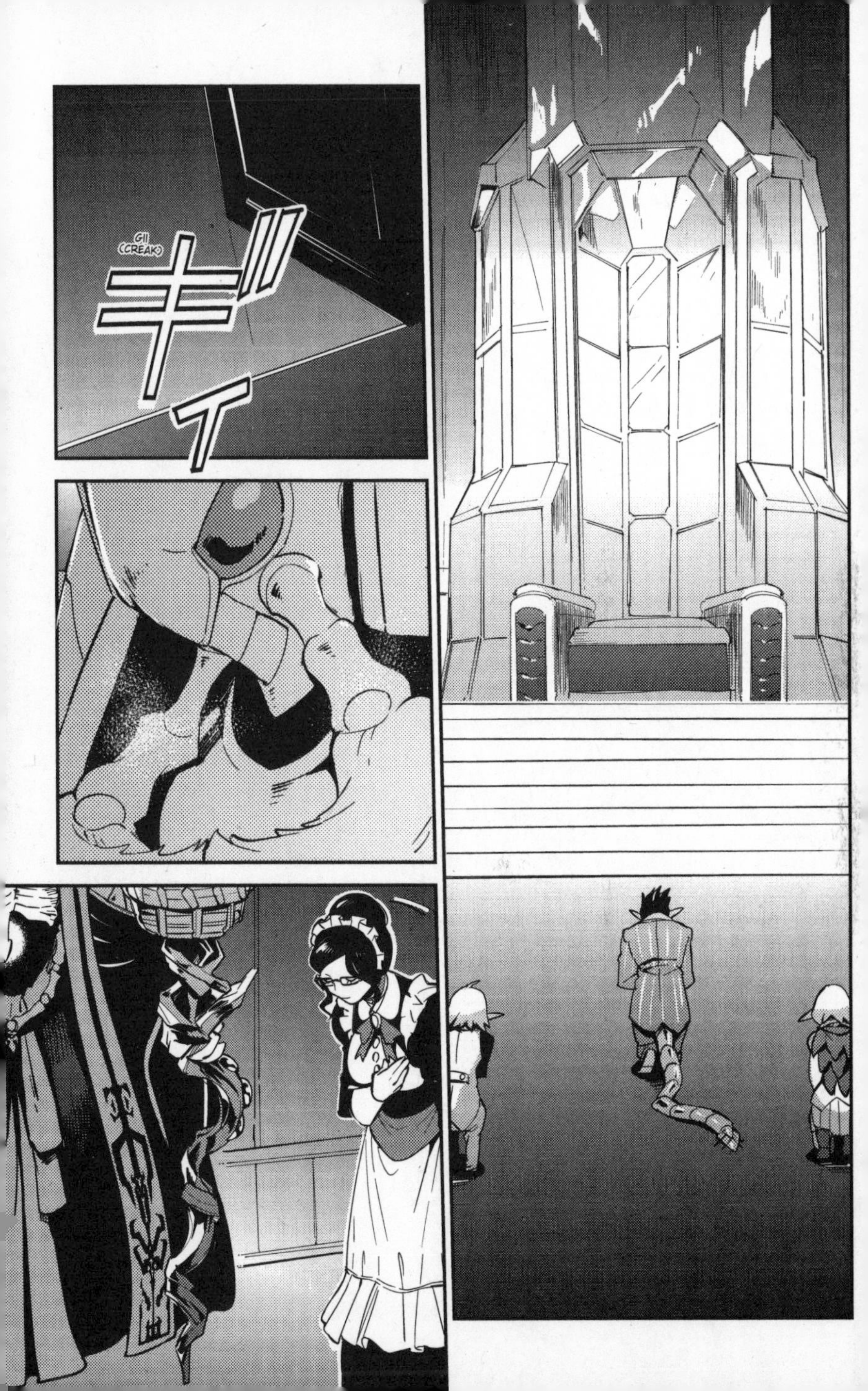
GII
(CREAK)

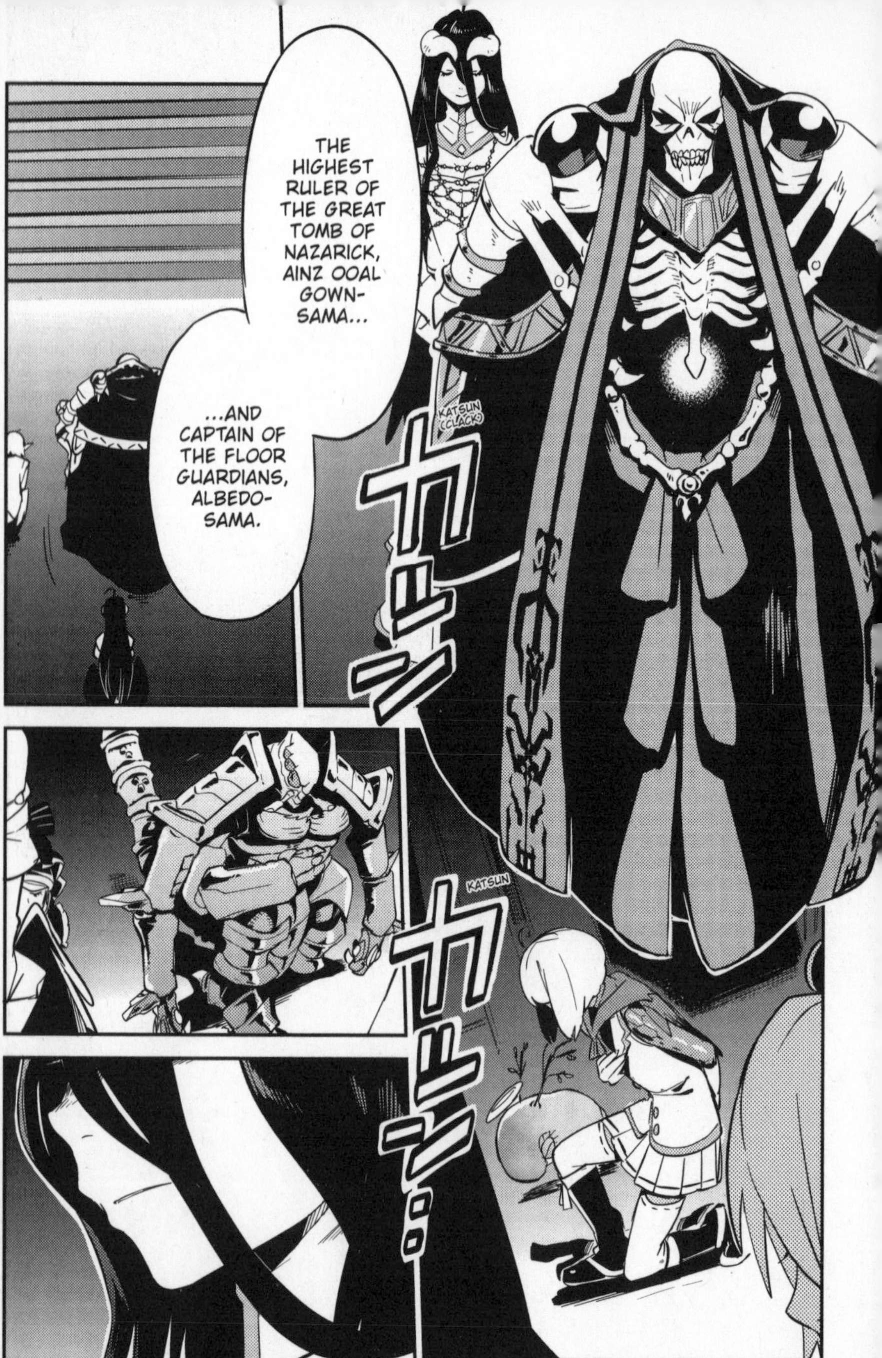
THE HIGHEST RULER OF THE GREAT TOMB OF NAZARICK, AINZ OOAL GOWN-SAMA...
...AND CAPTAIN OF THE FLOOR GUARDIANS, ALBEDO-SAMA.
KATSUN (CLACK)
カッン
KATSUN
カッン...

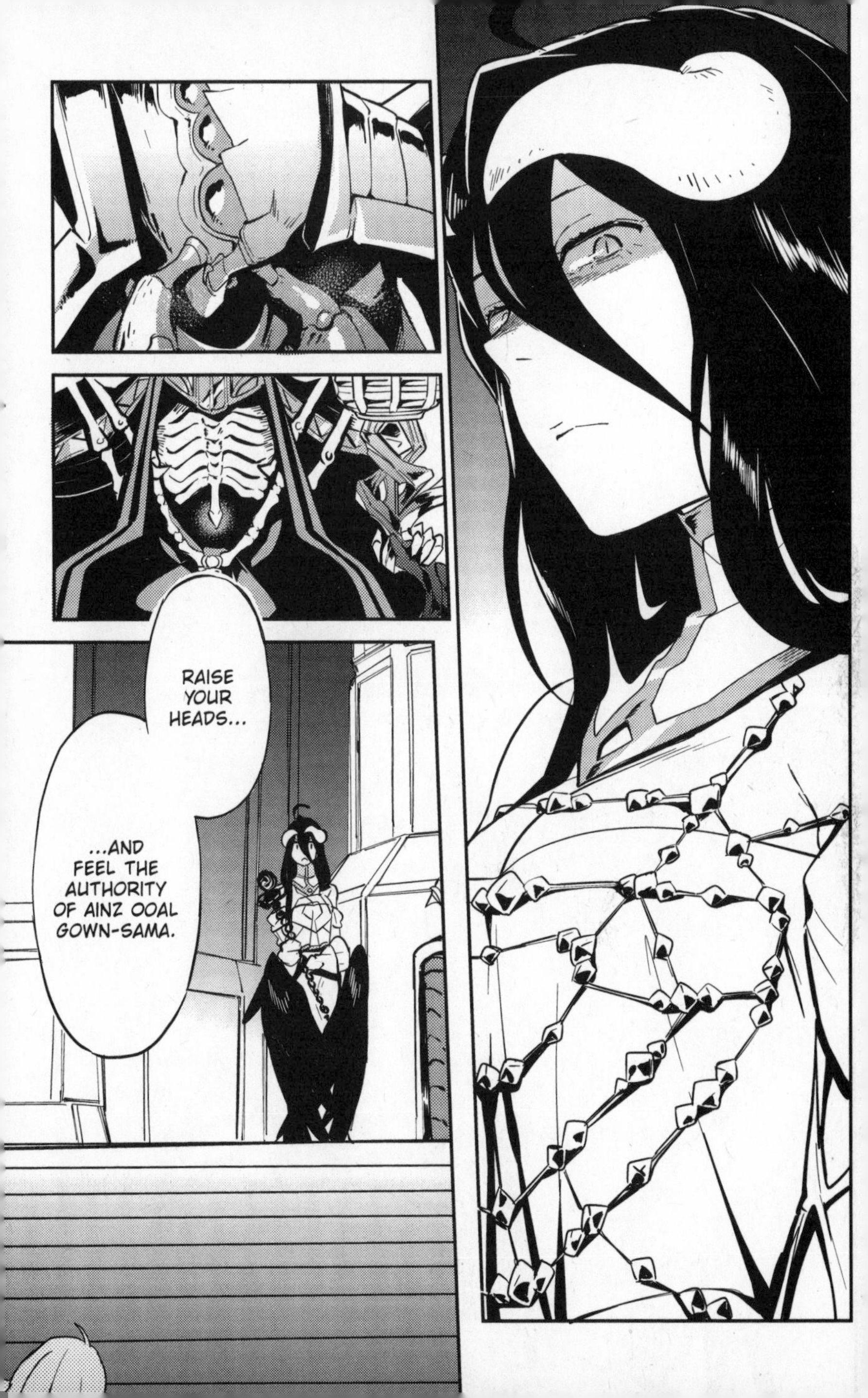
RAISE YOUR HEADS...
...AND FEEL THE AUTHORITY OF AINZ OOAL GOWN-SAMA.

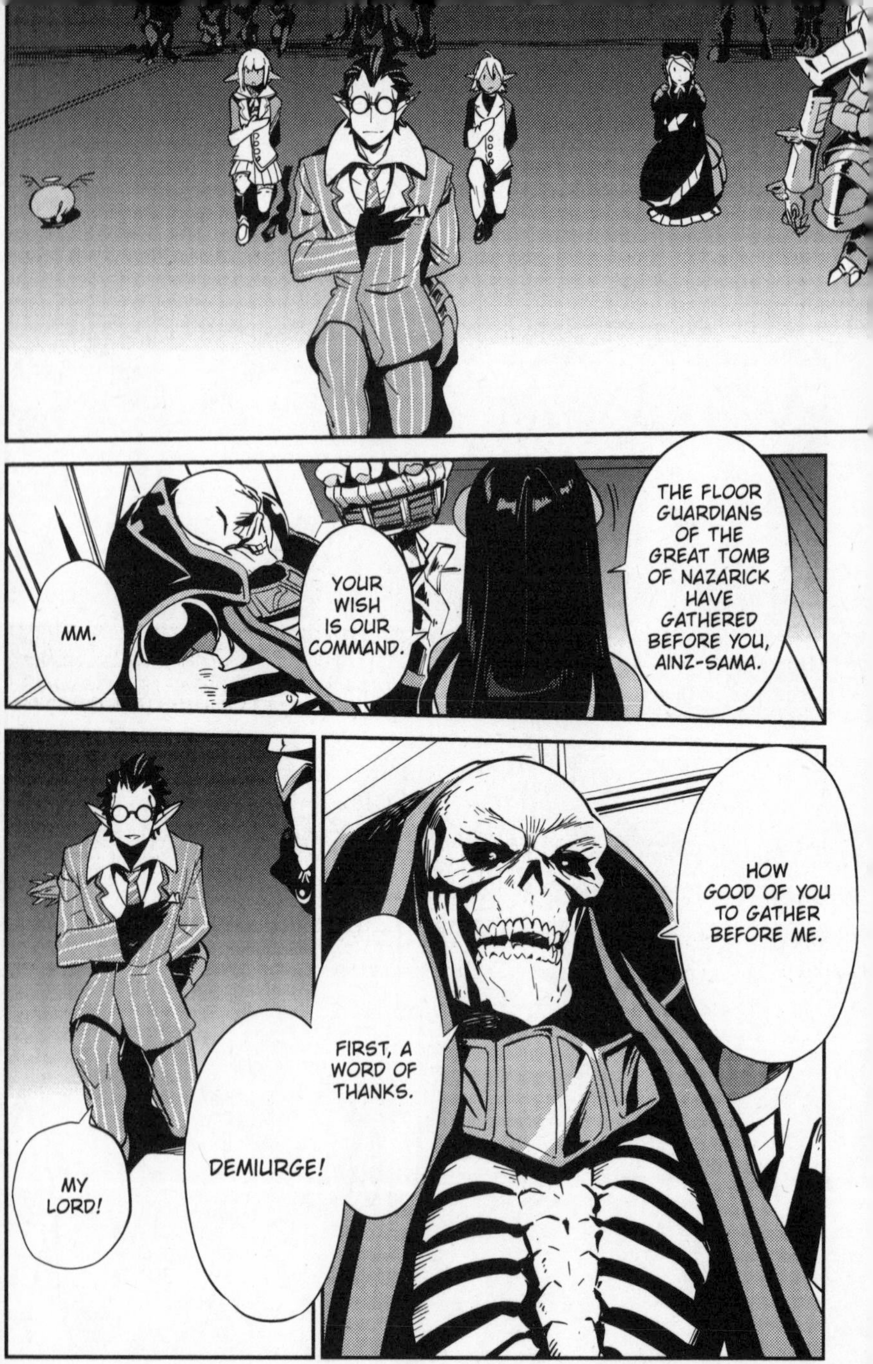
THE FLOOR GUARDIANS OF THE GREAT TOMB OF NAZARICK HAVE GATHERED BEFORE YOU, AINZ-SAMA.
YOUR WISH IS OUR COMMAND.
MM.
HOW GOOD OF YOU TO GATHER BEFORE ME.
FIRST, A WORD OF THANKS.
DEMIURGE!
MY LORD!

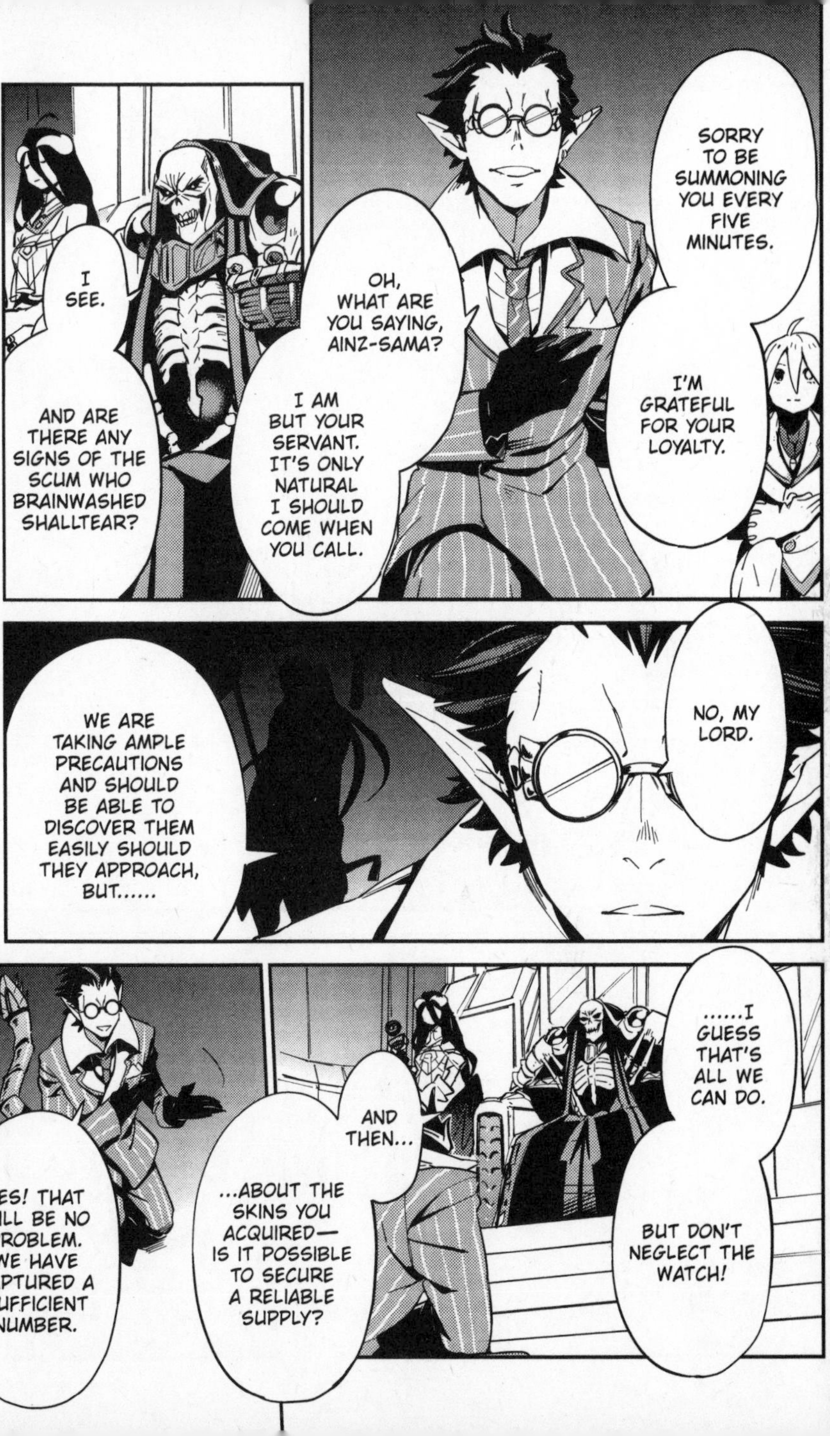
SORRY TO BE SUMMONING YOU EVERY FIVE MINUTES.
OH, WHAT ARE YOU SAYING, AINZ-SAMA?
I AM BUT YOUR SERVANT. IT'S ONLY NATURAL I SHOULD COME WHEN YOU CALL.
I'M GRATEFUL FOR YOUR LOYALTY.
I SEE.
AND ARE THERE ANY SIGNS OF THE SCUM WHO BRAINWASHED SHALLTEAR?
NO, MY LORD.
WE ARE TAKING AMPLE PRECAUTIONS AND SHOULD BE ABLE TO DISCOVER THEM EASILY SHOULD THEY APPROACH, BUT......
......I GUESS THAT'S ALL WE CAN DO.
BUT DON'T NEGLECT THE WATCH!
AND THEN...
...ABOUT THE SKINS YOU ACQUIRED— IS IT POSSIBLE TO SECURE A RELIABLE SUPPLY?
YES! THAT WILL BE NO PROBLEM. WE HAVE CAPTURED A SUFFICIENT NUMBER.

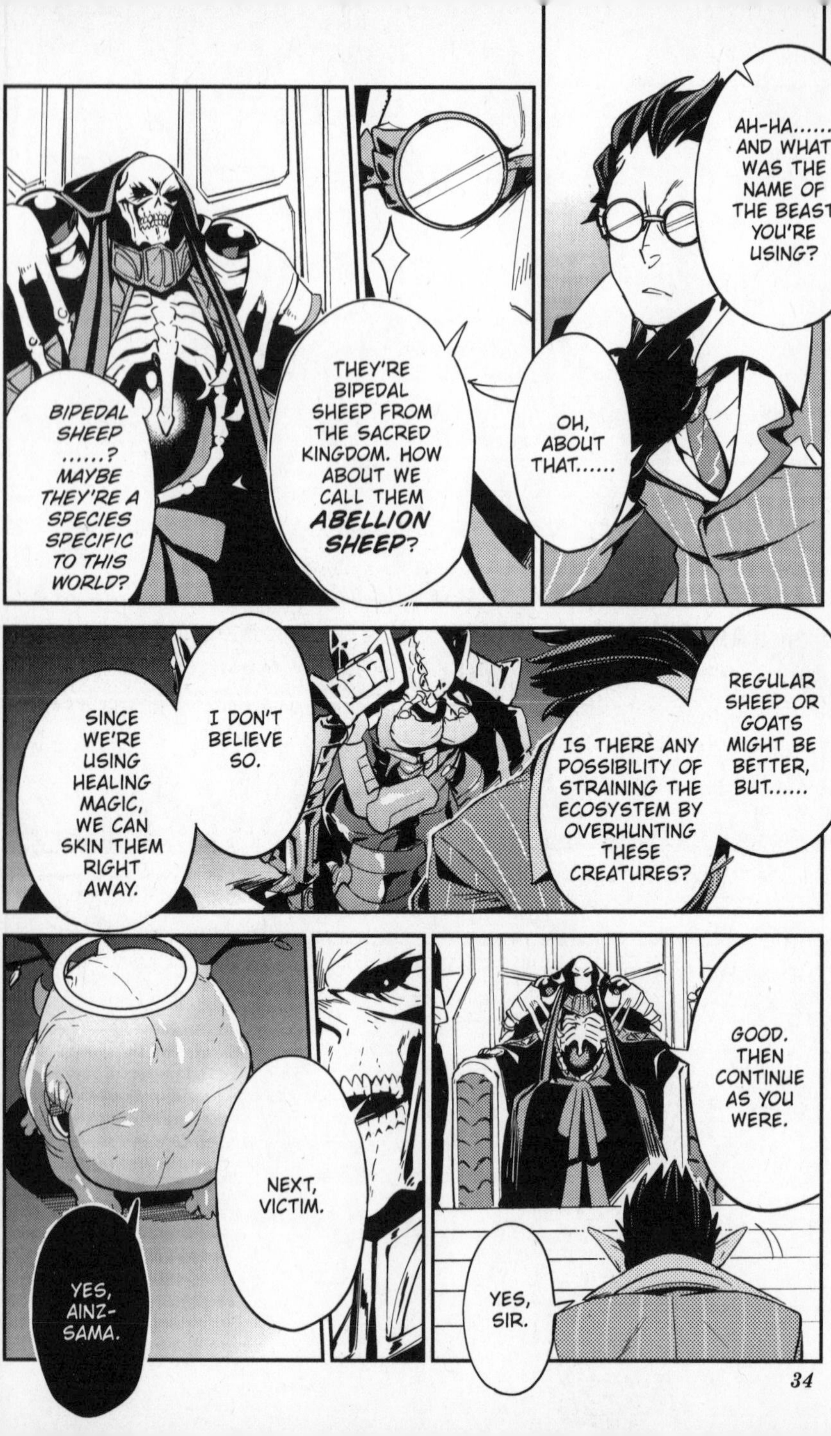
AH-HA...... AND WHAT WAS THE NAME OF THE BEAST YOU'RE USING?
OH, ABOUT THAT......
THEY'RE BIPEDAL SHEEP FROM THE SACRED KINGDOM. HOW ABOUT WE CALL THEM ABELLION SHEEP?
BIPEDAL SHEEP ......? MAYBE THEY'RE A SPECIES SPECIFIC TO THIS WORLD?
REGULAR SHEEP OR GOATS MIGHT BE BETTER, BUT......
IS THERE ANY POSSIBILITY OF STRAINING THE ECOSYSTEM BY OVERHUNTING THESE CREATURES?
I DON'T BELIEVE SO.
SINCE WE'RE USING HEALING MAGIC, WE CAN SKIN THEM RIGHT AWAY.
GOOD. THEN CONTINUE AS YOU WERE.
YES, SIR.
NEXT, VICTIM.
YES, AINZ-SAMA.

I'VE CALLED YOU FOR THE REASON YOU'RE THINKING.

SOMETHING UNIMAGINABLE HAS HAPPENED, AND WE'LL NEED YOUR SKILL TO PROTECT THE GUARDIANS AND ME.

YOU'LL DIE WHEN YOU USE IT, BUT I PROMISE TO RESURRECT YOU RIGHT AWAY.

SU (RUSTLE)

......THERE MAY COME A TIME WHEN WE NEED TO KILL YOU TO PREVENT OUR ENEMY'S ESCAPE.

FORGIVE US.

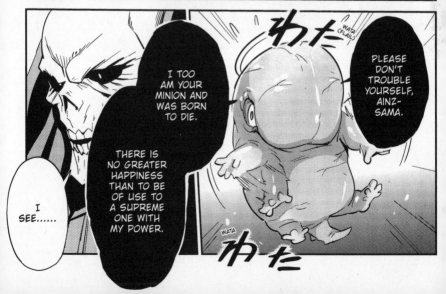

わた
WATA (FLAIL)

PLEASE DON'T TROUBLE YOURSELF, AINZ-SAMA.

I TOO AM YOUR MINION AND WAS BORN TO DIE.

THERE IS NO GREATER HAPPINESS THAN TO BE OF USE TO A SUPREME ONE WITH MY POWER.

I SEE......

わた
WATA

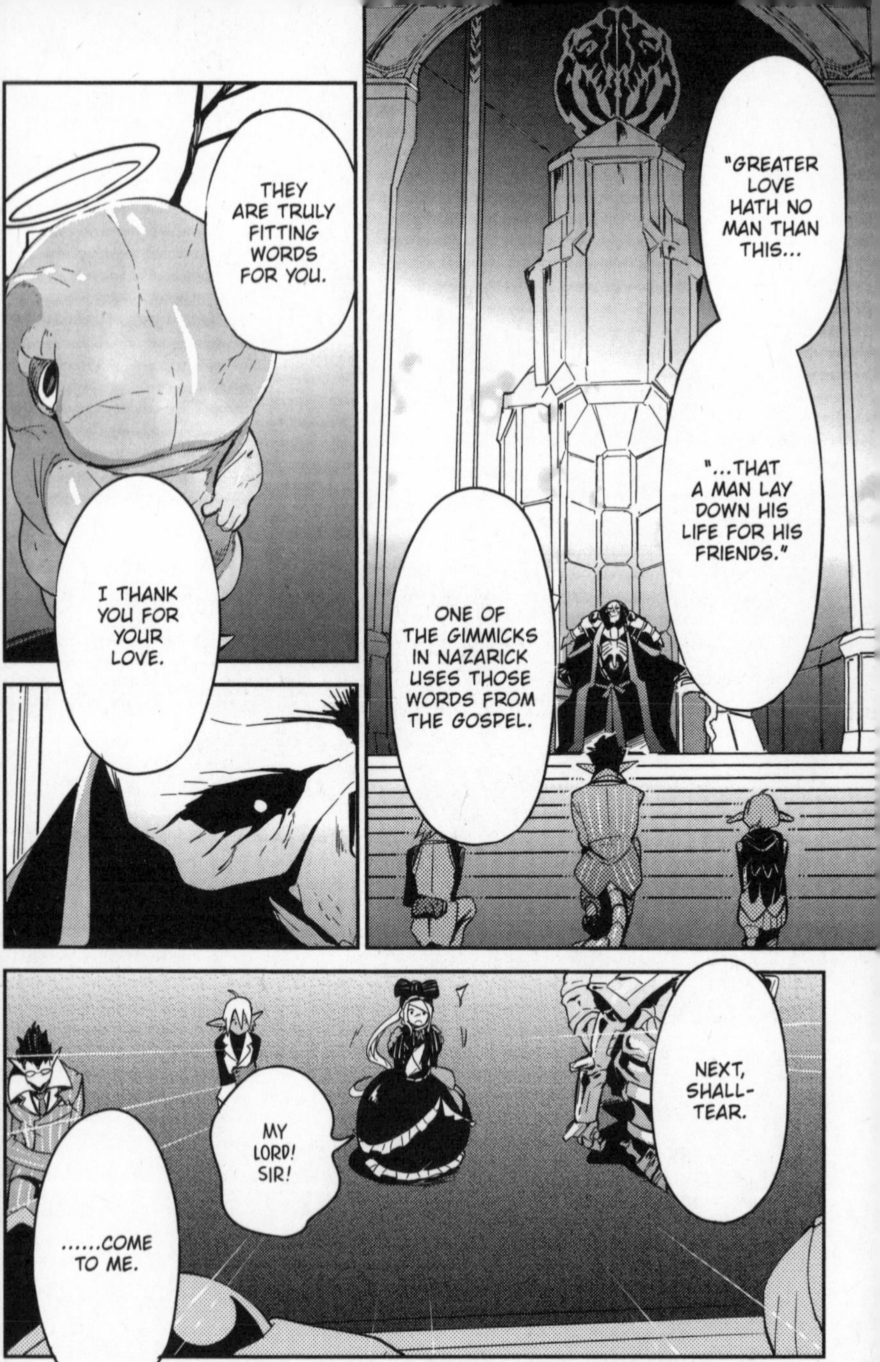
"GREATER LOVE HATH NO MAN THAN THIS...
"...THAT A MAN LAY DOWN HIS LIFE FOR HIS FRIENDS."
ONE OF THE GIMMICKS IN NAZARICK USES THOSE WORDS FROM THE GOSPEL.
THEY ARE TRULY FITTING WORDS FOR YOU.
I THANK YOU FOR YOUR LOVE.
NEXT, SHALL-TEAR.
MY LORD! SIR!
......COME TO ME.

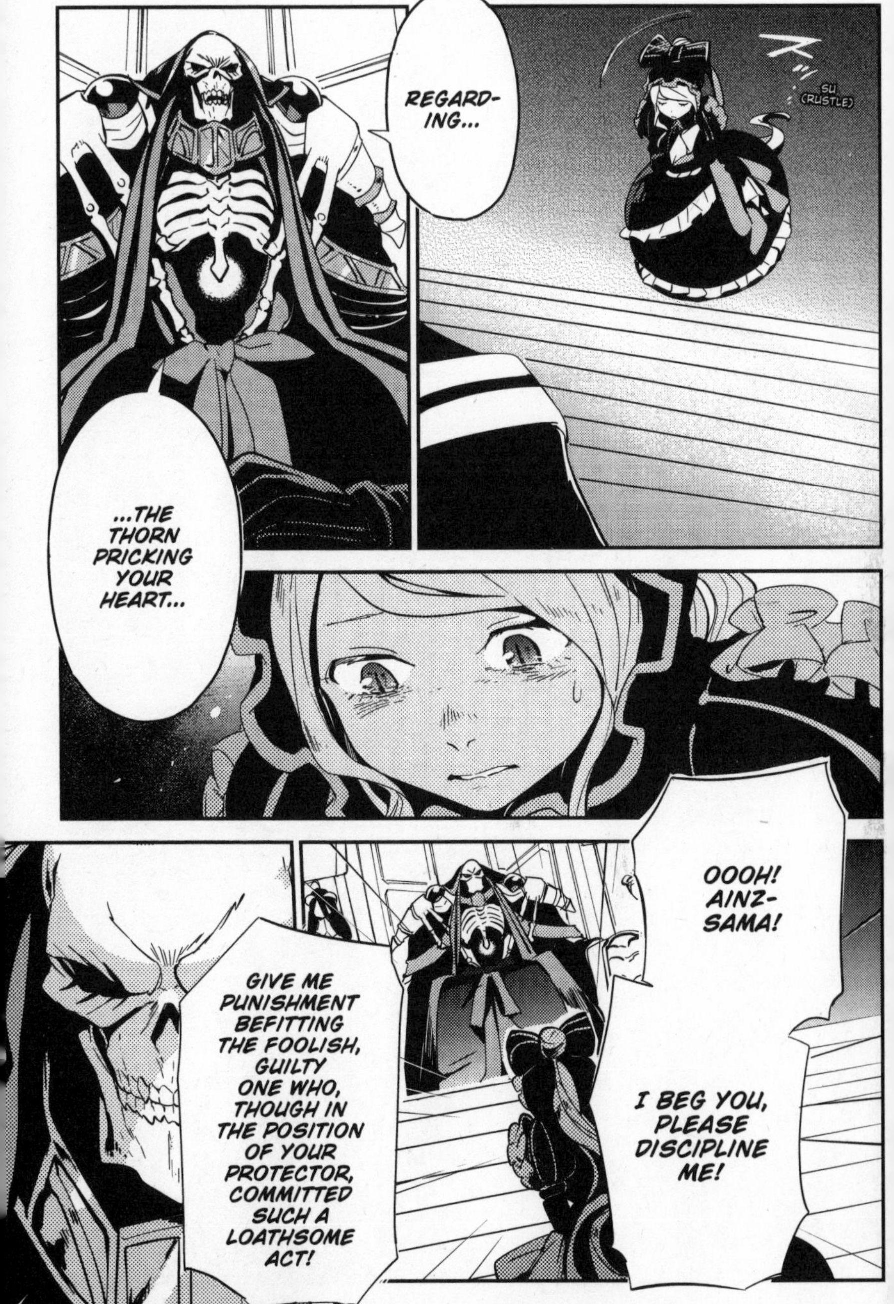
SU (RUSTLE)
REGARDING...
...THE THORN PRICKING YOUR HEART...
OOOH! AINZ-SAMA!
GIVE ME PUNISHMENT BEFITTING THE FOOLISH, GUILTY ONE WHO, THOUGH IN THE POSITION OF YOUR PROTECTOR, COMMITTED SUCH A LOATHSOME ACT!
I BEG YOU, PLEASE DISCIPLINE ME!

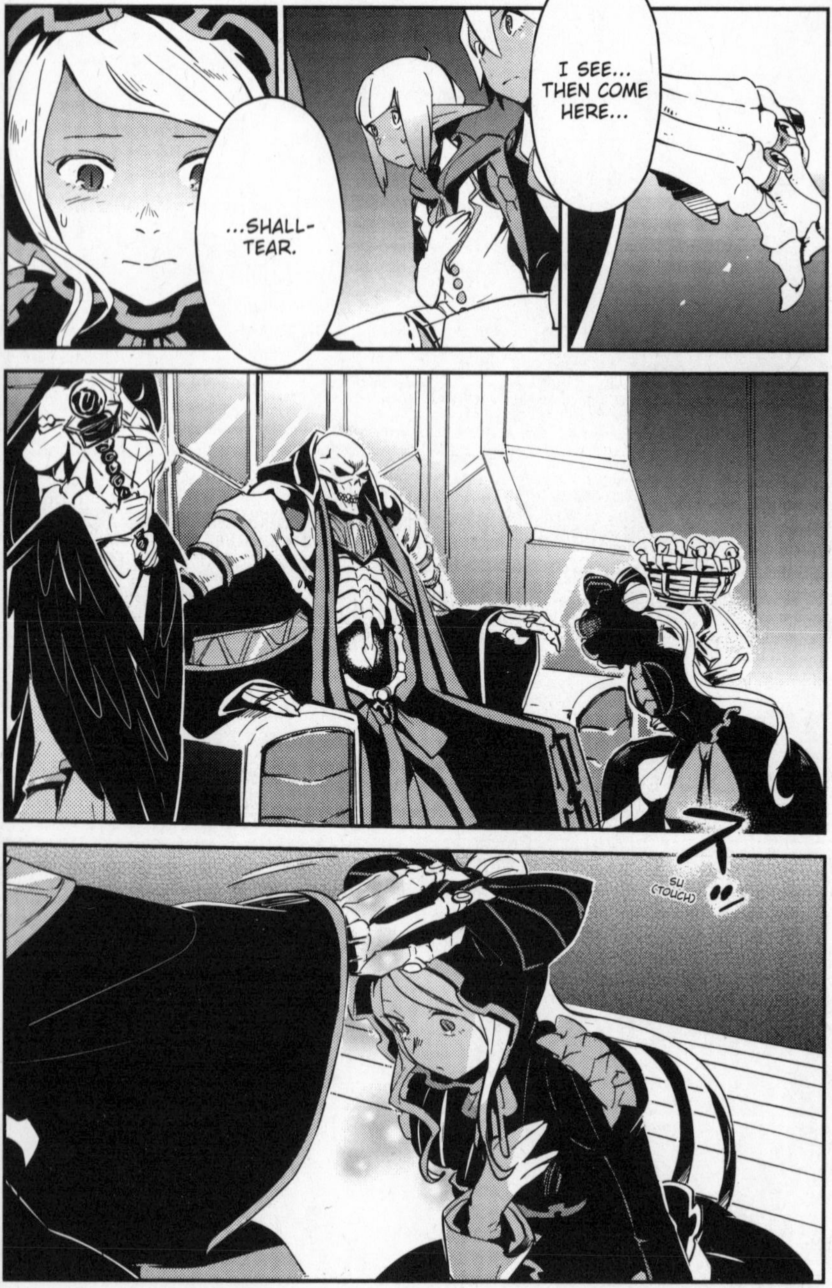
I SEE... THEN COME HERE...
...SHALL-TEAR.
SU (TOUCH)

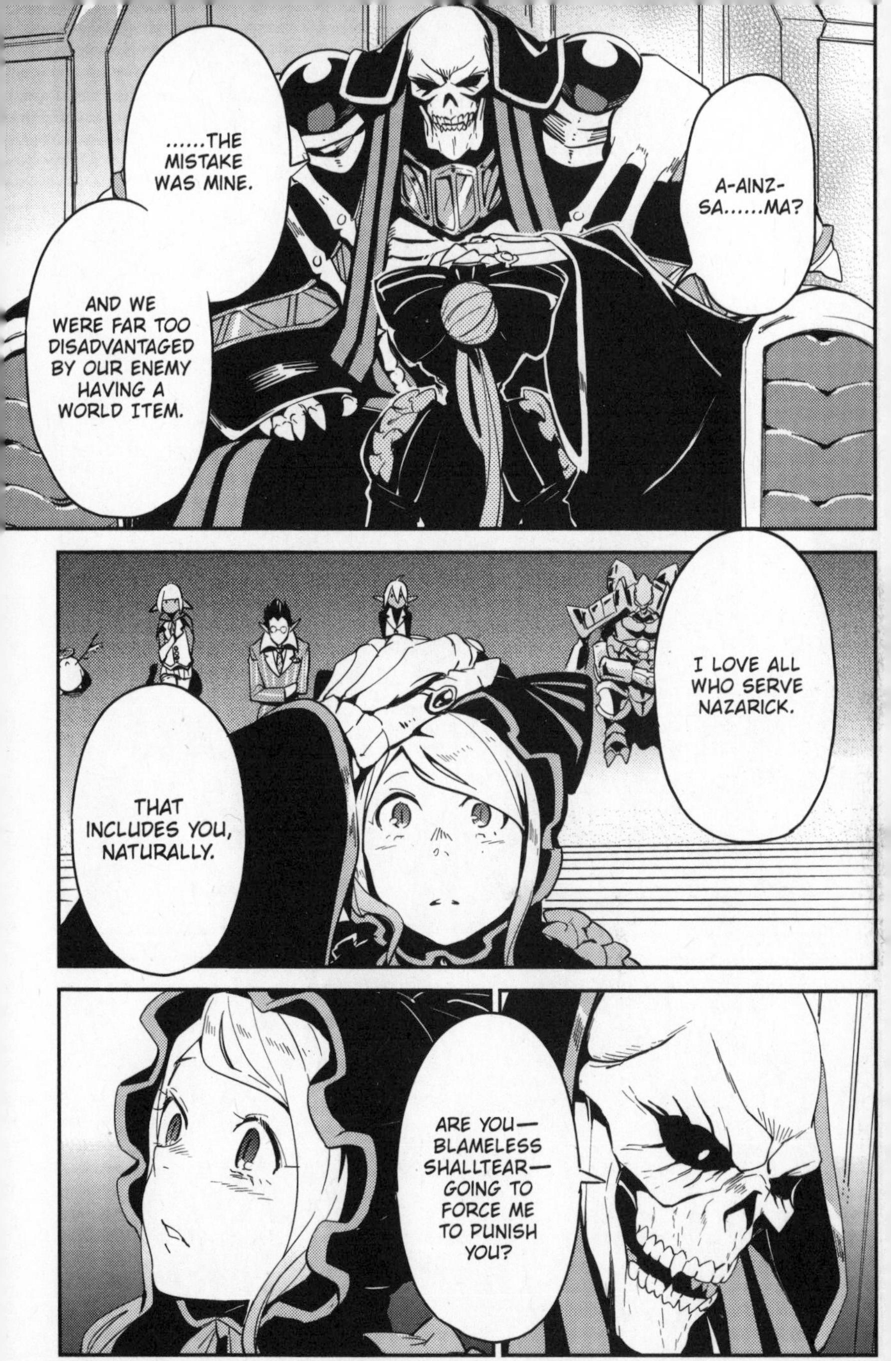
A-AINZ-SA......MA?
......THE MISTAKE WAS MINE.
AND WE WERE FAR TOO DISADVANTAGED BY OUR ENEMY HAVING A WORLD ITEM.
I LOVE ALL WHO SERVE NAZARICK.
THAT INCLUDES YOU, NATURALLY.
ARE YOU—BLAMELESS SHALLTEAR—GOING TO FORCE ME TO PUNISH YOU?

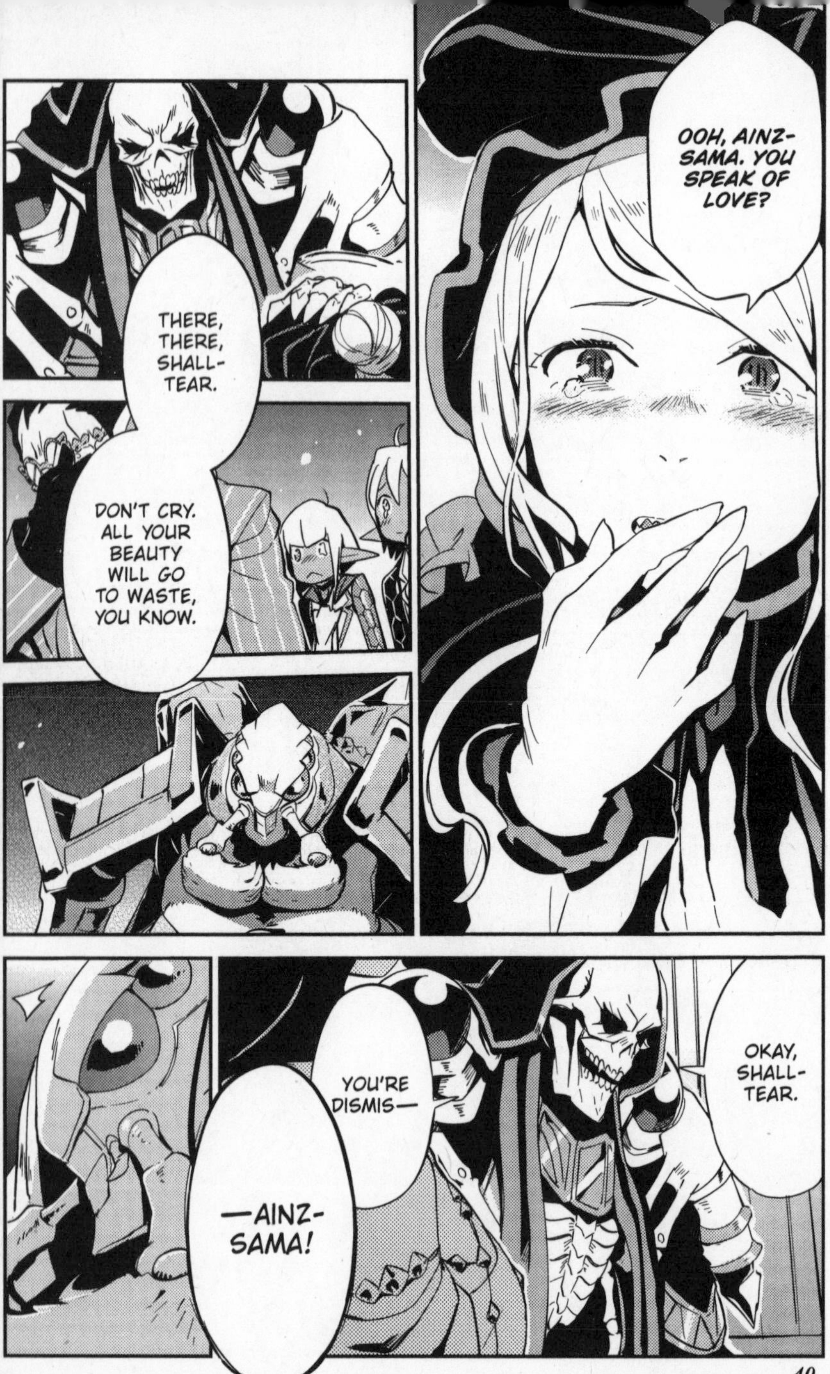
OOH, AINZ-SAMA. YOU SPEAK OF LOVE?
THERE, THERE, SHALL-TEAR.
DON'T CRY. ALL YOUR BEAUTY WILL GO TO WASTE, YOU KNOW.
OKAY, SHALL-TEAR.
YOU'RE DISMIS—
—AINZ-SAMA!

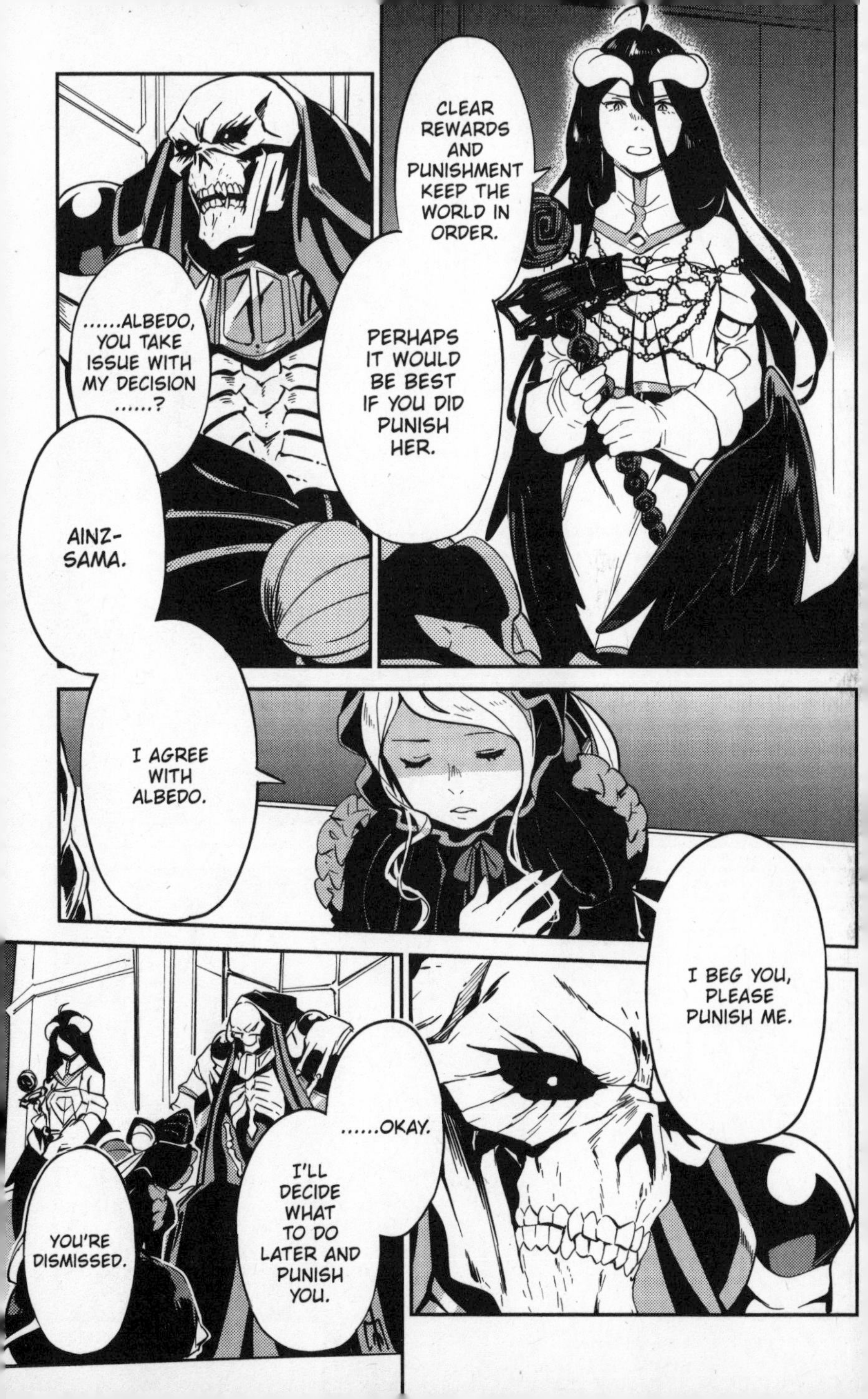
CLEAR REWARDS AND PUNISHMENT KEEP THE WORLD IN ORDER.
PERHAPS IT WOULD BE BEST IF YOU DID PUNISH HER.
......ALBEDO, YOU TAKE ISSUE WITH MY DECISION ......?
AINZ-SAMA.
I AGREE WITH ALBEDO.
I BEG YOU, PLEASE PUNISH ME.
......OKAY.
I'LL DECIDE WHAT TO DO LATER AND PUNISH YOU.
YOU'RE DISMISSED.

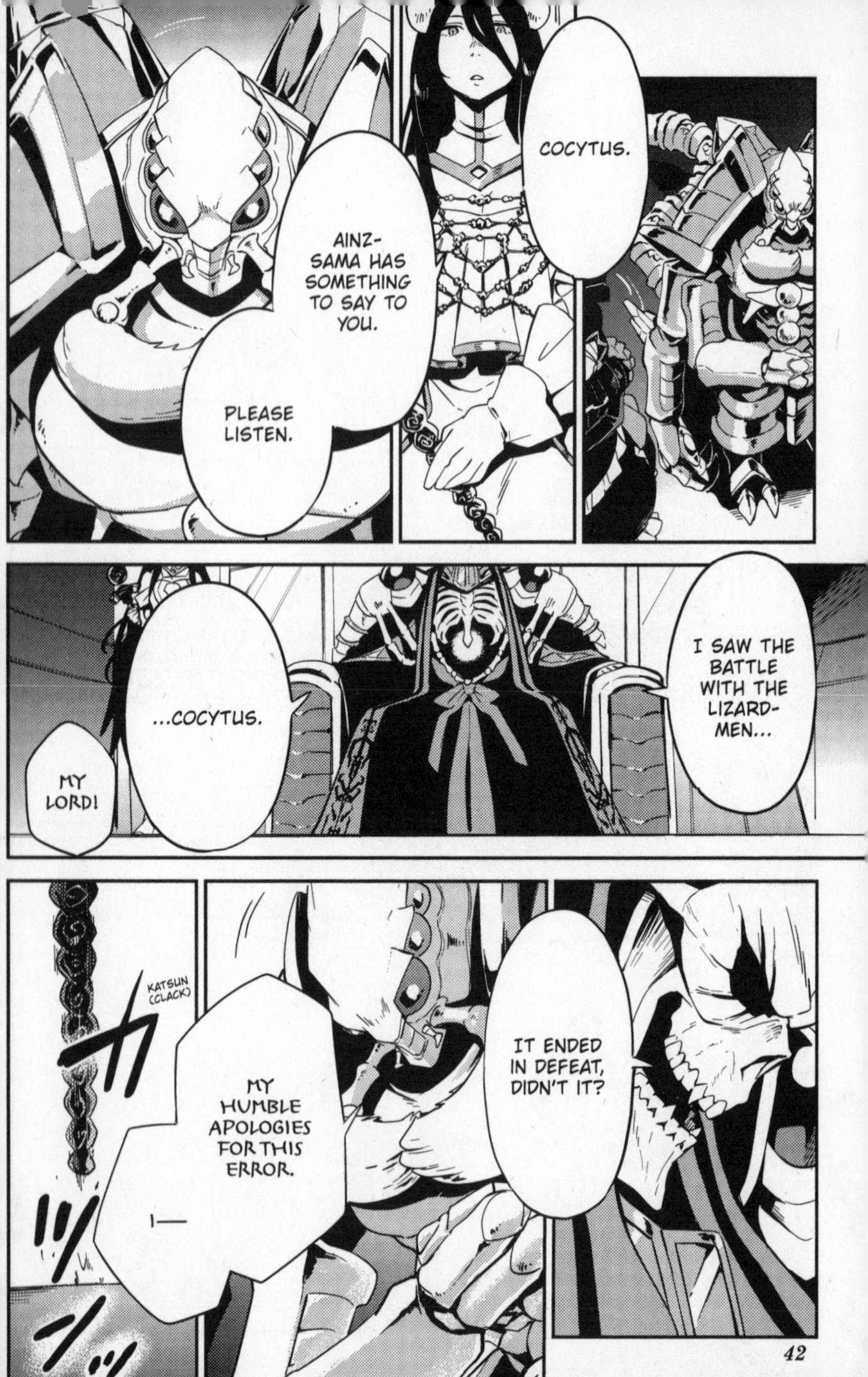
COCYTUS.
AINZ-SAMA HAS SOMETHING TO SAY TO YOU.
PLEASE LISTEN.
I SAW THE BATTLE WITH THE LIZARD-MEN...
...COCYTUS.
MY LORD!
IT ENDED IN DEFEAT, DIDN'T IT?
MY HUMBLE APOLOGIES FOR THIS ERROR.
I—
KATSUN (CLACK)

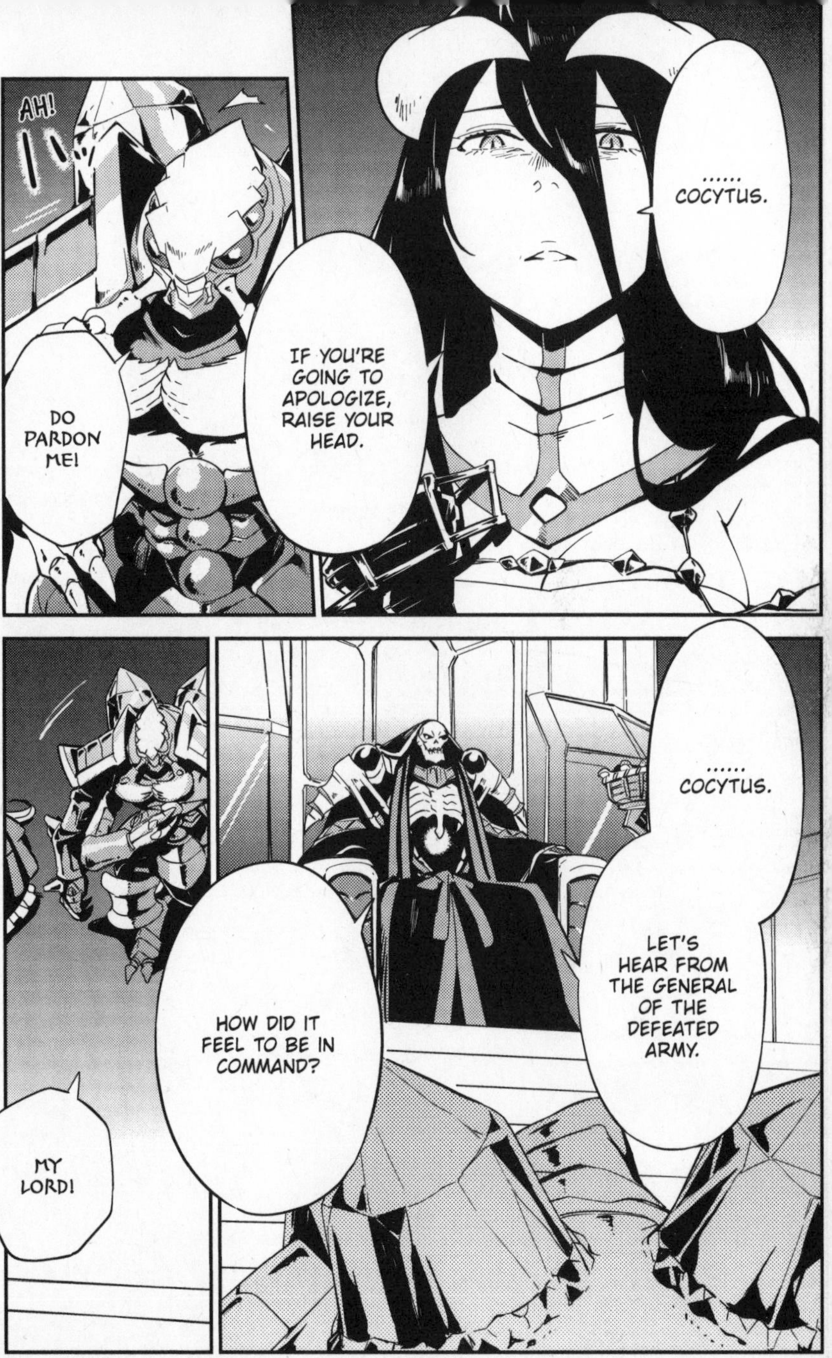
......
COCYTUS.
AH!
DO PARDON ME!
IF YOU'RE GOING TO APOLOGIZE, RAISE YOUR HEAD.
......
COCYTUS.
LET'S HEAR FROM THE GENERAL OF THE DEFEATED ARMY.
HOW DID IT FEEL TO BE IN COMMAND?
MY LORD!

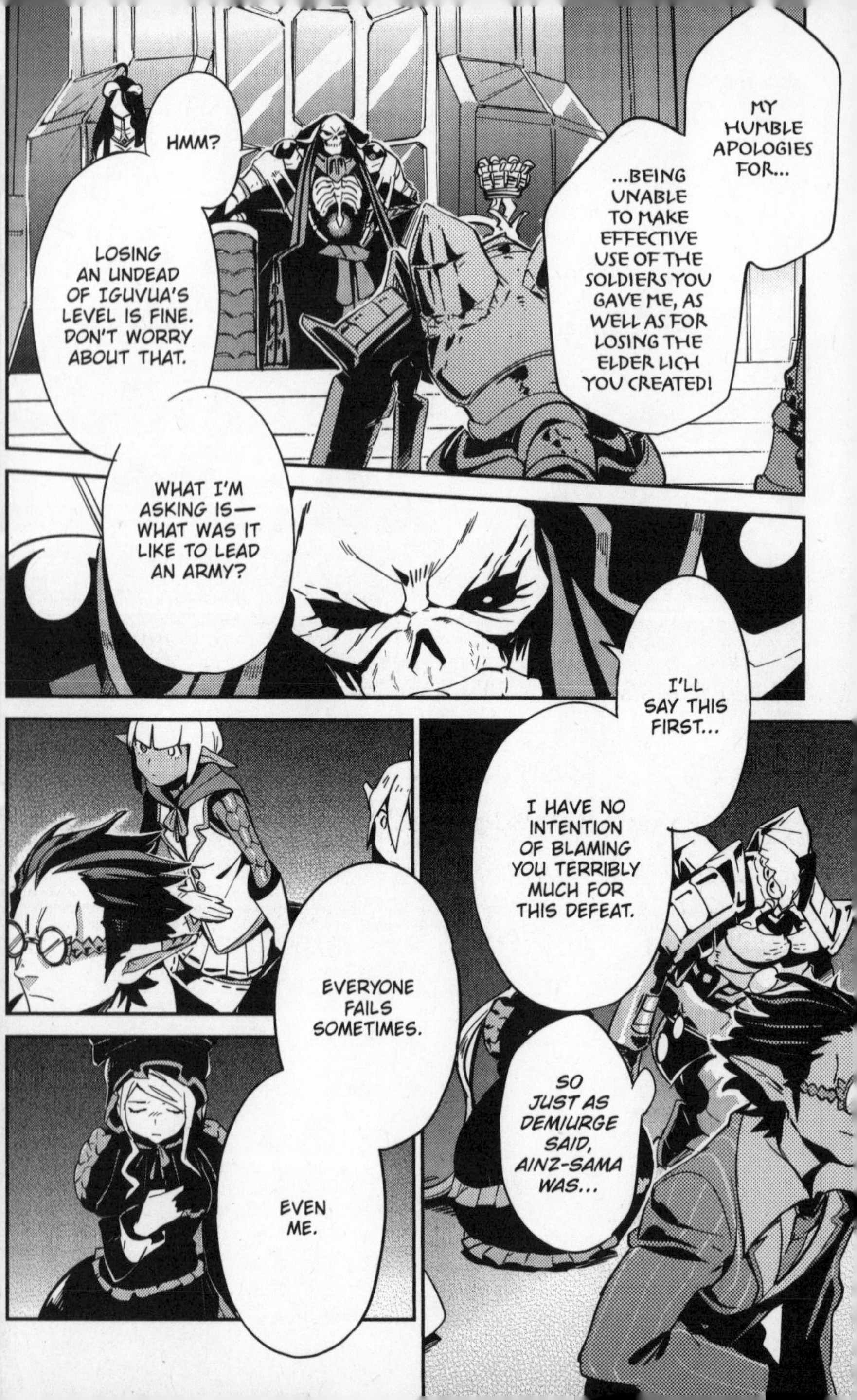
MY HUMBLE APOLOGIES FOR...
...BEING UNABLE TO MAKE EFFECTIVE USE OF THE SOLDIERS YOU GAVE ME, AS WELL AS FOR LOSING THE ELDER LICH YOU CREATED!
HMM?
LOSING AN UNDEAD OF IGUVUA'S LEVEL IS FINE. DON'T WORRY ABOUT THAT.
WHAT I'M ASKING IS— WHAT WAS IT LIKE TO LEAD AN ARMY?
I'LL SAY THIS FIRST...
I HAVE NO INTENTION OF BLAMING YOU TERRIBLY MUCH FOR THIS DEFEAT.
EVERYONE FAILS SOMETIMES.
EVEN ME.
SO JUST AS DEMIURGE SAID, AINZ-SAMA WAS...

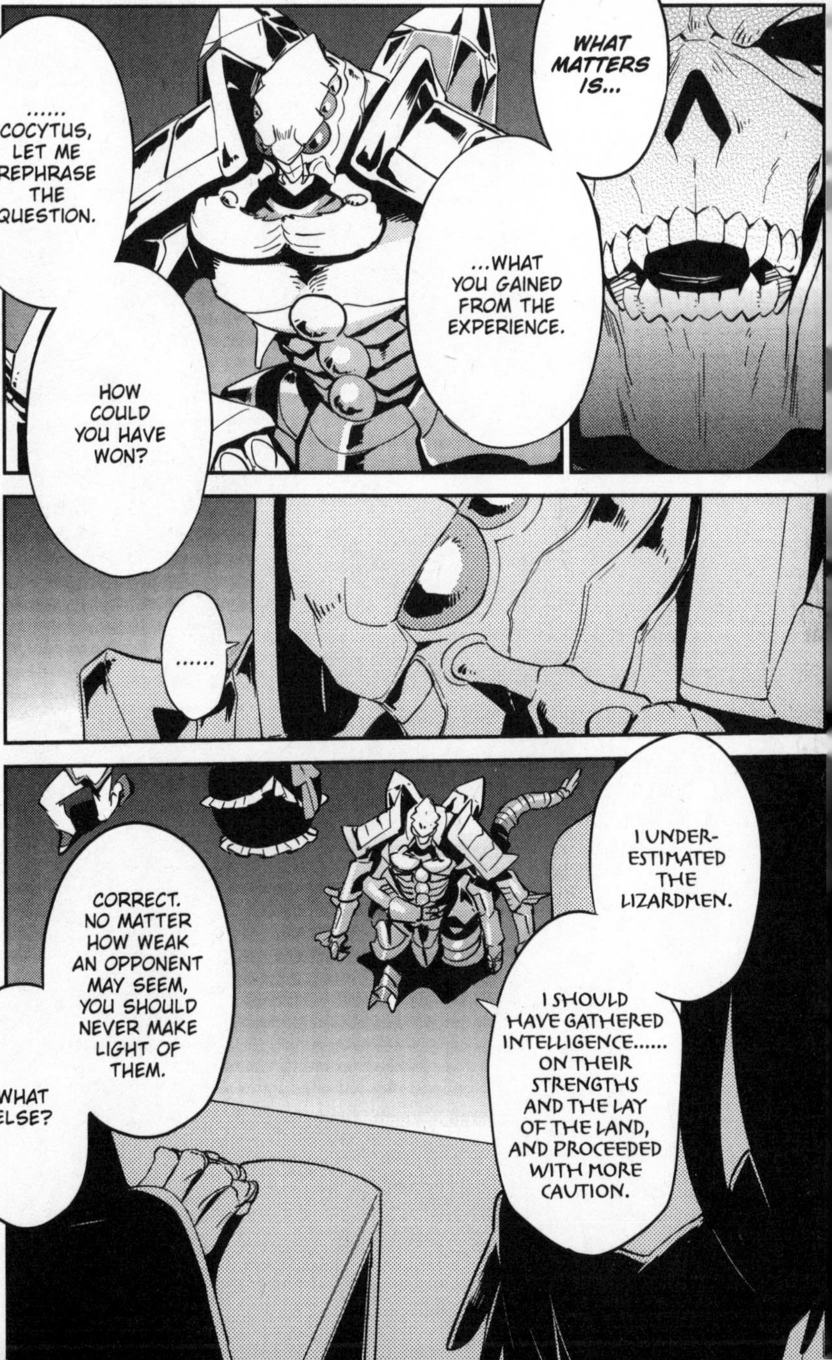
WHAT MATTERS IS...
...WHAT YOU GAINED FROM THE EXPERIENCE.
...... COCYTUS, LET ME REPHRASE THE QUESTION.
HOW COULD YOU HAVE WON?
......
I UNDER-ESTIMATED THE LIZARDMEN.
I SHOULD HAVE GATHERED INTELLIGENCE...... ON THEIR STRENGTHS AND THE LAY OF THE LAND, AND PROCEEDED WITH MORE CAUTION.
CORRECT. NO MATTER HOW WEAK AN OPPONENT MAY SEEM, YOU SHOULD NEVER MAKE LIGHT OF THEM.
WHAT ELSE?

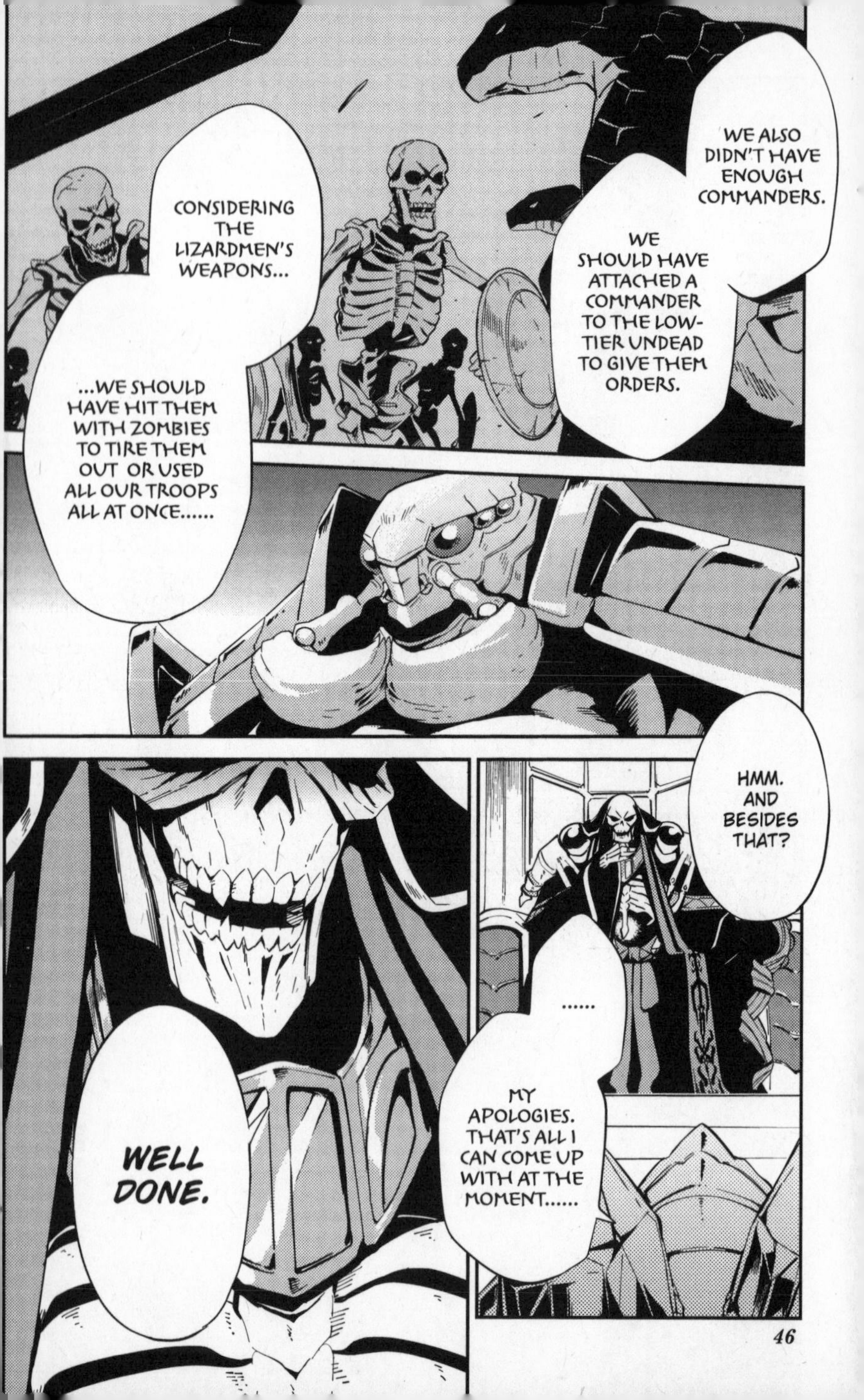
WE ALSO DIDN'T HAVE ENOUGH COMMANDERS.
WE SHOULD HAVE ATTACHED A COMMANDER TO THE LOW-TIER UNDEAD TO GIVE THEM ORDERS.
CONSIDERING THE LIZARDMEN'S WEAPONS...
...WE SHOULD HAVE HIT THEM WITH ZOMBIES TO TIRE THEM OUT OR USED ALL OUR TROOPS ALL AT ONCE......
HMM. AND BESIDES THAT?
......
MY APOLOGIES. THAT'S ALL I CAN COME UP WITH AT THE MOMENT......
WELL DONE.

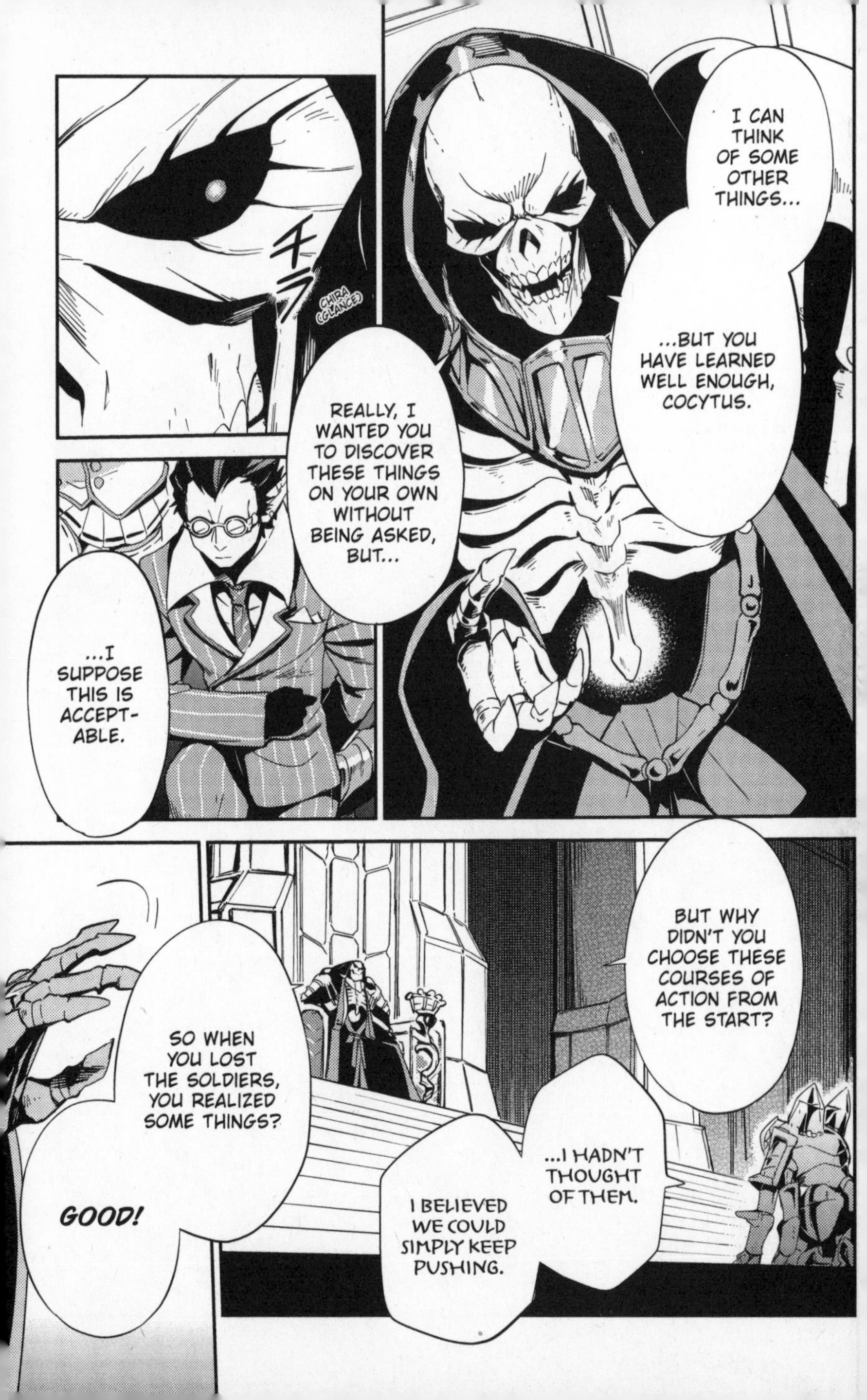
I CAN THINK OF SOME OTHER THINGS...
...BUT YOU HAVE LEARNED WELL ENOUGH, COCYTUS.
REALLY, I WANTED YOU TO DISCOVER THESE THINGS ON YOUR OWN WITHOUT BEING ASKED, BUT...
CHIRA (GLANCE)
...I SUPPOSE THIS IS ACCEPT-ABLE.
BUT WHY DIDN'T YOU CHOOSE THESE COURSES OF ACTION FROM THE START?
...I HADN'T THOUGHT OF THEM.
I BELIEVED WE COULD SIMPLY KEEP PUSHING.
SO WHEN YOU LOST THE SOLDIERS, YOU REALIZED SOME THINGS?
GOOD!

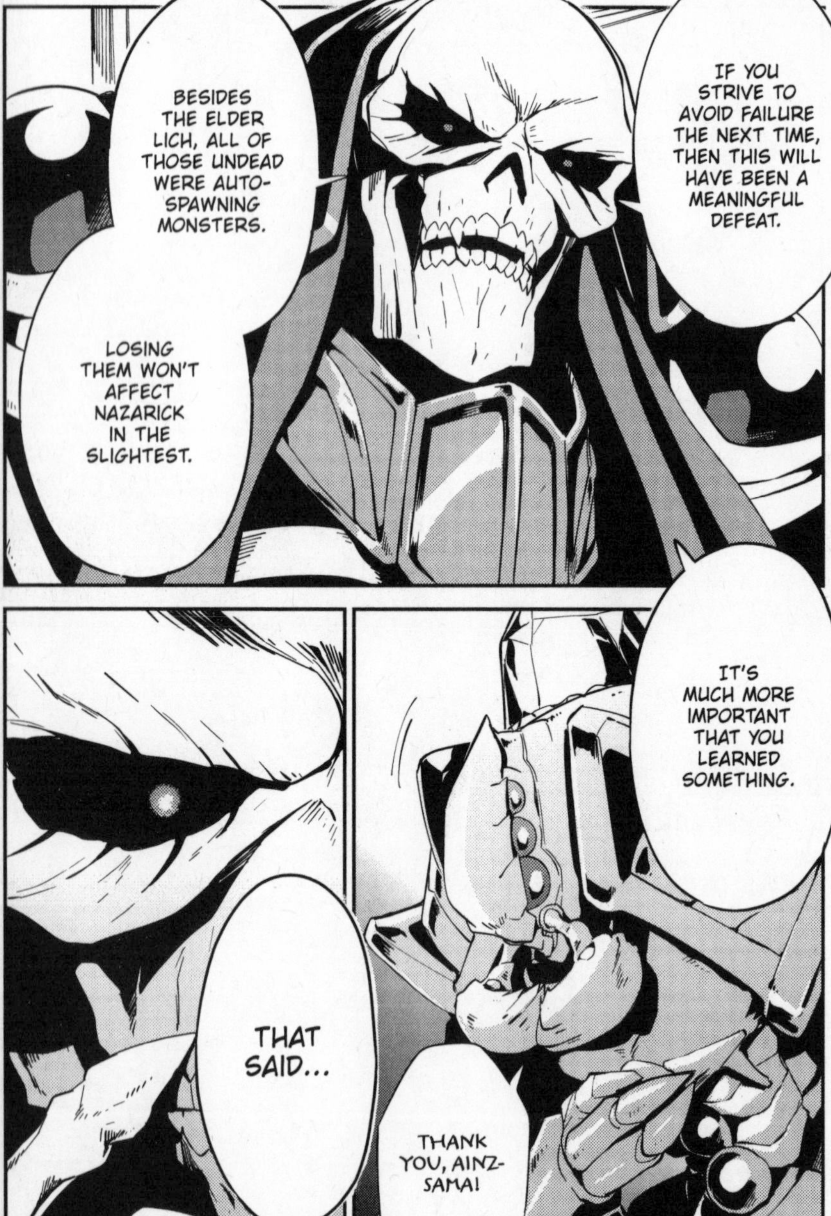
IF YOU STRIVE TO AVOID FAILURE THE NEXT TIME, THEN THIS WILL HAVE BEEN A MEANINGFUL DEFEAT.
BESIDES THE ELDER LICH, ALL OF THOSE UNDEAD WERE AUTO-SPAWNING MONSTERS.
LOSING THEM WON'T AFFECT NAZARICK IN THE SLIGHTEST.
IT'S MUCH MORE IMPORTANT THAT YOU LEARNED SOMETHING.
THANK YOU, AINZ-SAMA!
THAT SAID...

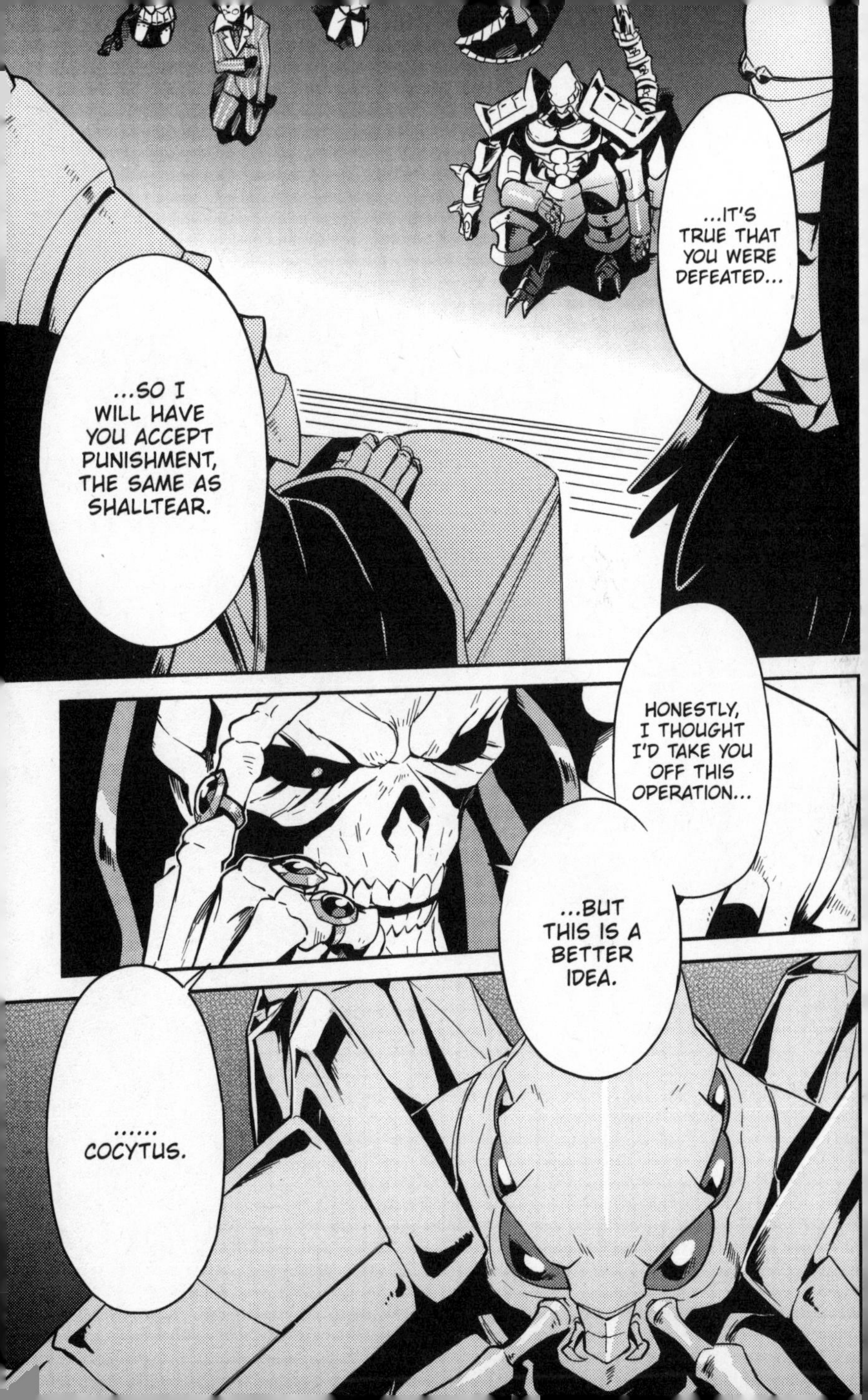
...IT'S TRUE THAT YOU WERE DEFEATED...
...SO I WILL HAVE YOU ACCEPT PUNISHMENT, THE SAME AS SHALLTEAR.
HONESTLY, I THOUGHT I'D TAKE YOU OFF THIS OPERATION...
...BUT THIS IS A BETTER IDEA.
...... COCYTUS.

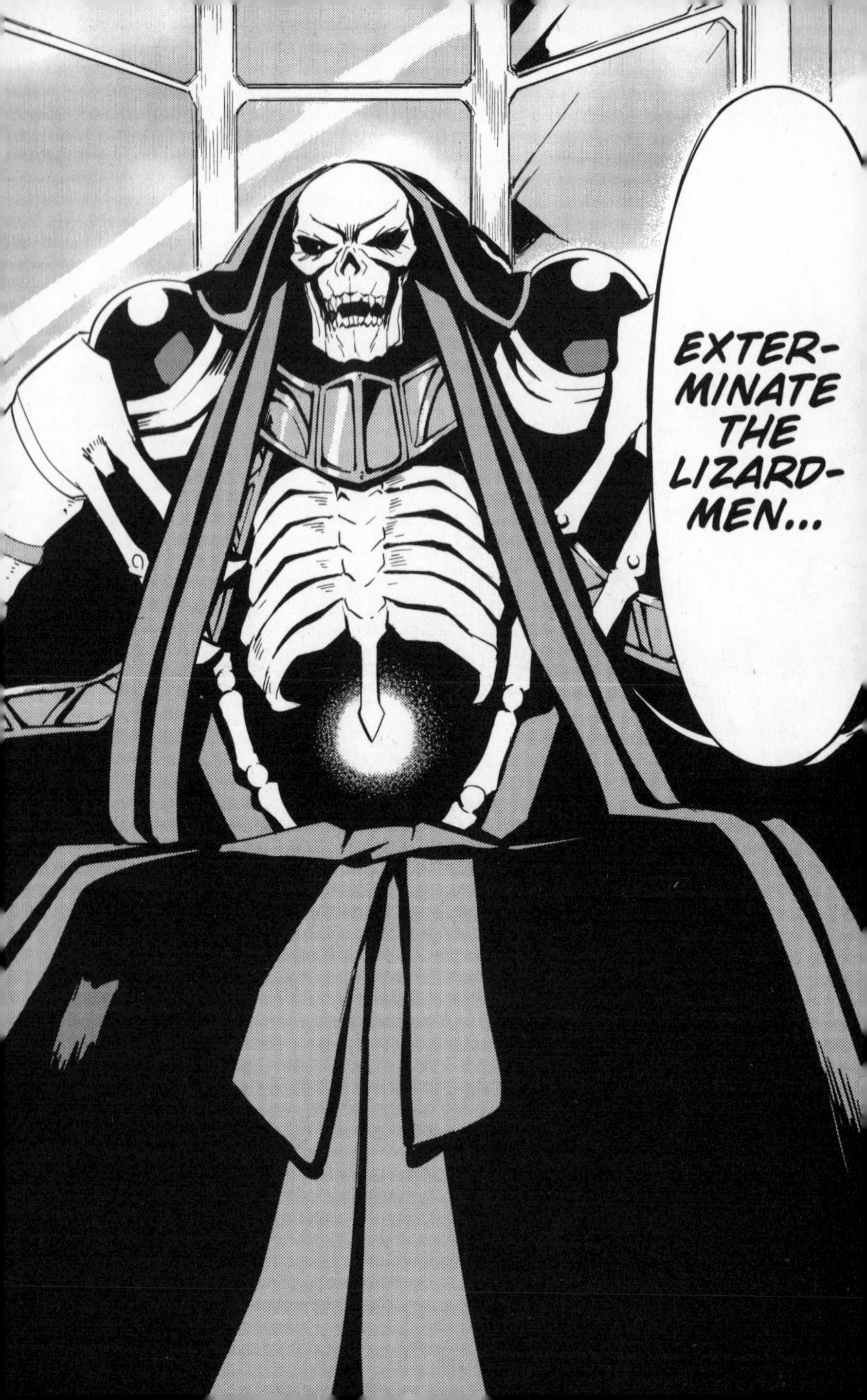
EXTER-MINATE THE LIZARD-MEN...

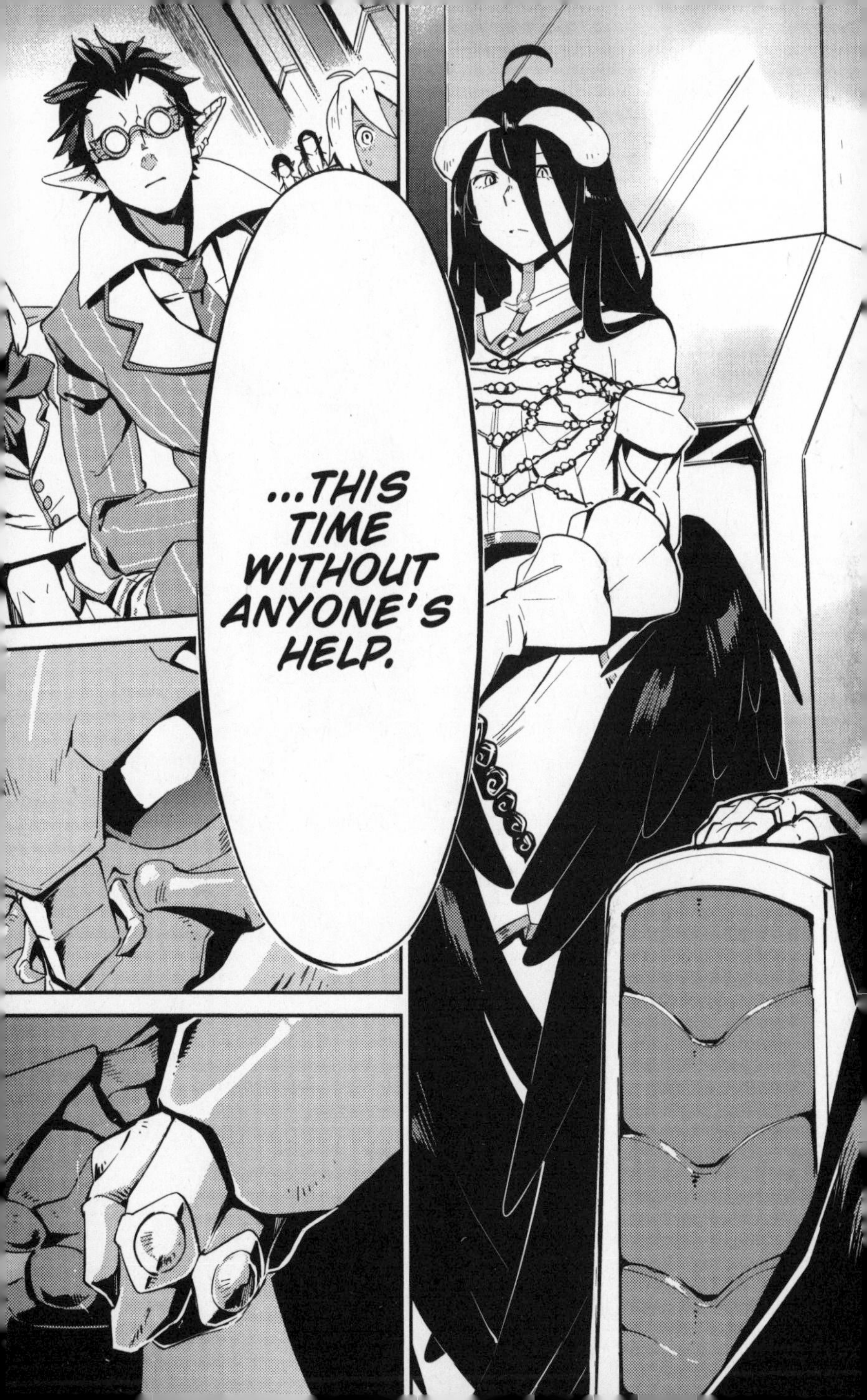
...THIS TIME WITHOUT ANYONE'S HELP.

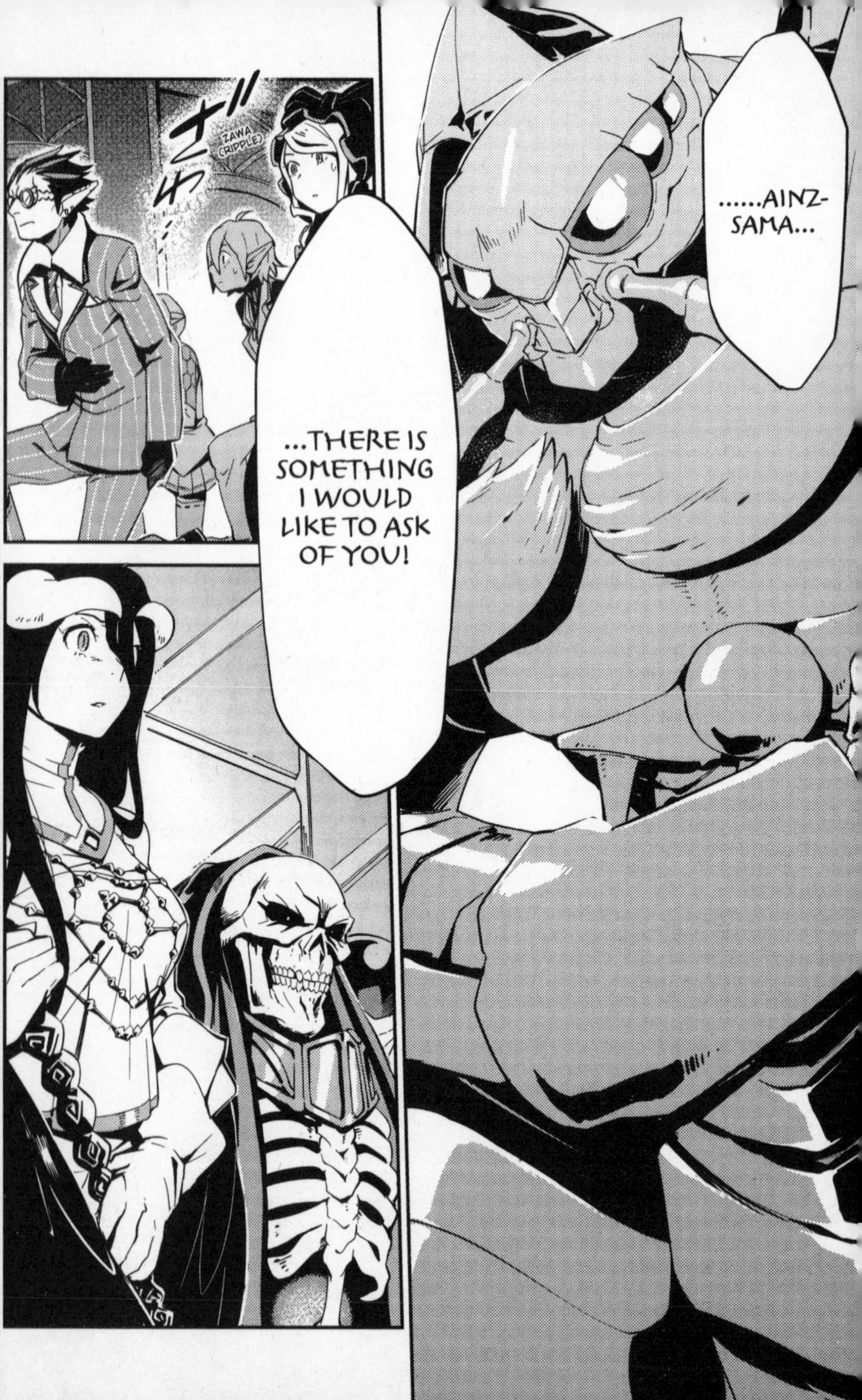
......AINZ-SAMA...
...THERE IS SOMETHING I WOULD LIKE TO ASK OF YOU!
ZAWA (RIPPLE)

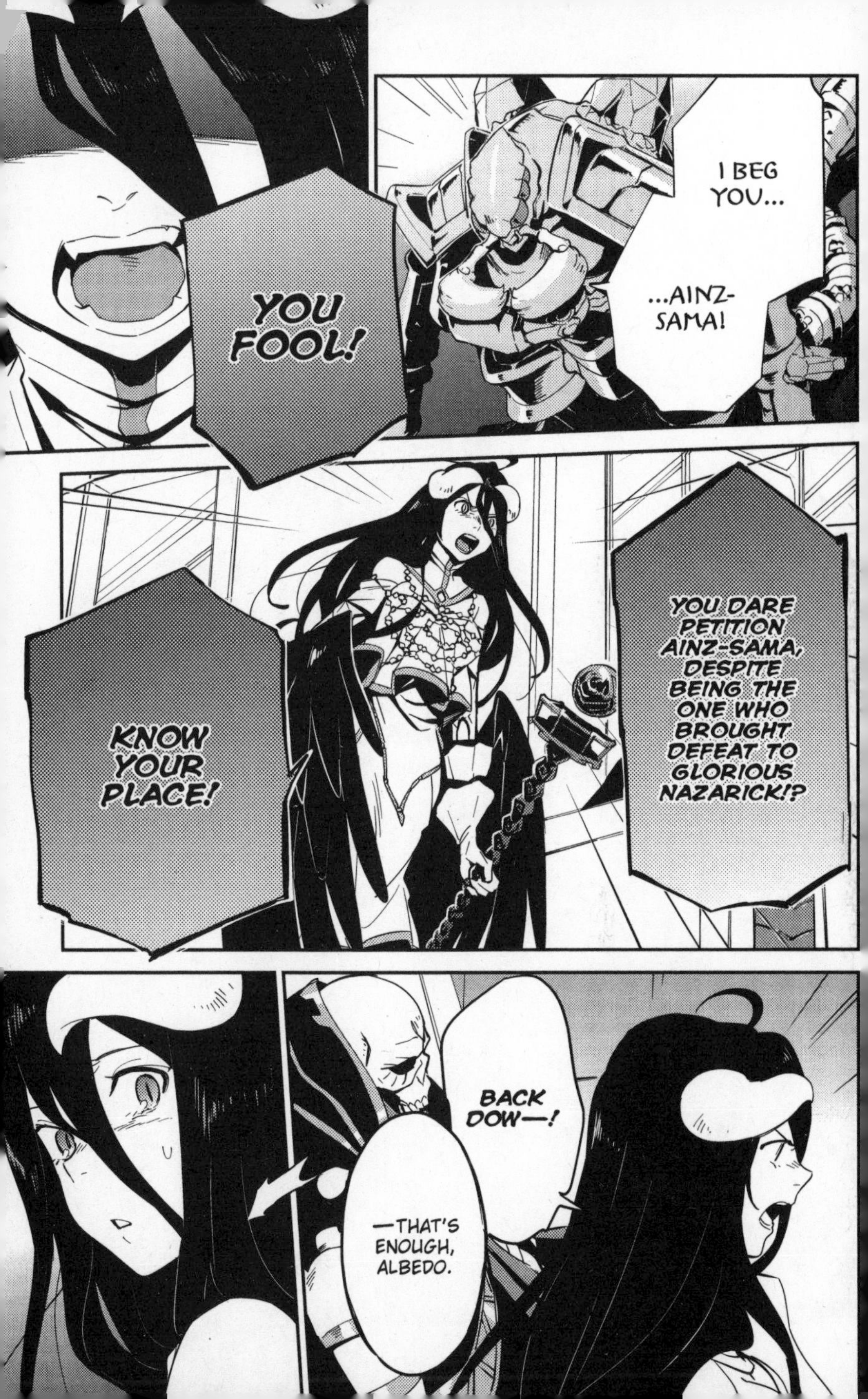
I BEG YOU...
...AINZ-SAMA!
YOU FOOL!
YOU DARE PETITION AINZ-SAMA, DESPITE BEING THE ONE WHO BROUGHT DEFEAT TO GLORIOUS NAZARICK!?
KNOW YOUR PLACE!
BACK DOW—!
—THAT'S ENOUGH, ALBEDO.

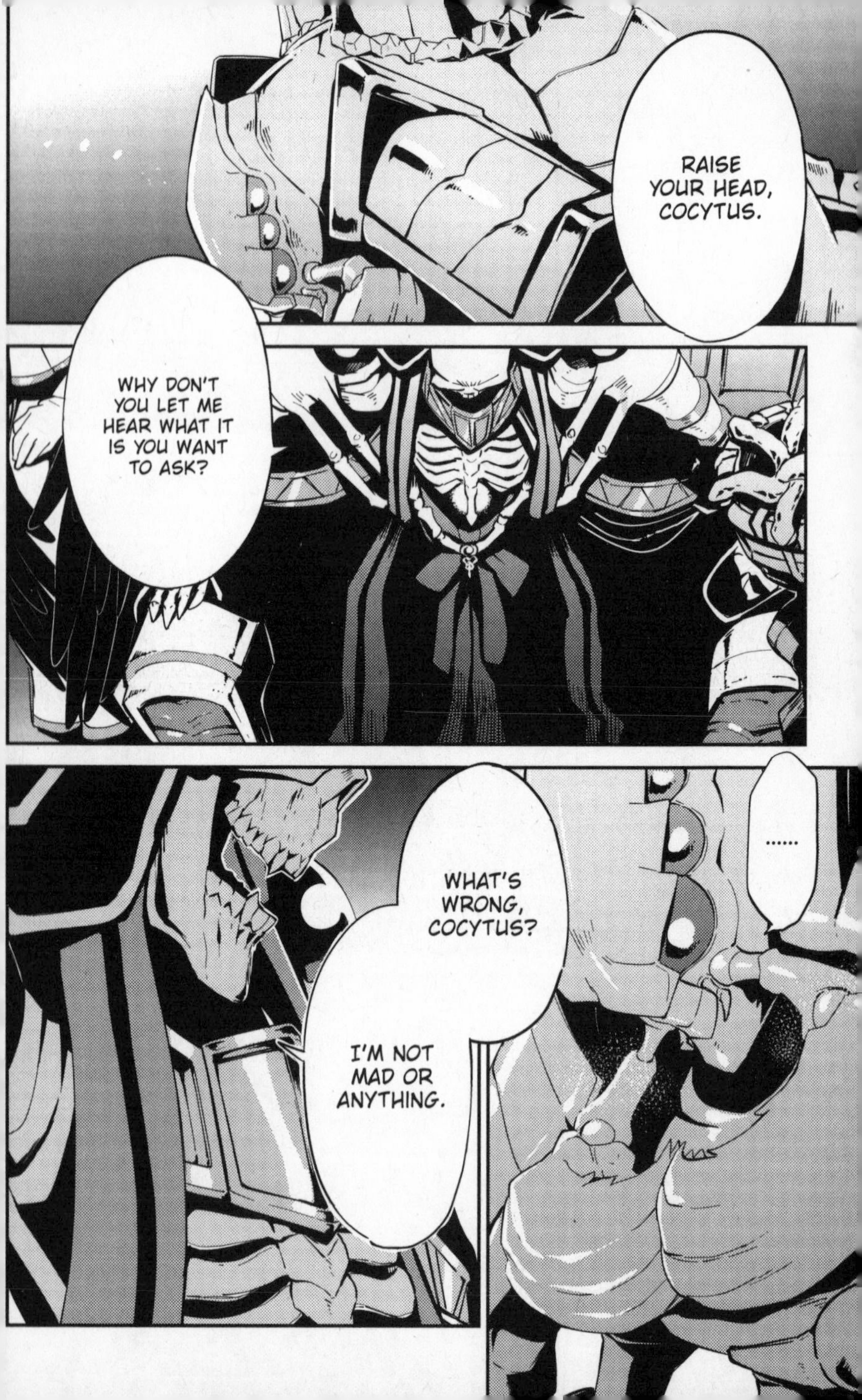
RAISE YOUR HEAD, COCYTUS.
WHY DON'T YOU LET ME HEAR WHAT IT IS YOU WANT TO ASK?
......
WHAT'S WRONG, COCYTUS?
I'M NOT MAD OR ANYTHING.

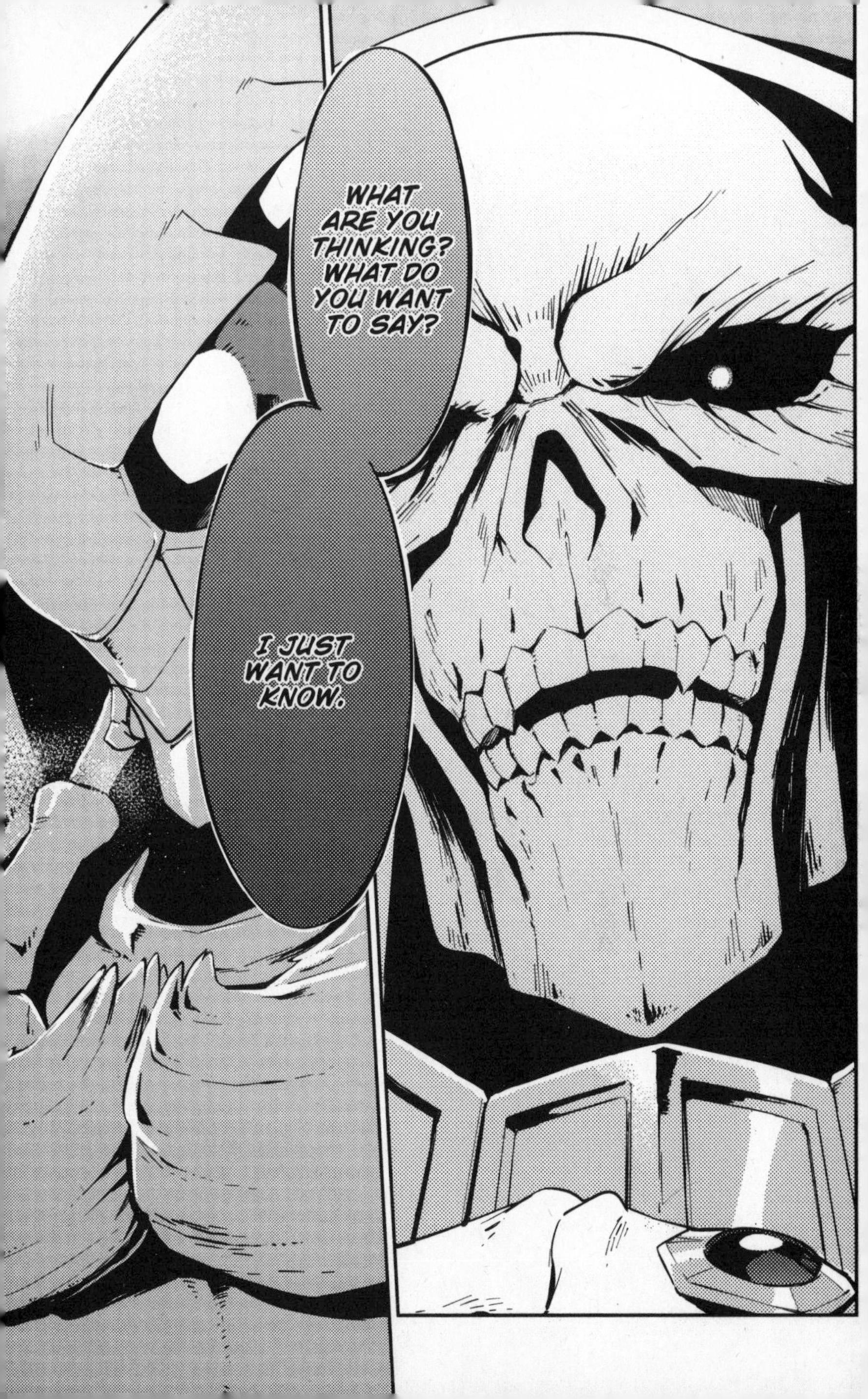
WHAT ARE YOU THINKING? WHAT DO YOU WANT TO SAY?
I JUST WANT TO KNOW.

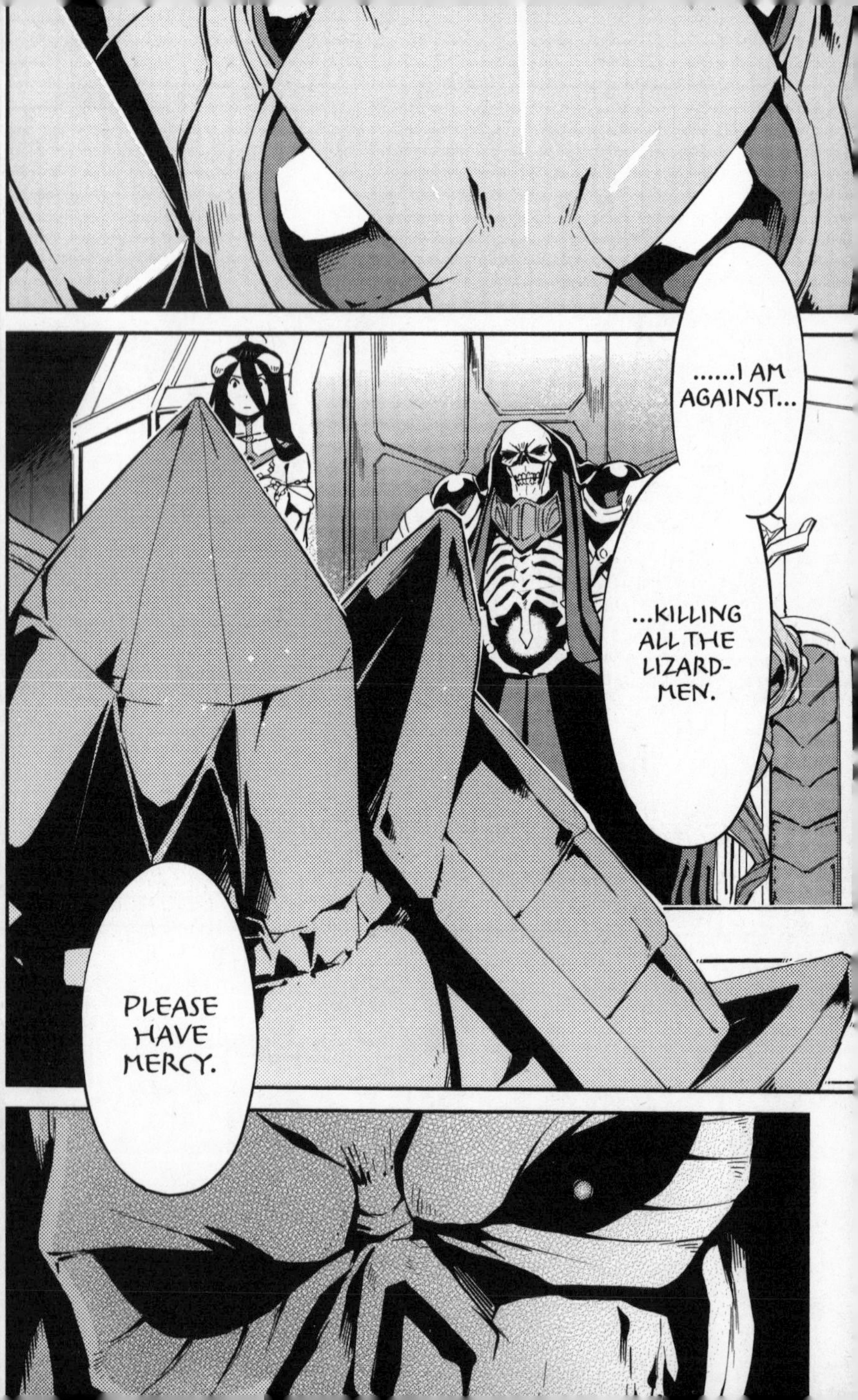
......I AM AGAINST...
...KILLING ALL THE LIZARD-MEN.
PLEASE HAVE MERCY.

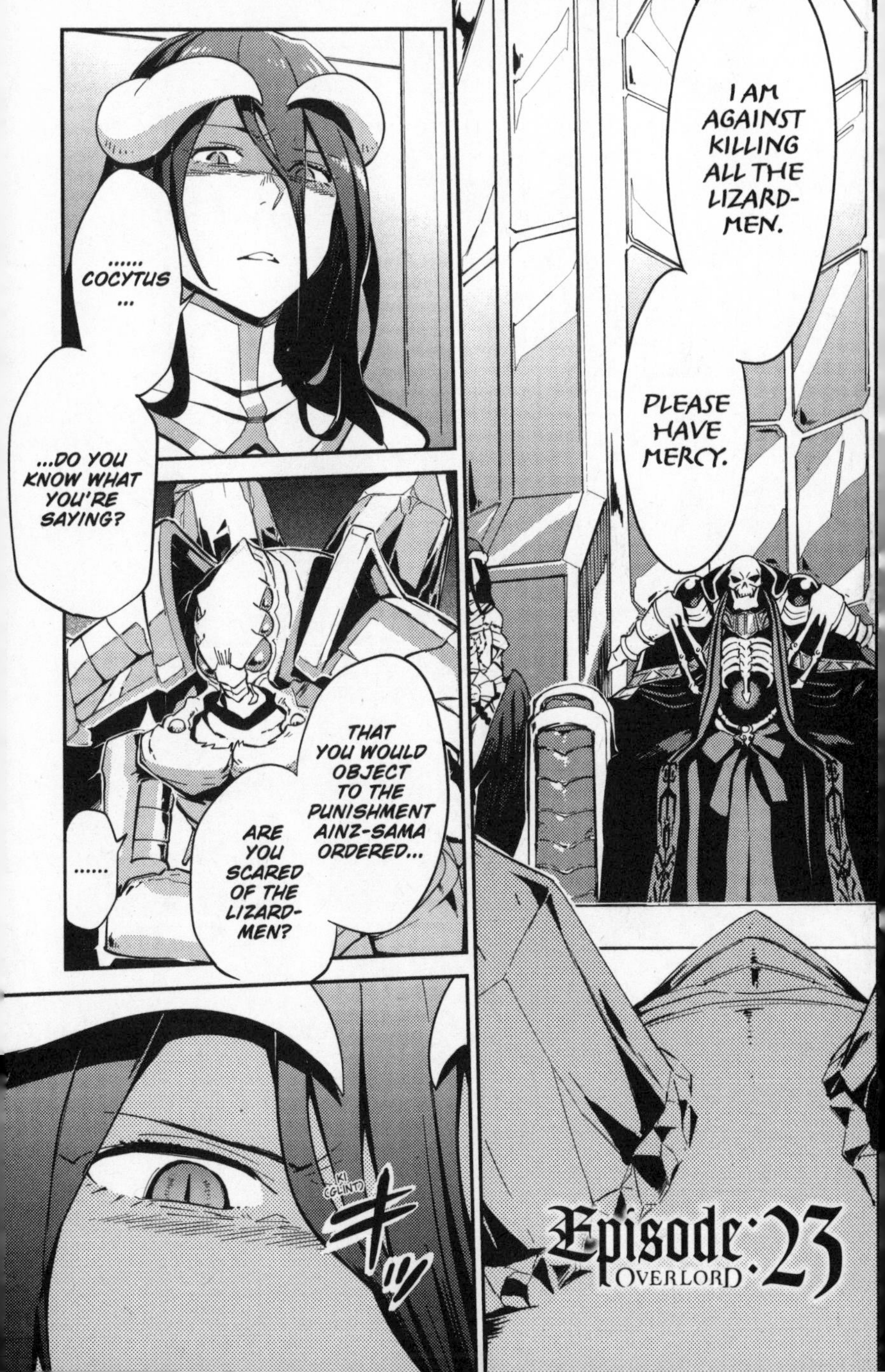
I AM AGAINST KILLING ALL THE LIZARD-MEN.
PLEASE HAVE MERCY.
...... COCYTUS ...
...DO YOU KNOW WHAT YOU'RE SAYING?
THAT YOU WOULD OBJECT TO THE PUNISHMENT AINZ-SAMA ORDERED...
ARE YOU SCARED OF THE LIZARD-MEN?
......
Episode: 23
OVERLORD
KI (GLINT)

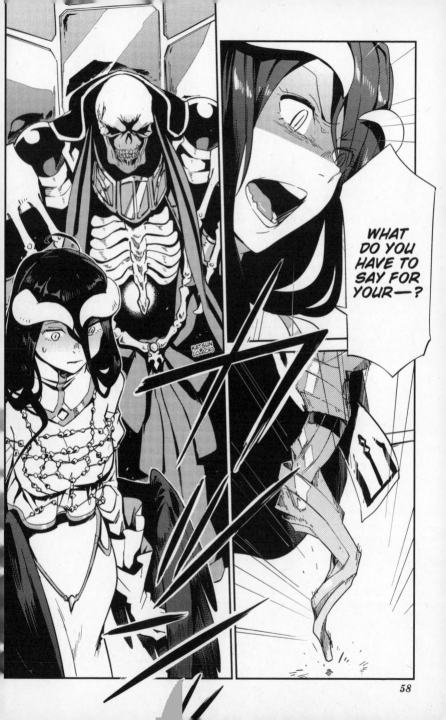

WHAT DO YOU HAVE TO SAY FOR YOUR—?

KATSUN (CLACK)

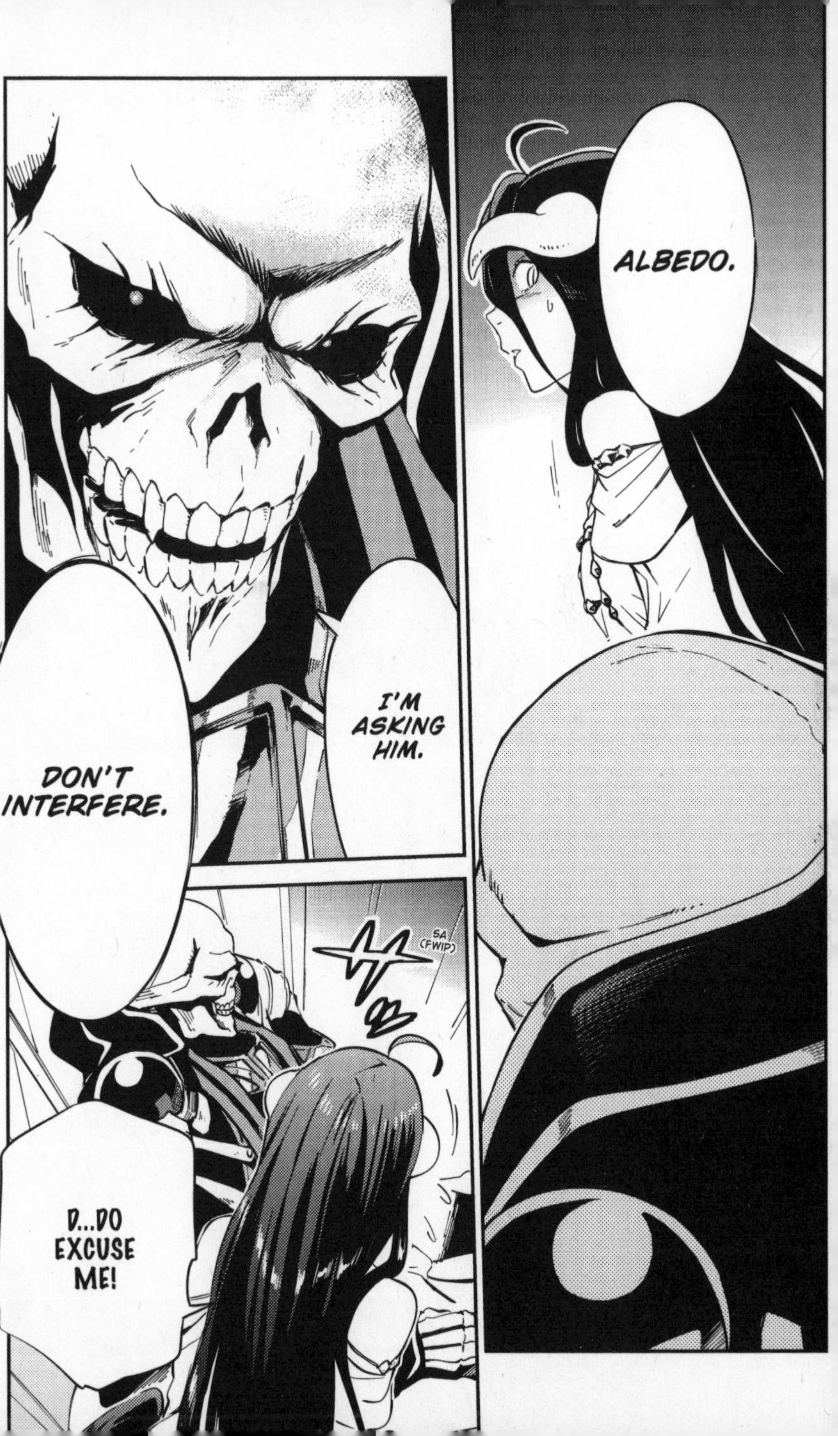
ALBEDO.
I'M ASKING HIM.
DON'T INTERFERE.
SA (FWIP)
D...DO EXCUSE ME!

COCYTUS.

YOU MUST HAVE A REASON FOR THIS REQUEST.

MY LORD!

SOME BENEFIT TO THE GREAT TOMB OF NAZARICK?

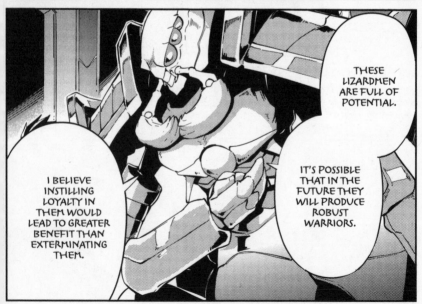

THESE LIZARDMEN ARE FULL OF POTENTIAL.

IT'S POSSIBLE THAT IN THE FUTURE THEY WILL PRODUCE ROBUST WARRIORS.

I BELIEVE INSTILLING LOYALTY IN THEM WOULD LEAD TO GREATER BENEFIT THAN EXTERMINATING THEM.

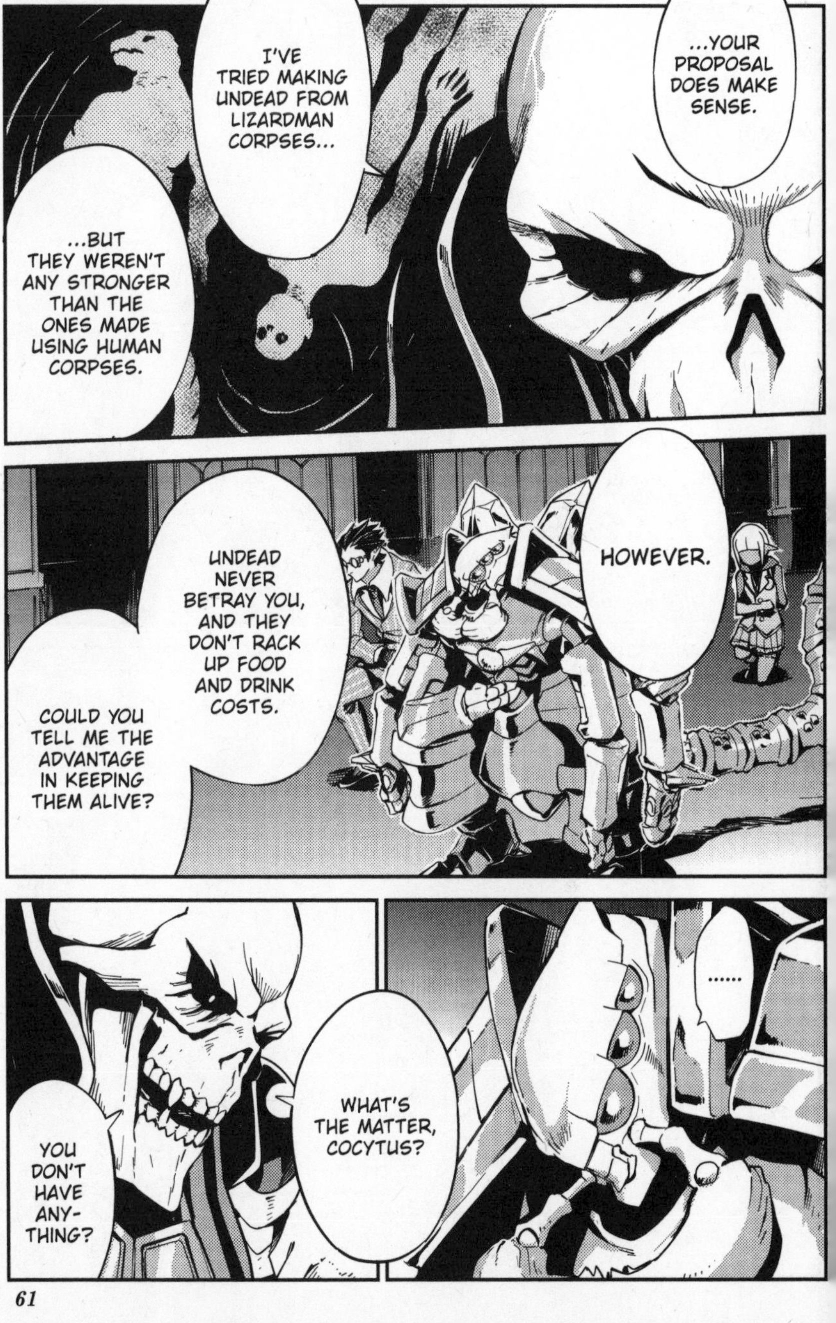
...YOUR PROPOSAL DOES MAKE SENSE.
I'VE TRIED MAKING UNDEAD FROM LIZARDMAN CORPSES...
...BUT THEY WEREN'T ANY STRONGER THAN THE ONES MADE USING HUMAN CORPSES.
HOWEVER.
UNDEAD NEVER BETRAY YOU, AND THEY DON'T RACK UP FOOD AND DRINK COSTS.
COULD YOU TELL ME THE ADVANTAGE IN KEEPING THEM ALIVE?
......
WHAT'S THE MATTER, COCYTUS?
YOU DON'T HAVE ANY-THING?

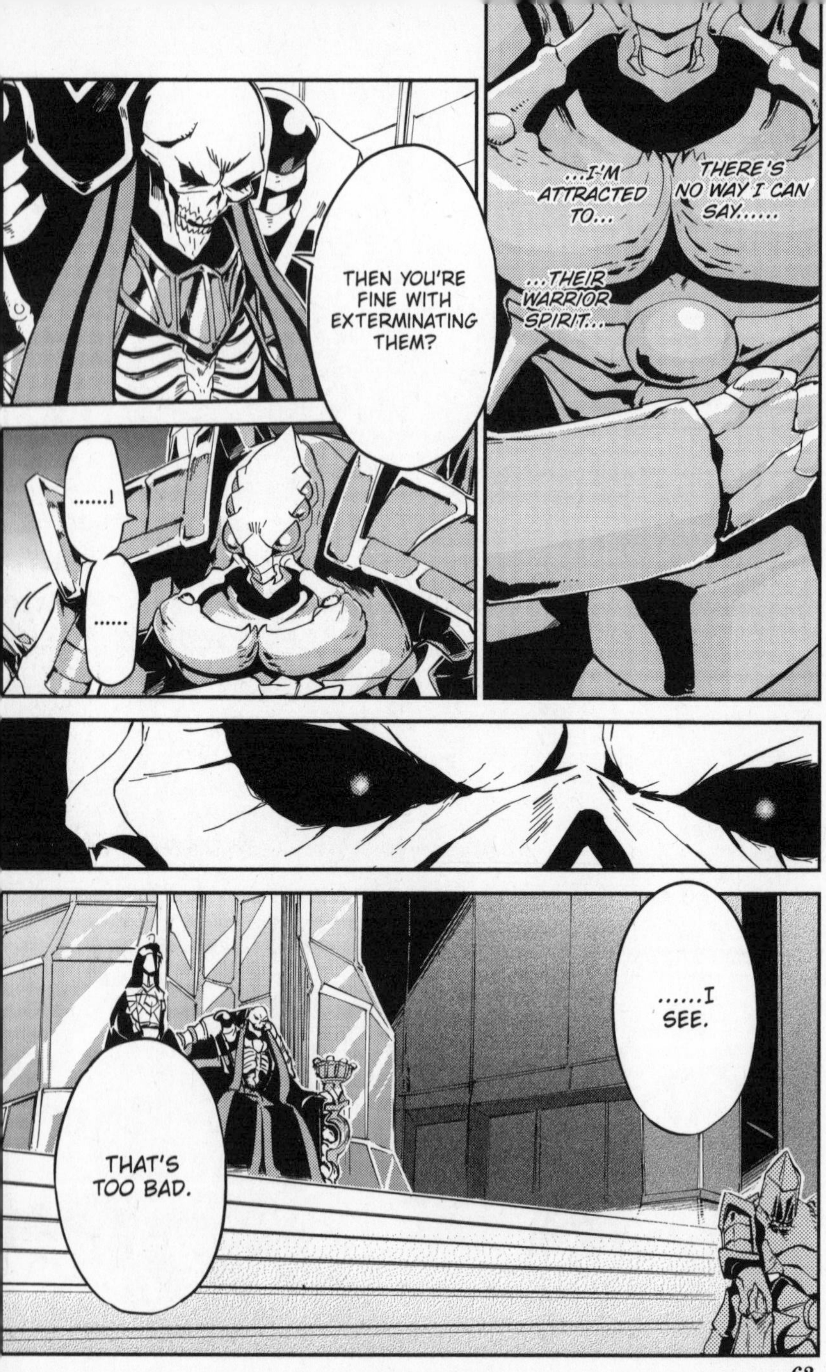
THERE'S NO WAY I CAN SAY......
...I'M ATTRACTED TO...
...THEIR WARRIOR SPIRIT...
THEN YOU'RE FINE WITH EXTERMINATING THEM?
......!
......
......I SEE.
THAT'S TOO BAD.

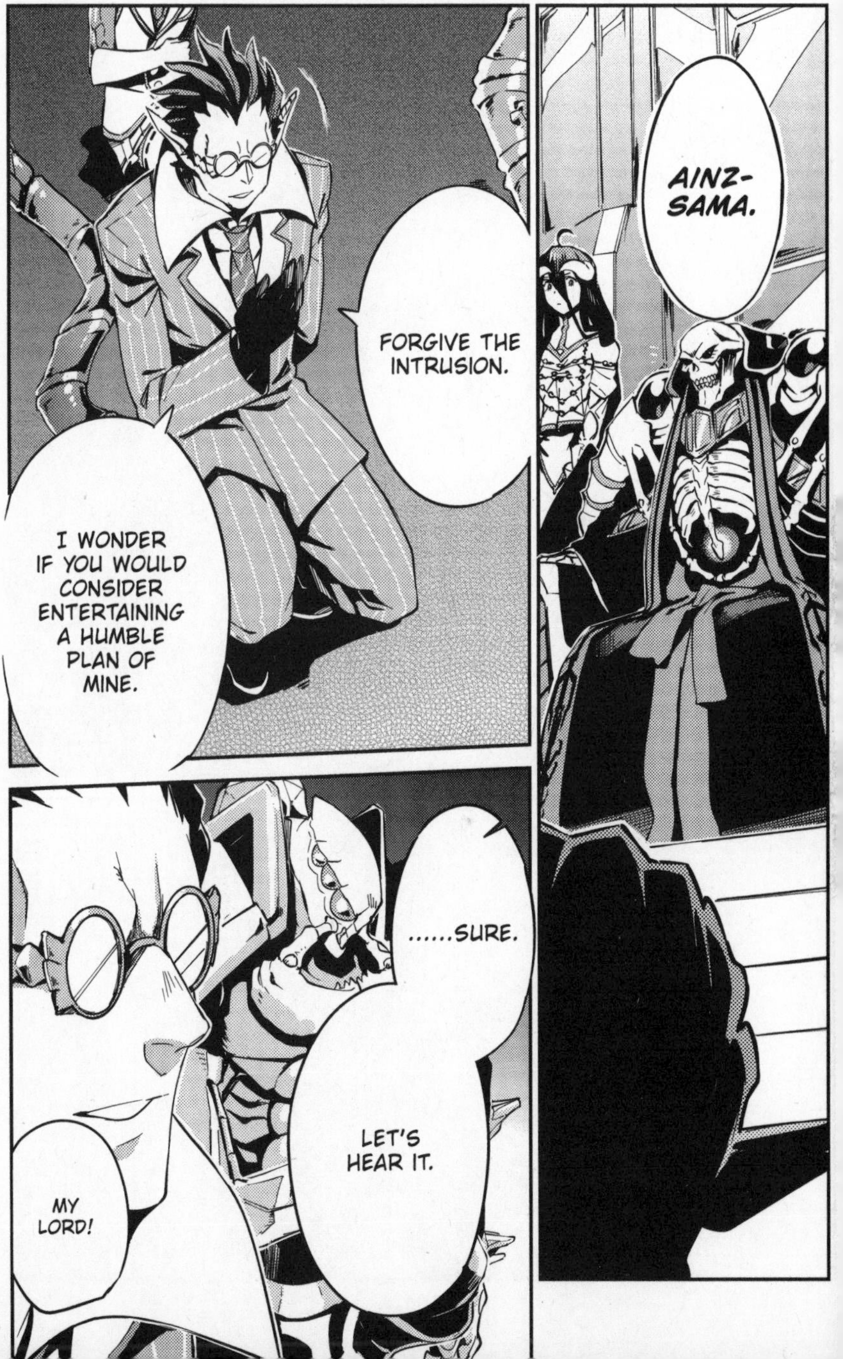
AINZ-SAMA.
FORGIVE THE INTRUSION.
I WONDER IF YOU WOULD CONSIDER ENTERTAINING A HUMBLE PLAN OF MINE.
......SURE.
LET'S HEAR IT.
MY LORD!

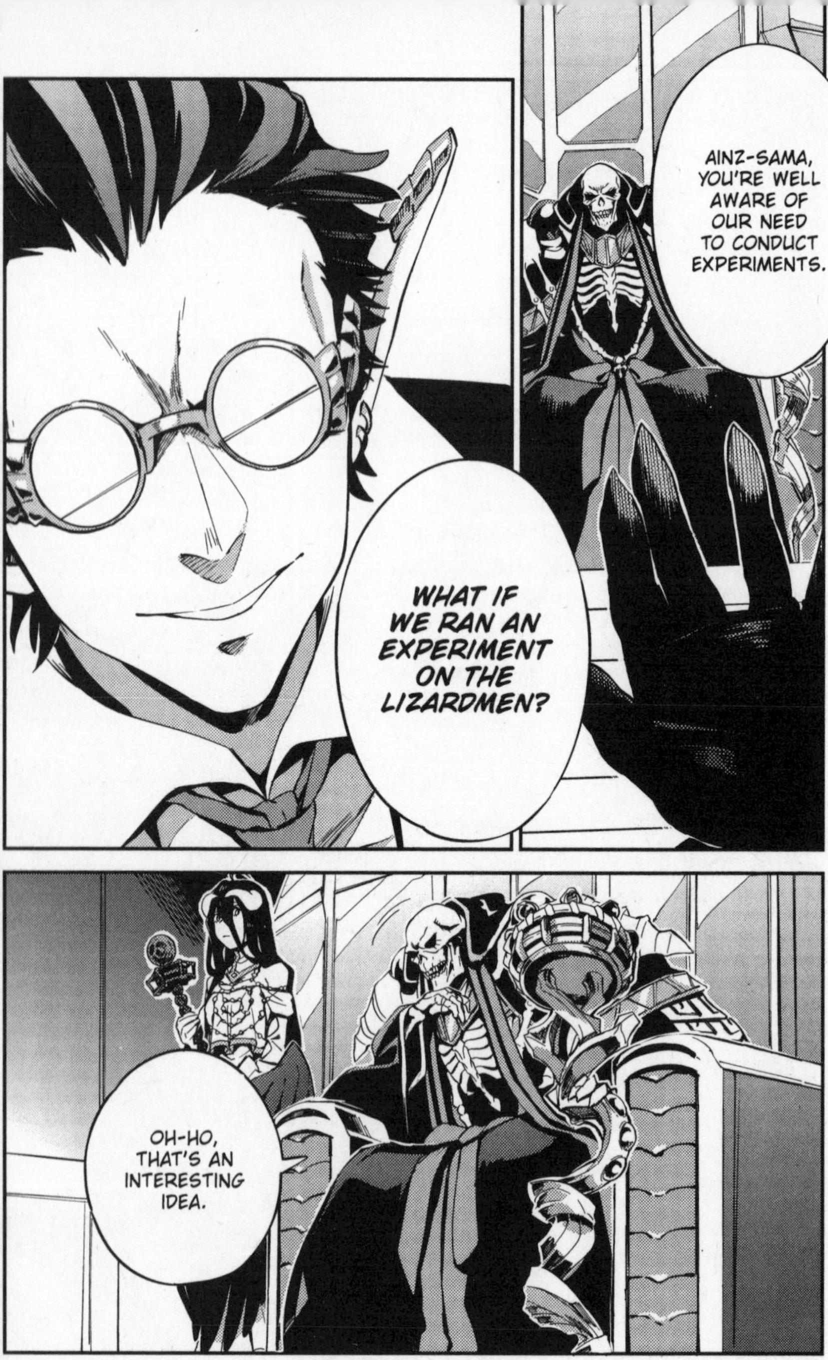
AINZ-SAMA, YOU'RE WELL AWARE OF OUR NEED TO CONDUCT EXPERIMENTS.
WHAT IF WE RAN AN EXPERIMENT ON THE LIZARDMEN?
OH-HO, THAT'S AN INTERESTING IDEA.

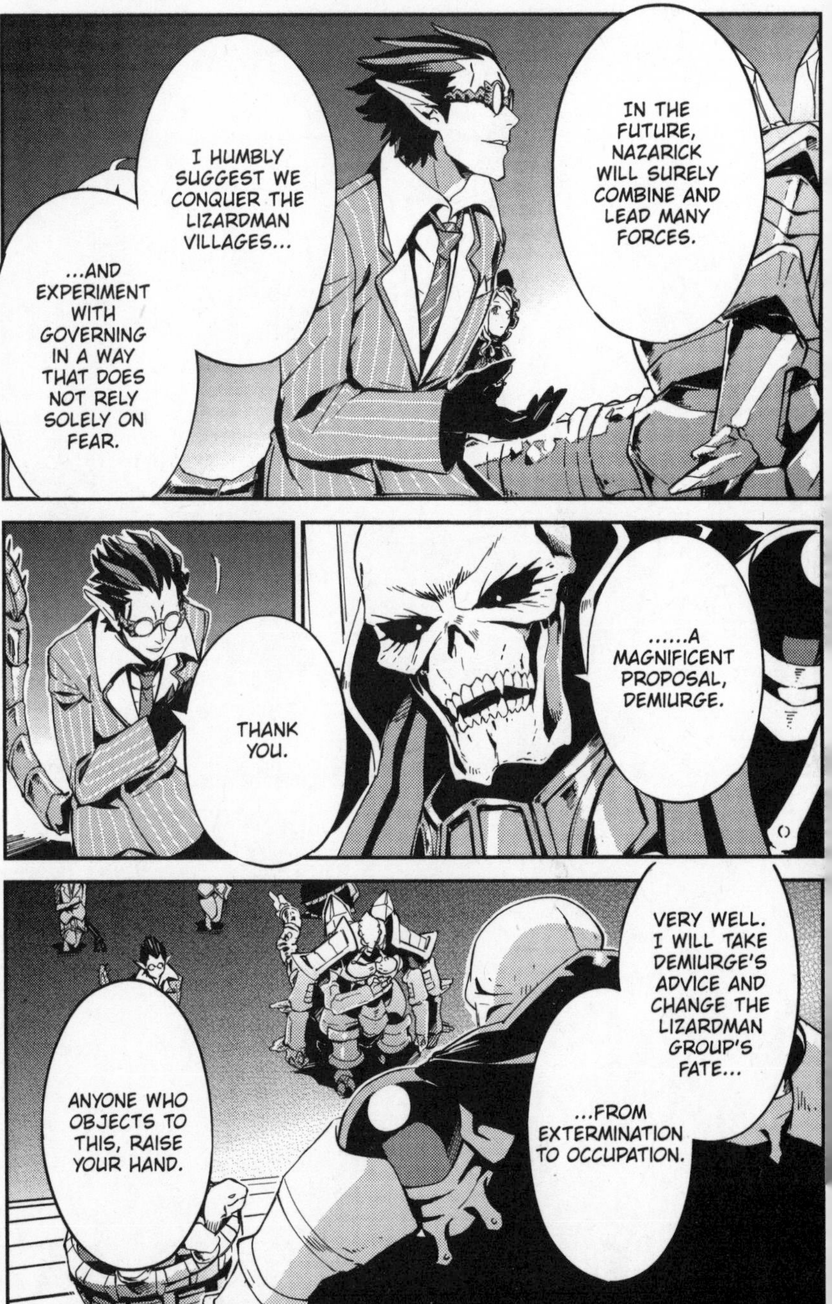
IN THE FUTURE, NAZARICK WILL SURELY COMBINE AND LEAD MANY FORCES.
I HUMBLY SUGGEST WE CONQUER THE LIZARDMAN VILLAGES...
...AND EXPERIMENT WITH GOVERNING IN A WAY THAT DOES NOT RELY SOLELY ON FEAR.
......A MAGNIFICENT PROPOSAL, DEMIURGE.
THANK YOU.
VERY WELL. I WILL TAKE DEMIURGE'S ADVICE AND CHANGE THE LIZARDMAN GROUP'S FATE...
...FROM EXTERMINATION TO OCCUPATION.
ANYONE WHO OBJECTS TO THIS, RAISE YOUR HAND.

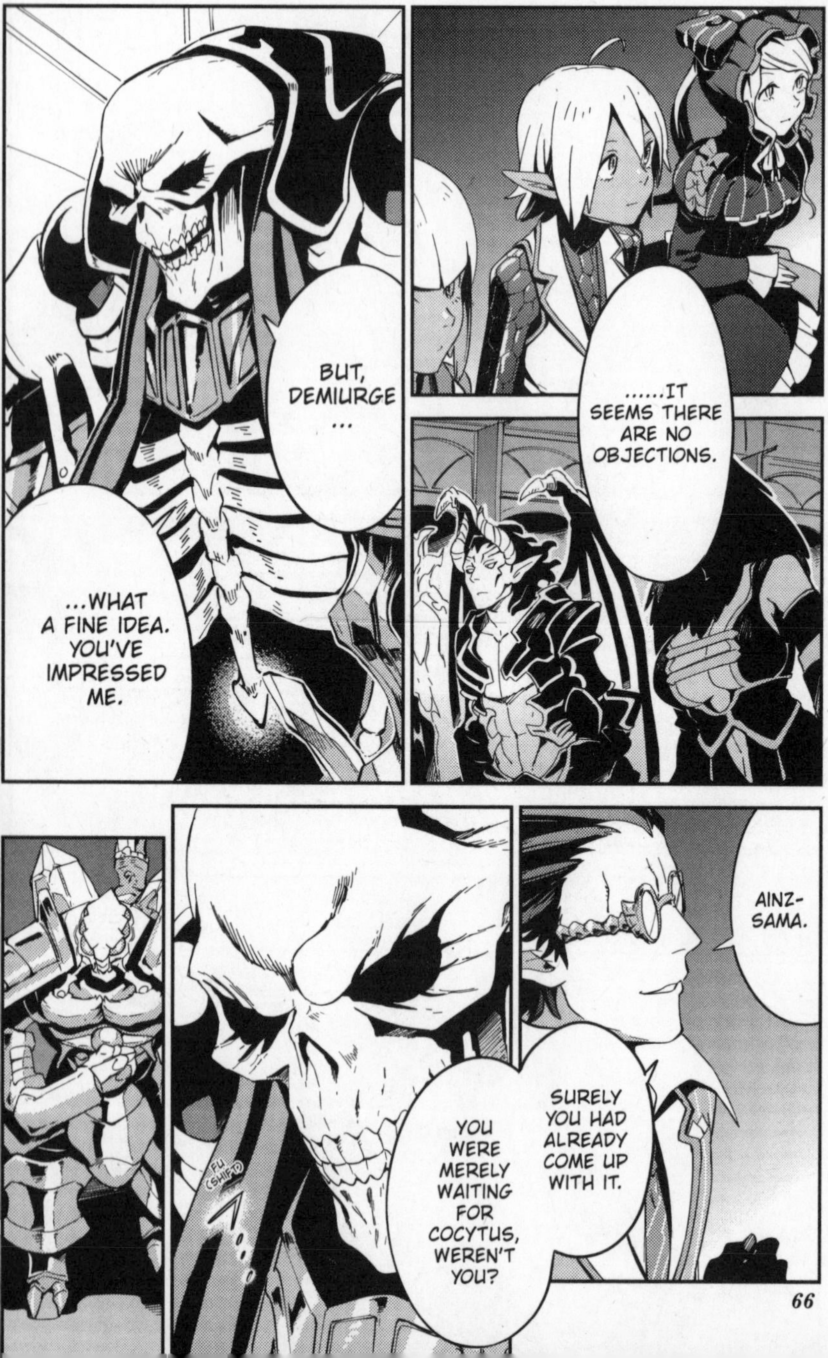
......IT SEEMS THERE ARE NO OBJECTIONS.
BUT, DEMIURGE ...
...WHAT A FINE IDEA. YOU'VE IMPRESSED ME.
AINZ-SAMA.
SURELY YOU HAD ALREADY COME UP WITH IT.
YOU WERE MERELY WAITING FOR COCYTUS, WEREN'T YOU?
FU (SHIFT)

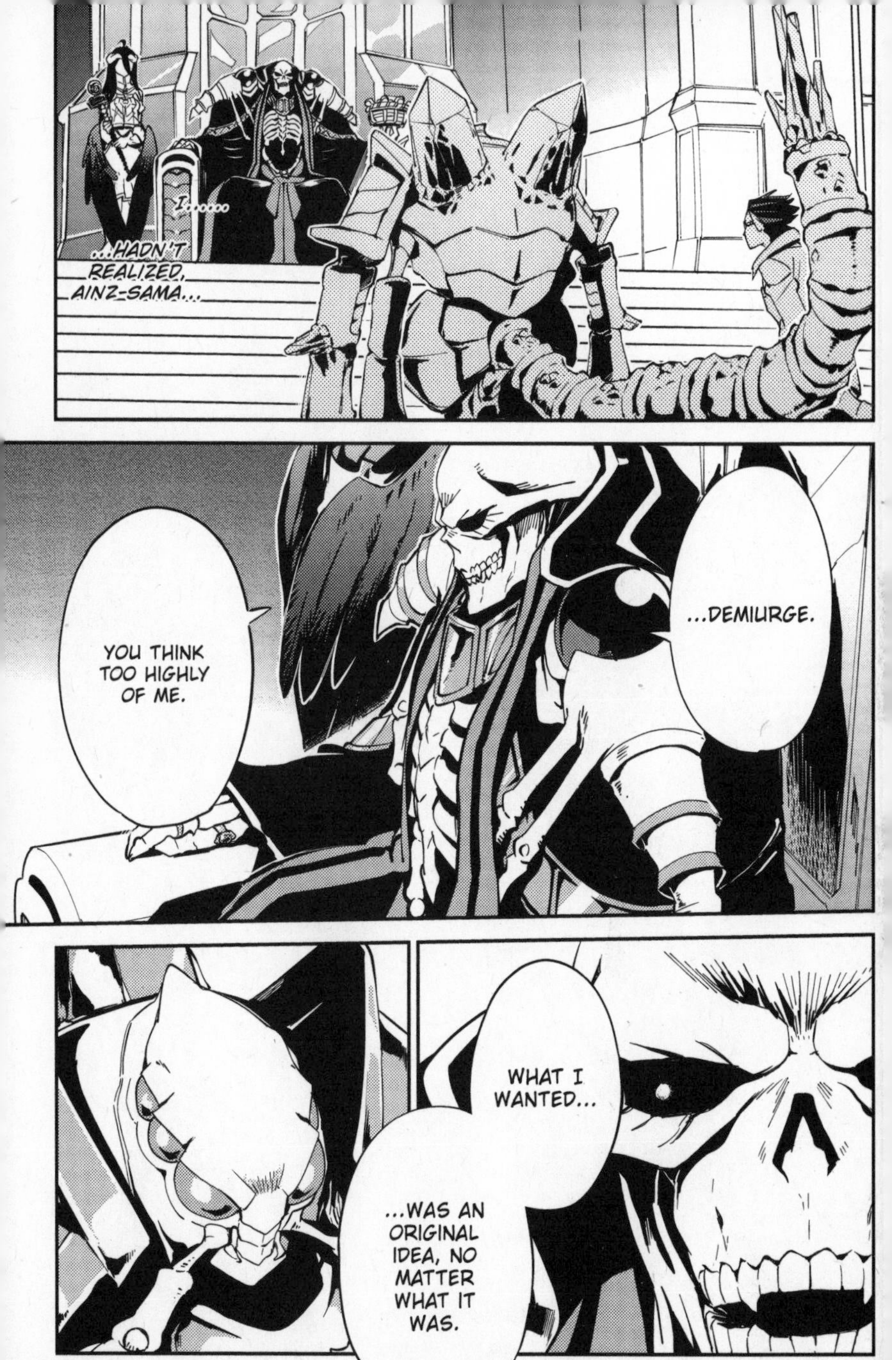
I......
...HADN'T REALIZED, AINZ-SAMA...
...DEMIURGE.
YOU THINK TOO HIGHLY OF ME.
WHAT I WANTED...
...WAS AN ORIGINAL IDEA, NO MATTER WHAT IT WAS.

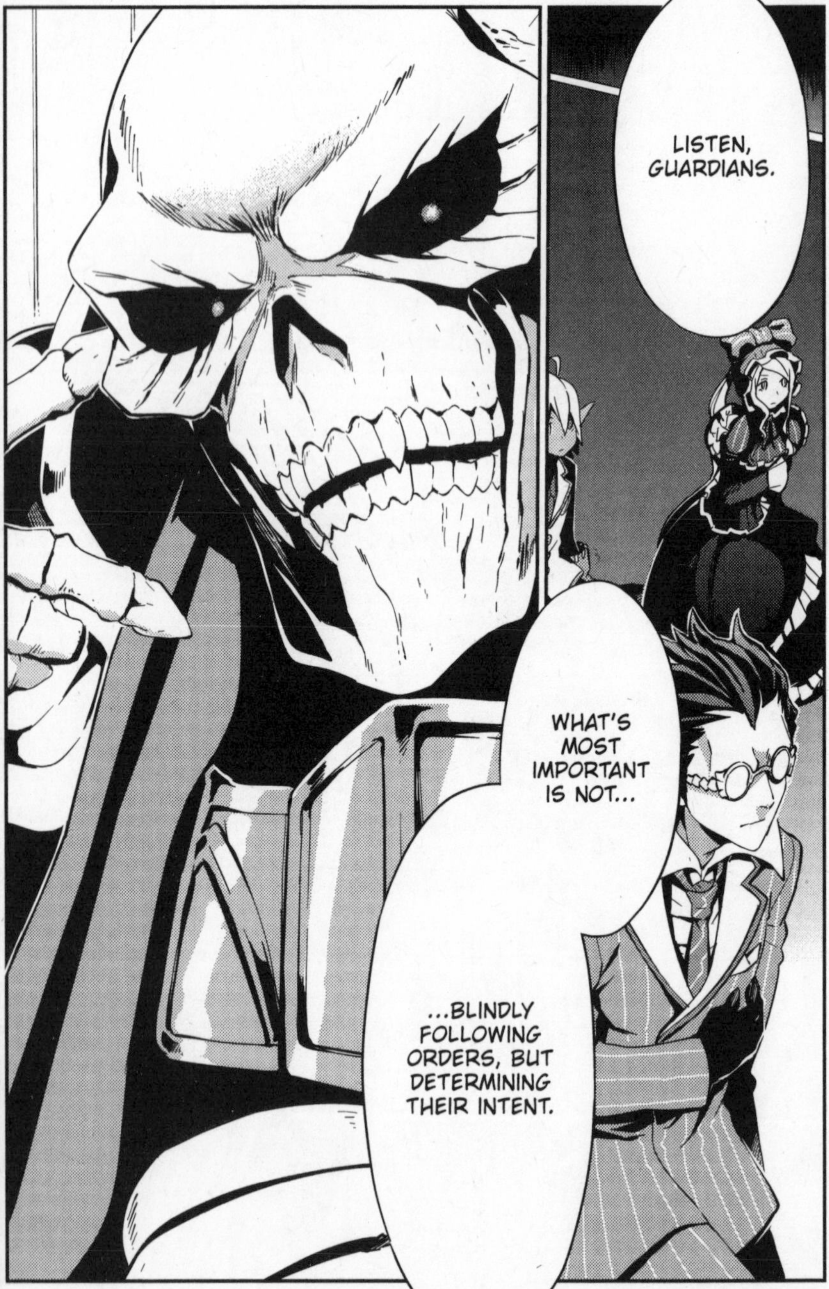
LISTEN, GUARDIANS.
WHAT'S MOST IMPORTANT IS NOT...
...BLINDLY FOLLOWING ORDERS, BUT DETERMINING THEIR INTENT.

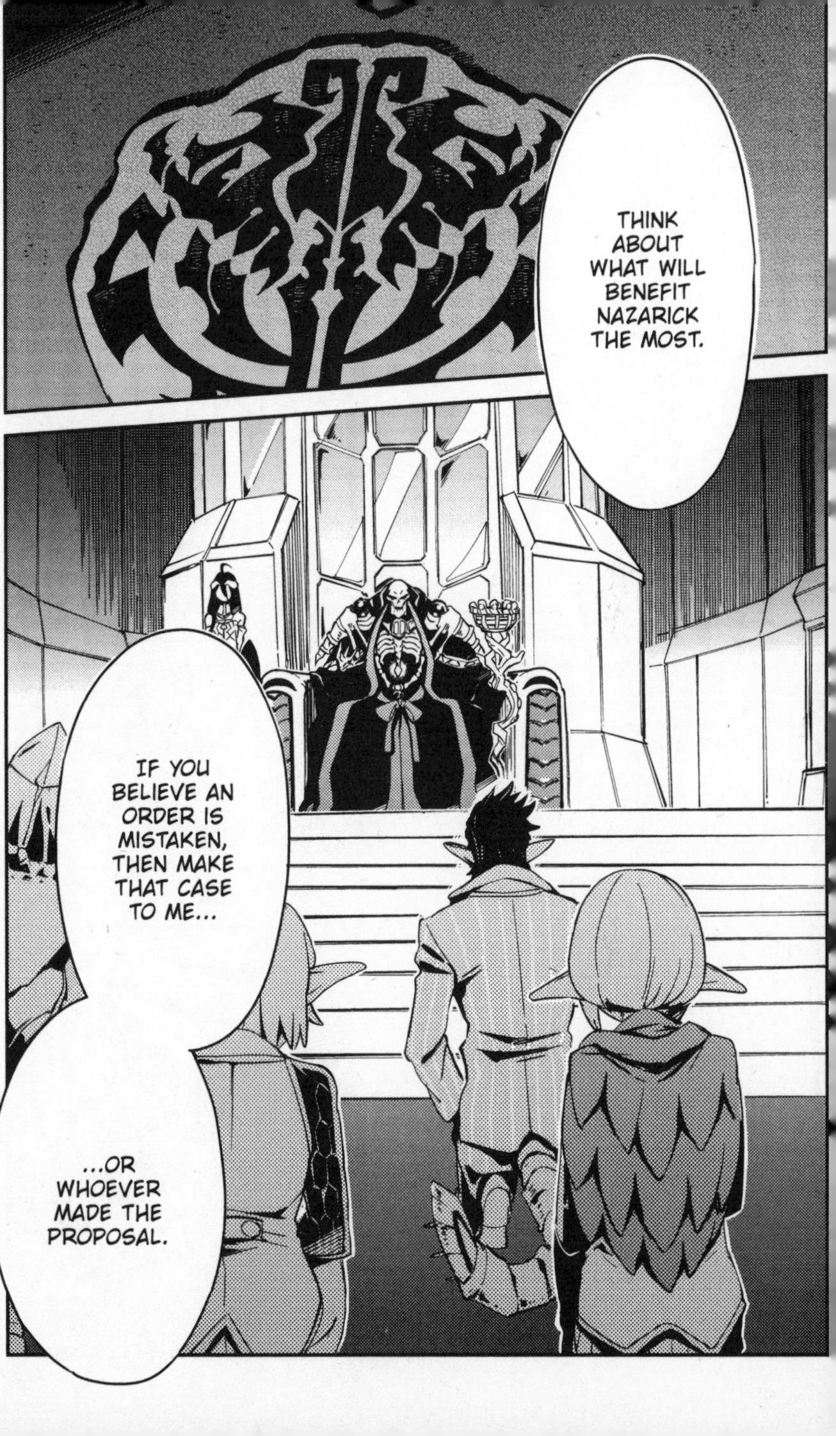
THINK ABOUT WHAT WILL BENEFIT NAZARICK THE MOST.
IF YOU BELIEVE AN ORDER IS MISTAKEN, THEN MAKE THAT CASE TO ME...
...OR WHOEVER MADE THE PROPOSAL.

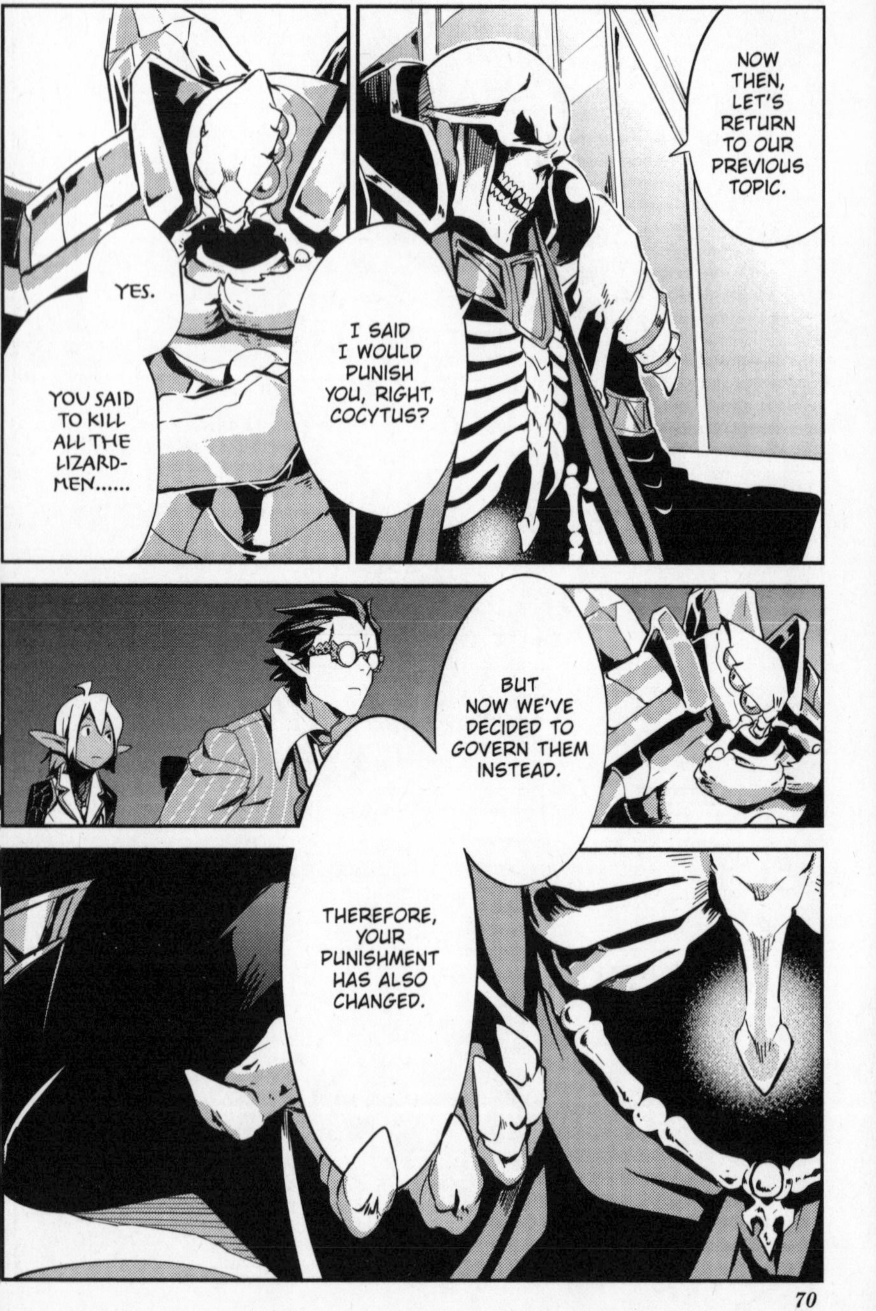
NOW THEN, LET'S RETURN TO OUR PREVIOUS TOPIC.
I SAID I WOULD PUNISH YOU, RIGHT, COCYTUS?
YES.
YOU SAID TO KILL ALL THE LIZARD-MEN......
BUT NOW WE'VE DECIDED TO GOVERN THEM INSTEAD.
THEREFORE, YOUR PUNISHMENT HAS ALSO CHANGED.

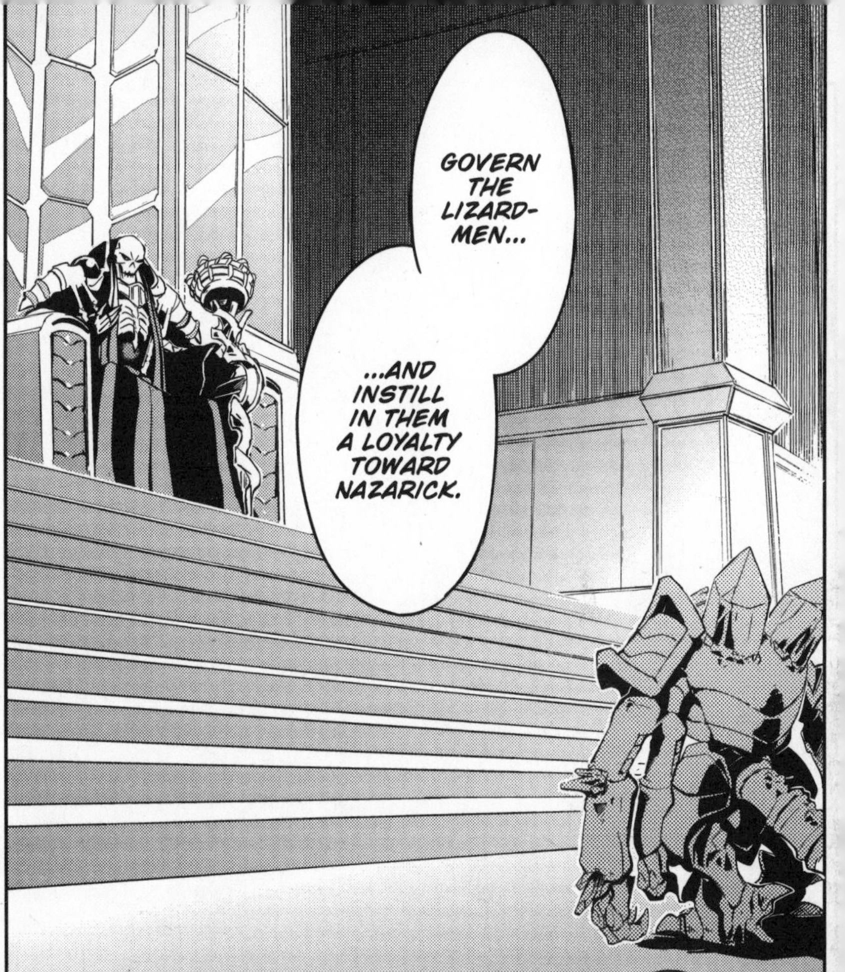
GOVERN THE LIZARD-MEN...
...AND INSTILL IN THEM A LOYALTY TOWARD NAZARICK.
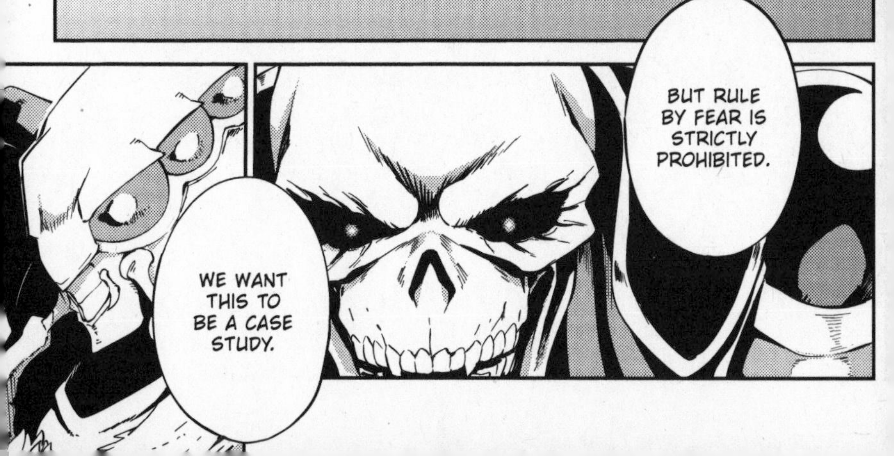
BUT RULE BY FEAR IS STRICTLY PROHIBITED.
WE WANT THIS TO BE A CASE STUDY.

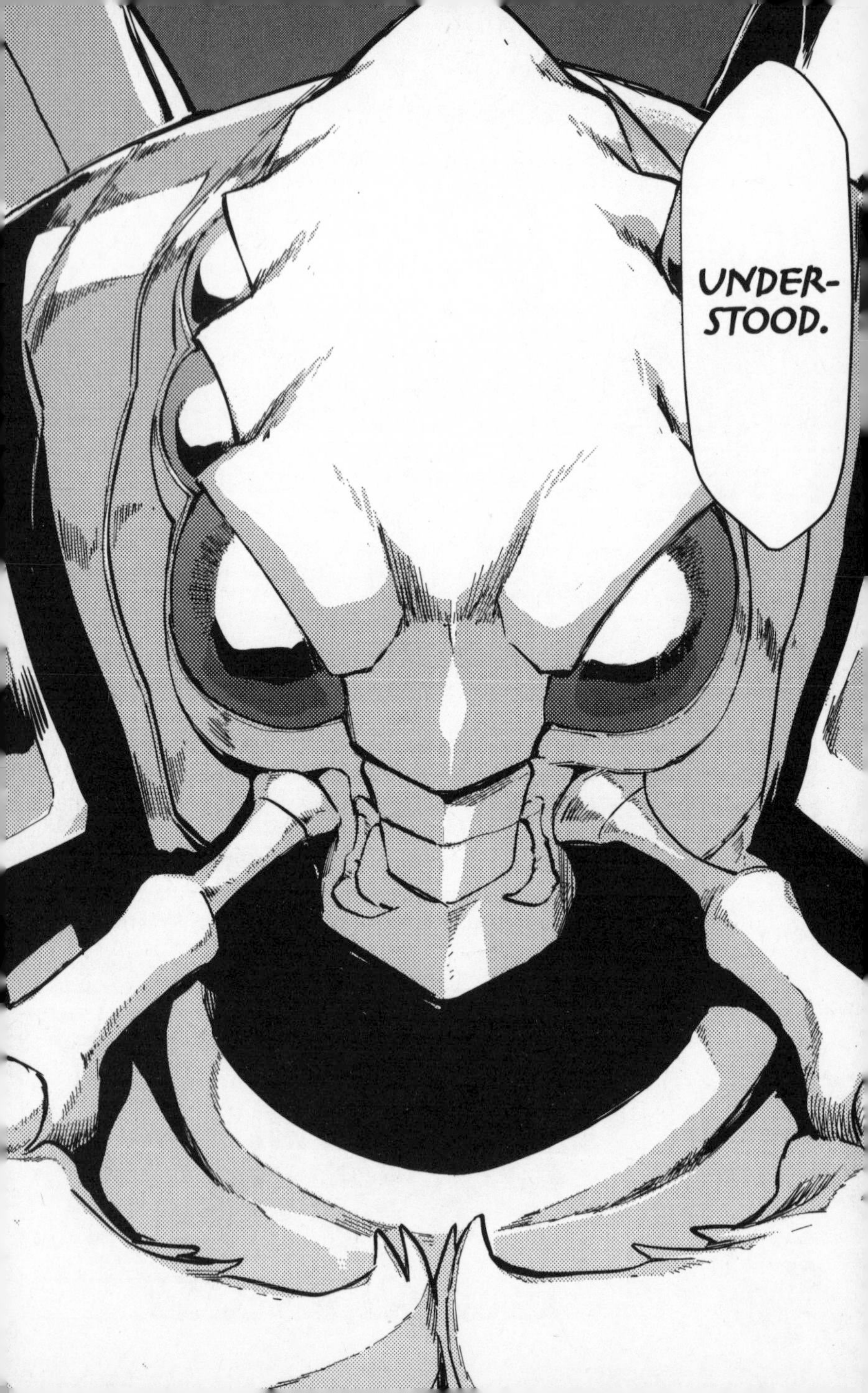
UNDER-
STOOD.

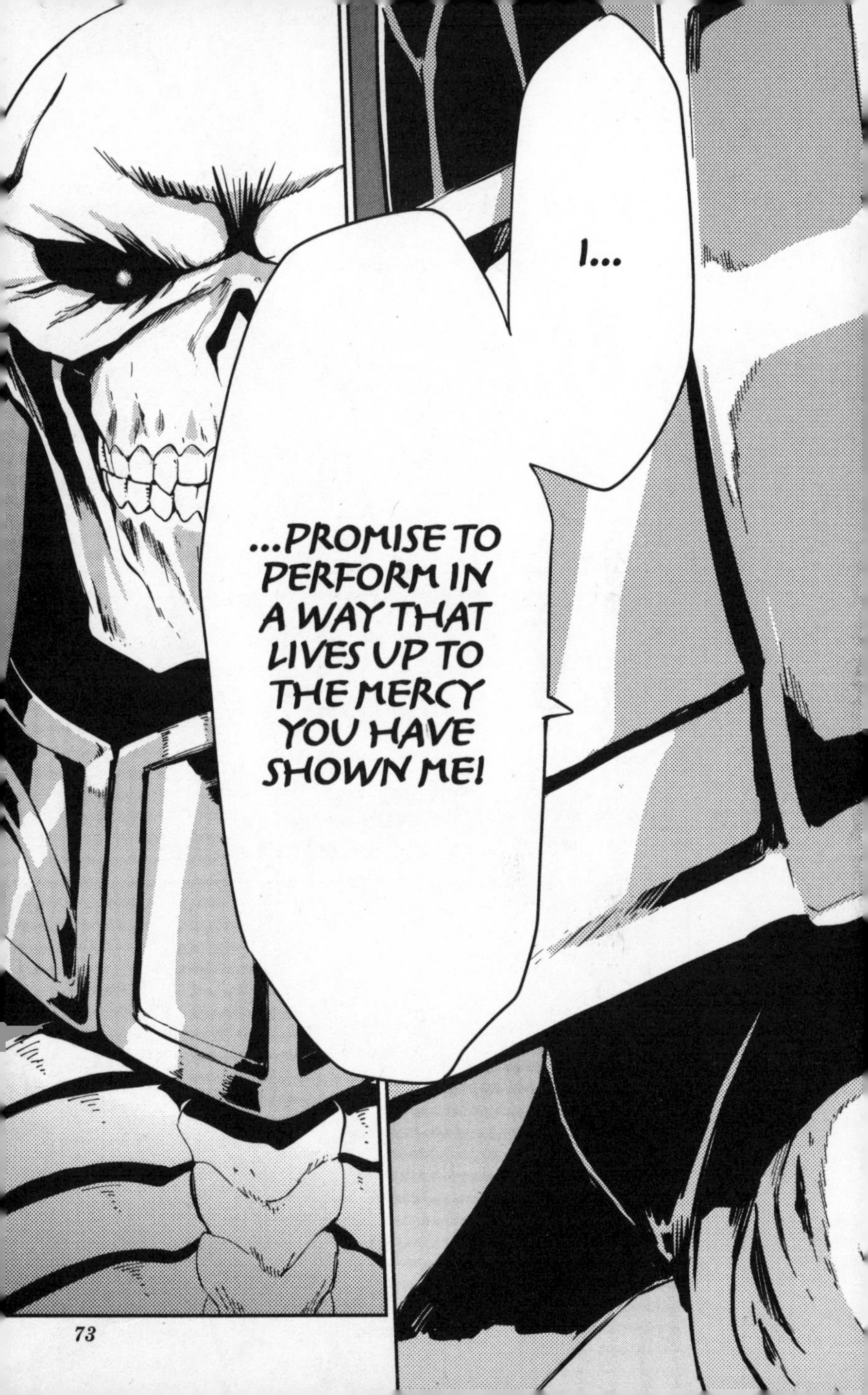
I...
...PROMISE TO PERFORM IN A WAY THAT LIVES UP TO THE MERCY YOU HAVE SHOWN ME!

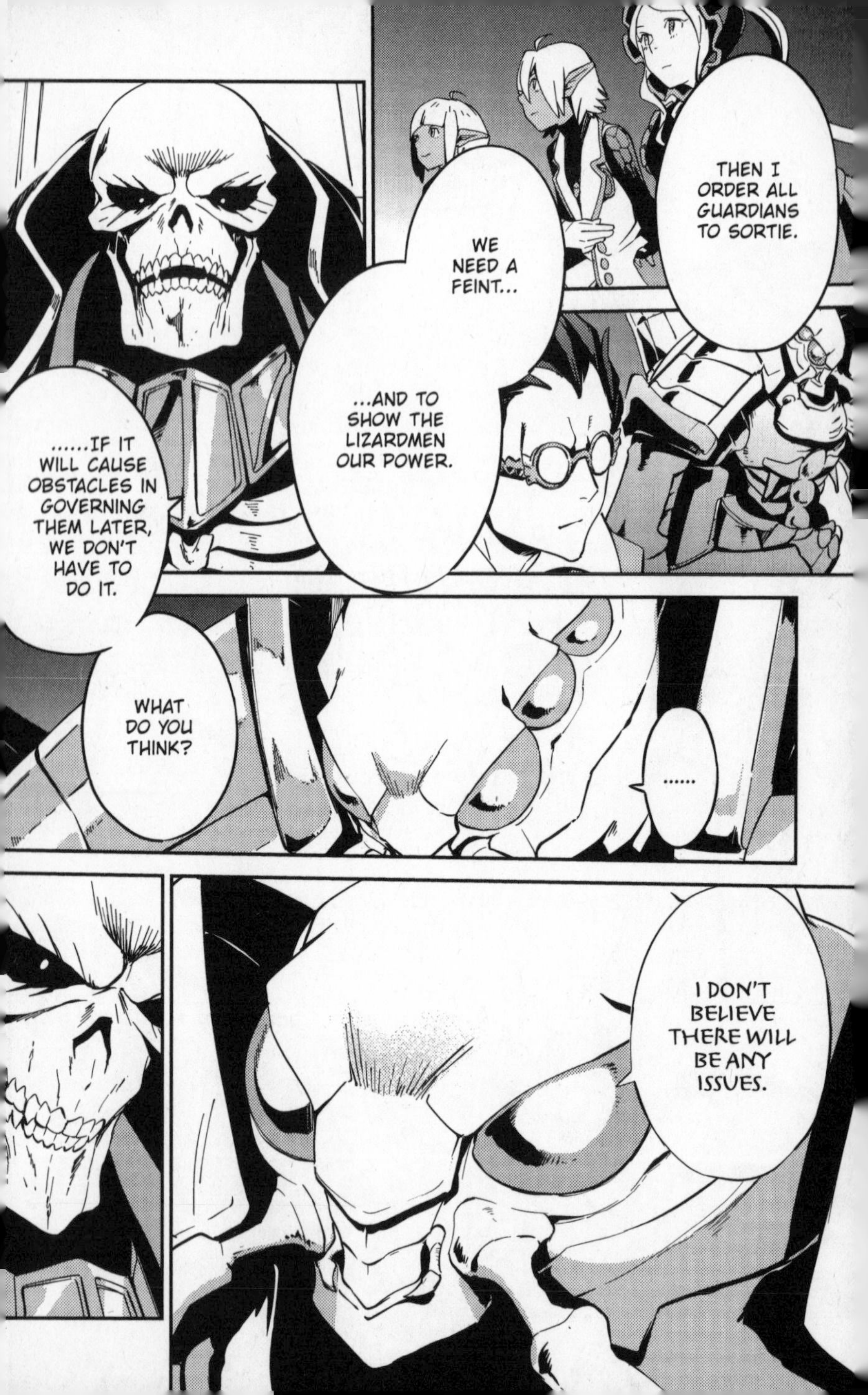
THEN I ORDER ALL GUARDIANS TO SORTIE.
WE NEED A FEINT...
...AND TO SHOW THE LIZARDMEN OUR POWER.
......IF IT WILL CAUSE OBSTACLES IN GOVERNING THEM LATER, WE DON'T HAVE TO DO IT.
WHAT DO YOU THINK?
......
I DON'T BELIEVE THERE WILL BE ANY ISSUES.

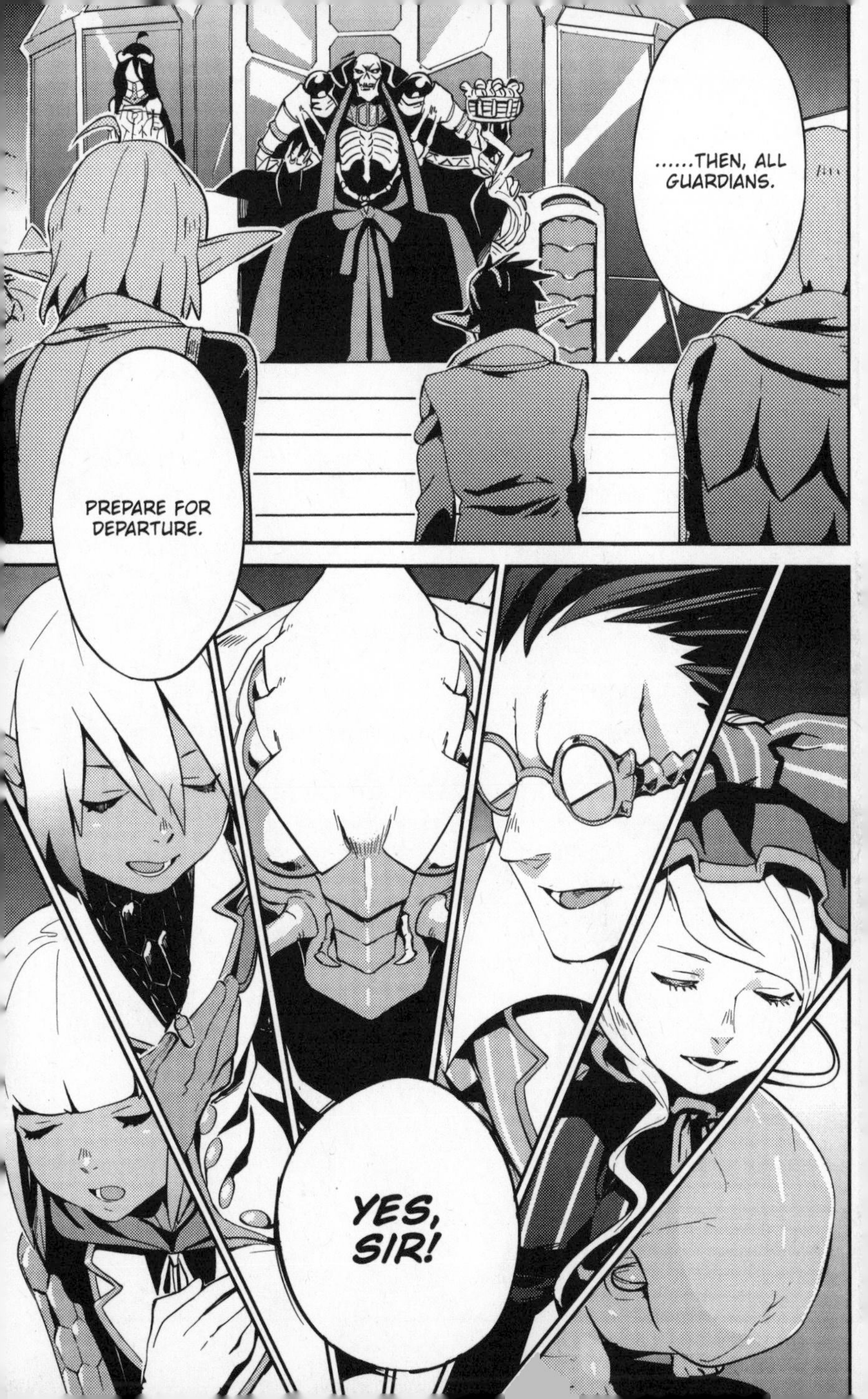
......THEN, ALL GUARDIANS.
PREPARE FOR DEPARTURE.
YES, SIR!

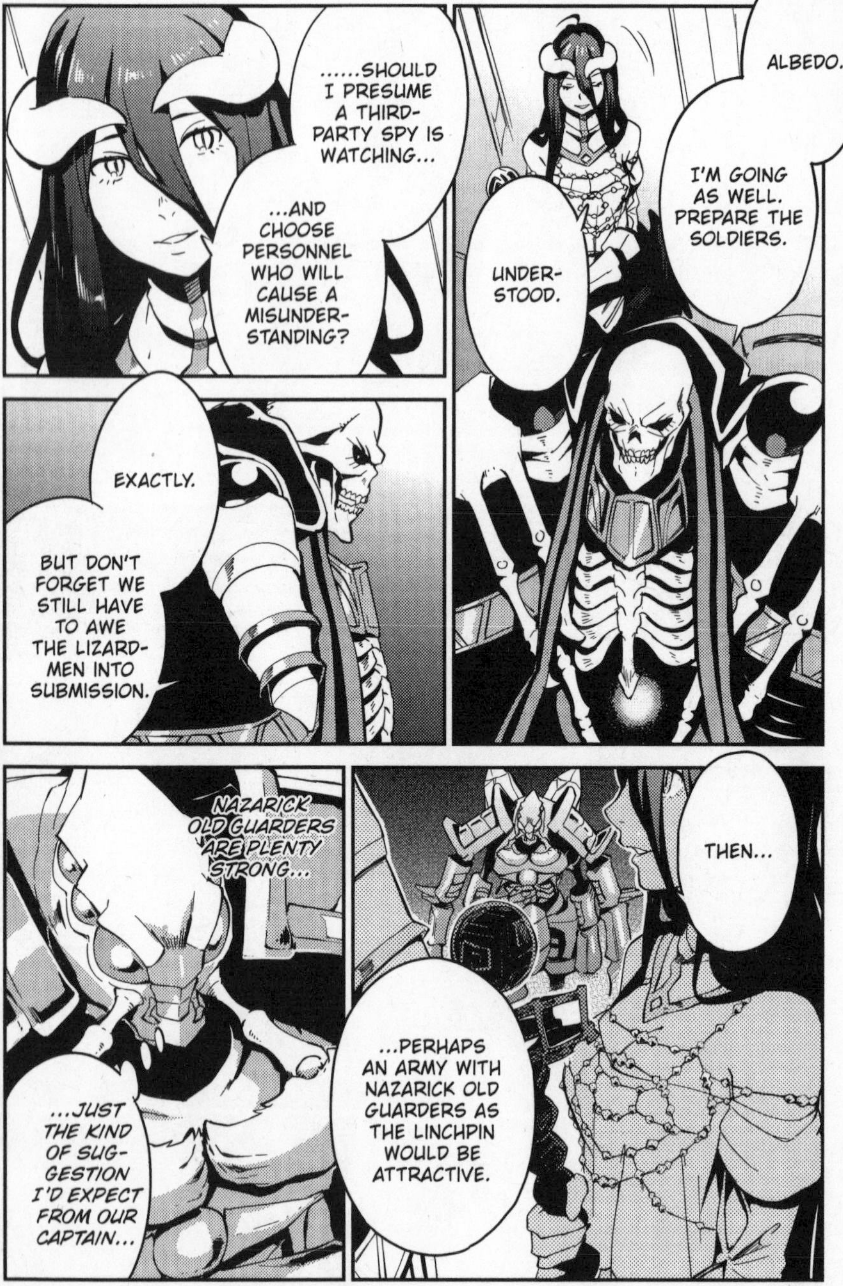
ALBEDO.
I'M GOING AS WELL. PREPARE THE SOLDIERS.
UNDERSTOOD.
......SHOULD I PRESUME A THIRD-PARTY SPY IS WATCHING...
...AND CHOOSE PERSONNEL WHO WILL CAUSE A MISUNDERSTANDING?
EXACTLY.
BUT DON'T FORGET WE STILL HAVE TO AWE THE LIZARDMEN INTO SUBMISSION.
THEN...
...PERHAPS AN ARMY WITH NAZARICK OLD GUARDERS AS THE LINCHPIN WOULD BE ATTRACTIVE.
NAZARICK OLD GUARDERS ARE PLENTY STRONG...
...JUST THE KIND OF SUGGESTION I'D EXPECT FROM OUR CAPTAIN...

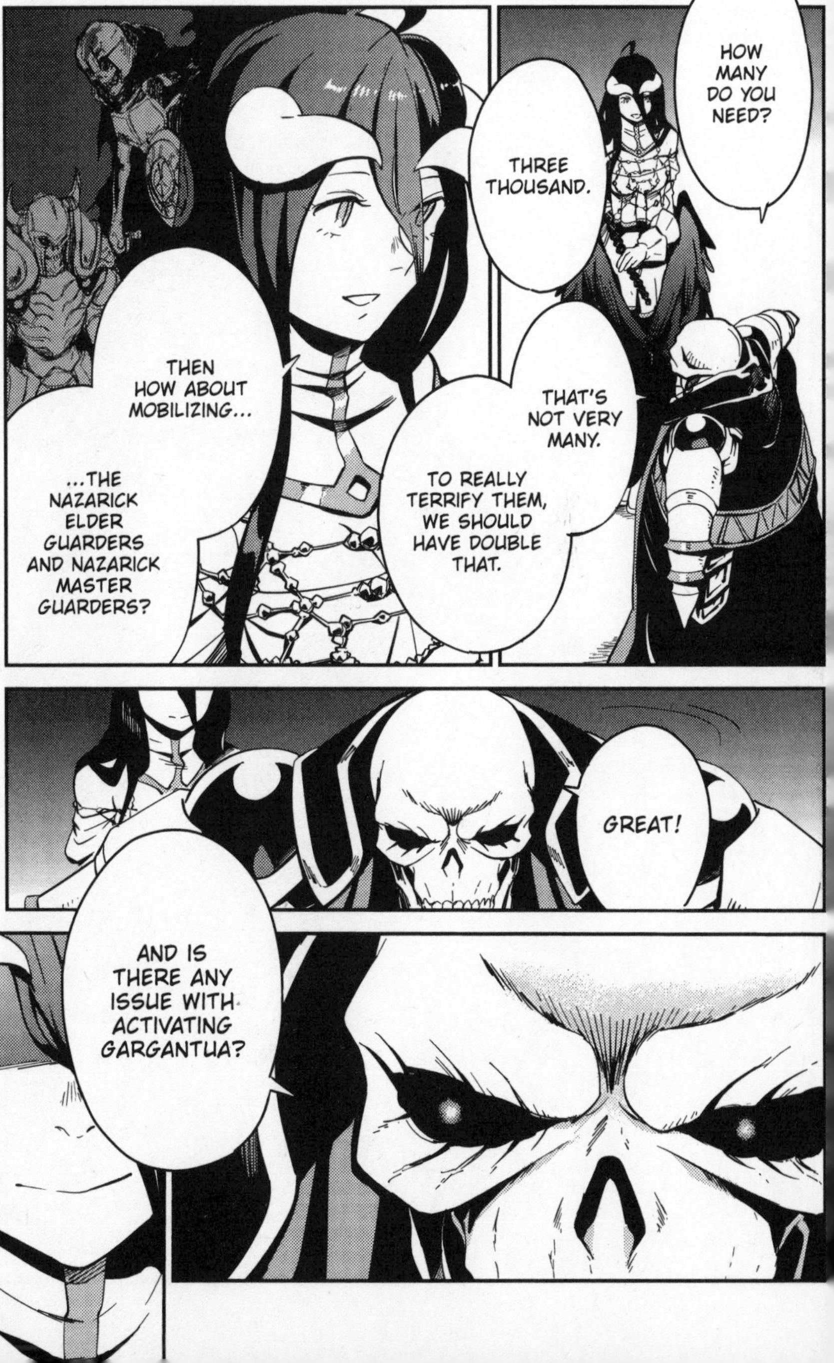

HOW MANY DO YOU NEED?
THREE THOUSAND.
THAT'S NOT VERY MANY.
TO REALLY TERRIFY THEM, WE SHOULD HAVE DOUBLE THAT.
THEN HOW ABOUT MOBILIZING...
...THE NAZARICK ELDER GUARDERS AND NAZARICK MASTER GUARDERS?
GREAT!
AND IS THERE ANY ISSUE WITH ACTIVATING GARGANTUA?

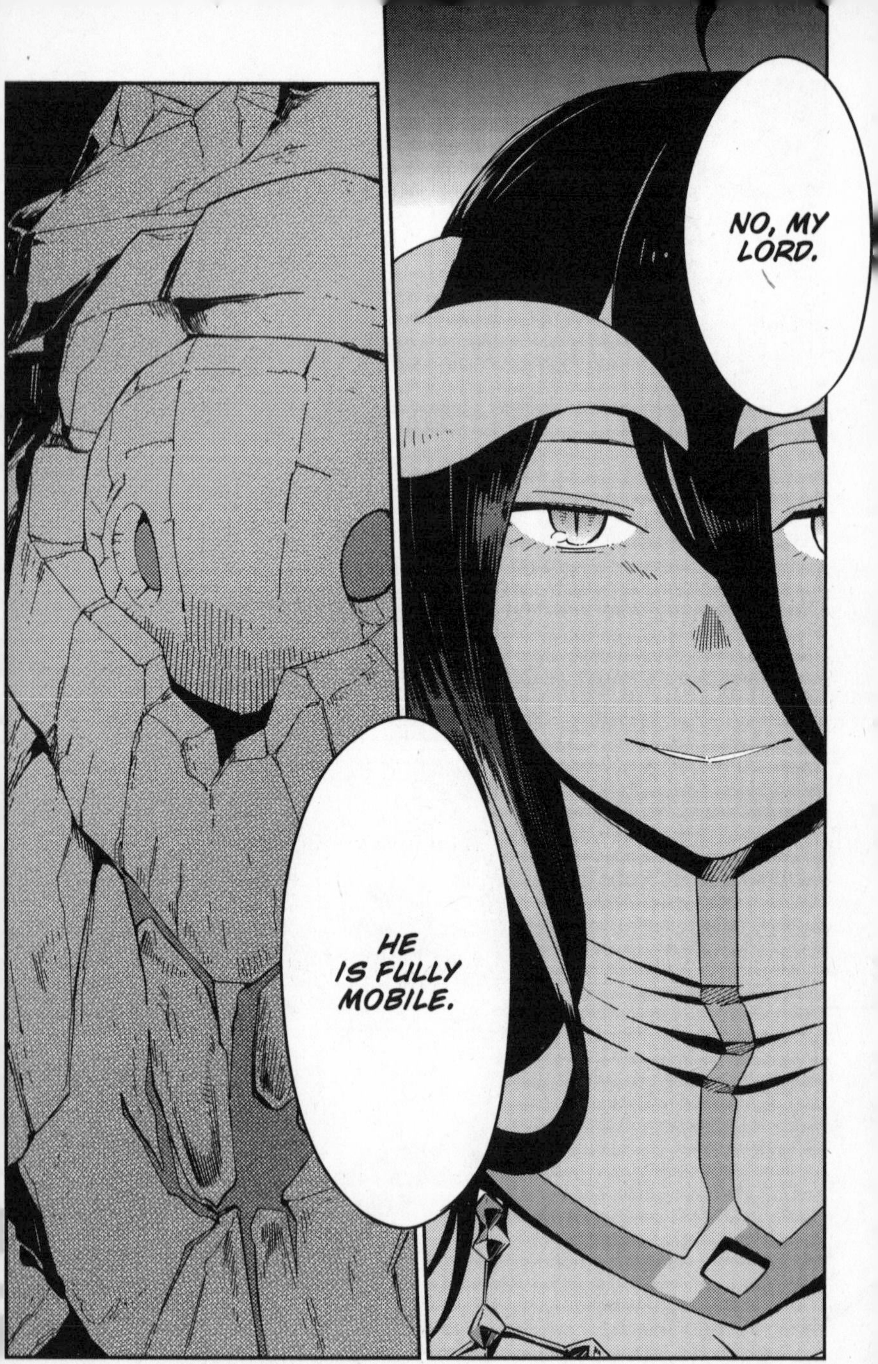
NO, MY LORD.
HE IS FULLY MOBILE.

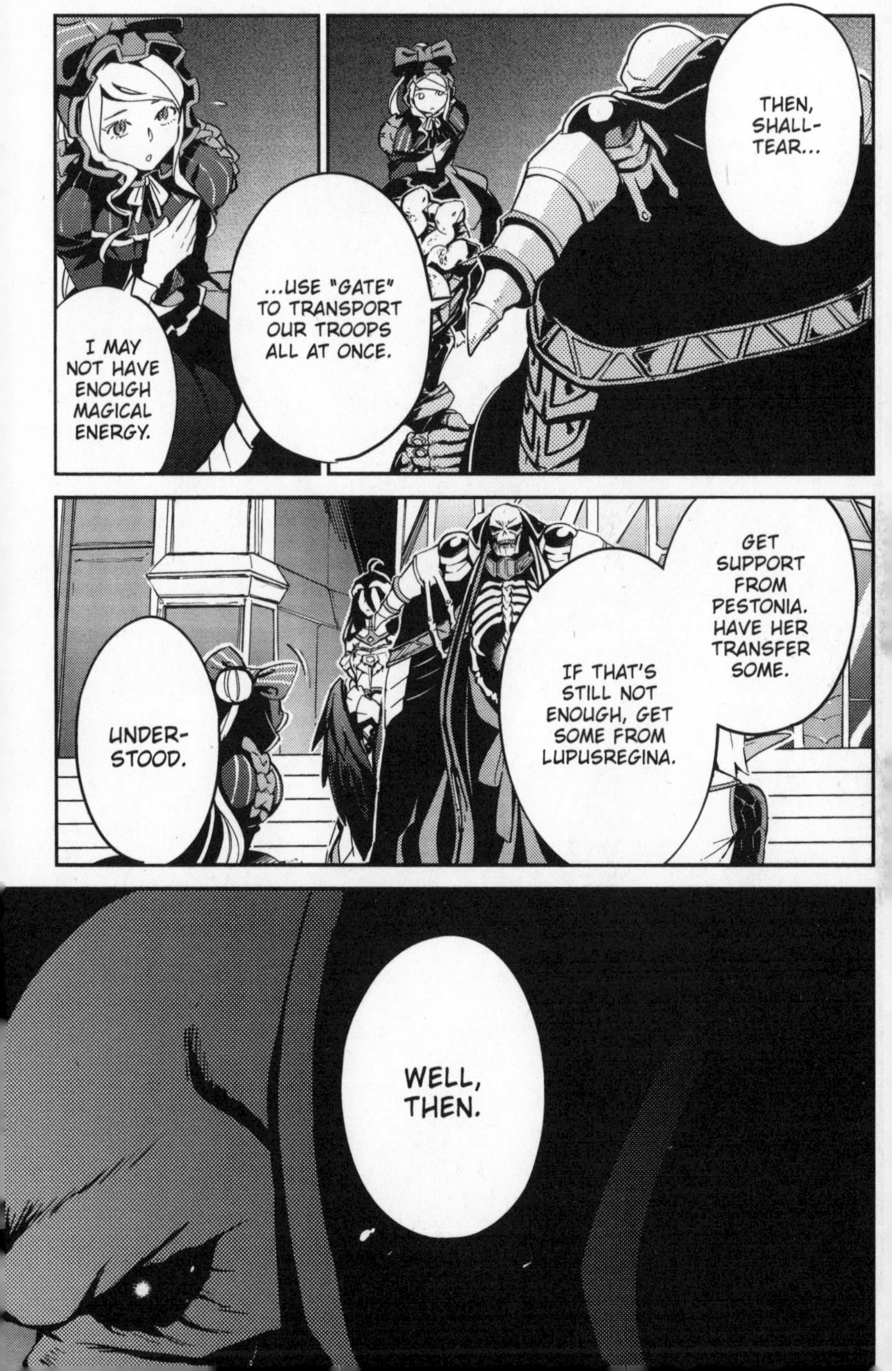
THEN, SHALL-TEAR...
...USE "GATE" TO TRANSPORT OUR TROOPS ALL AT ONCE.
I MAY NOT HAVE ENOUGH MAGICAL ENERGY.
GET SUPPORT FROM PESTONIA. HAVE HER TRANSFER SOME.
IF THAT'S STILL NOT ENOUGH, GET SOME FROM LUPUSREGINA.
UNDER-STOOD.
WELL, THEN.

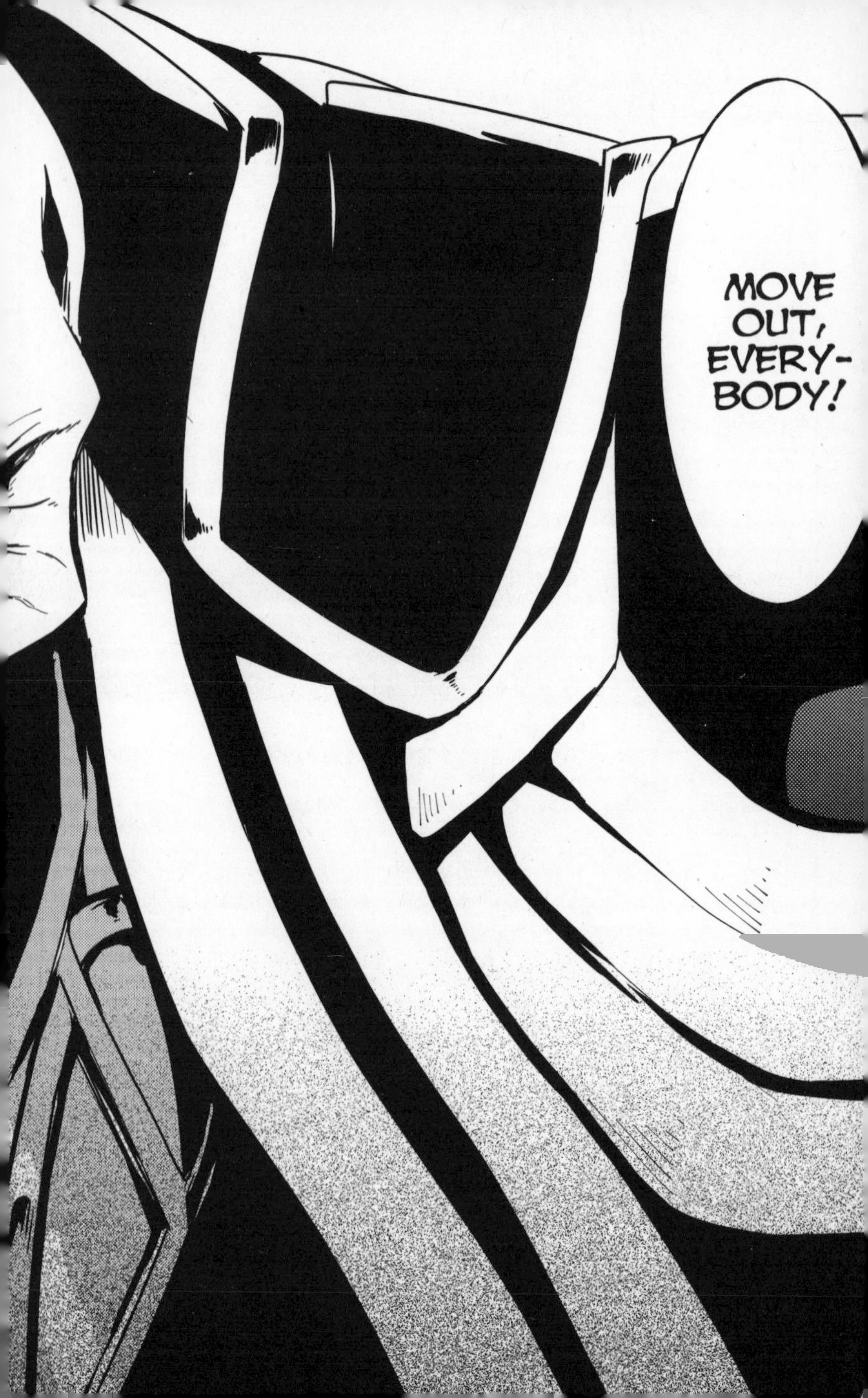
MOVE OUT, EVERY-BODY!

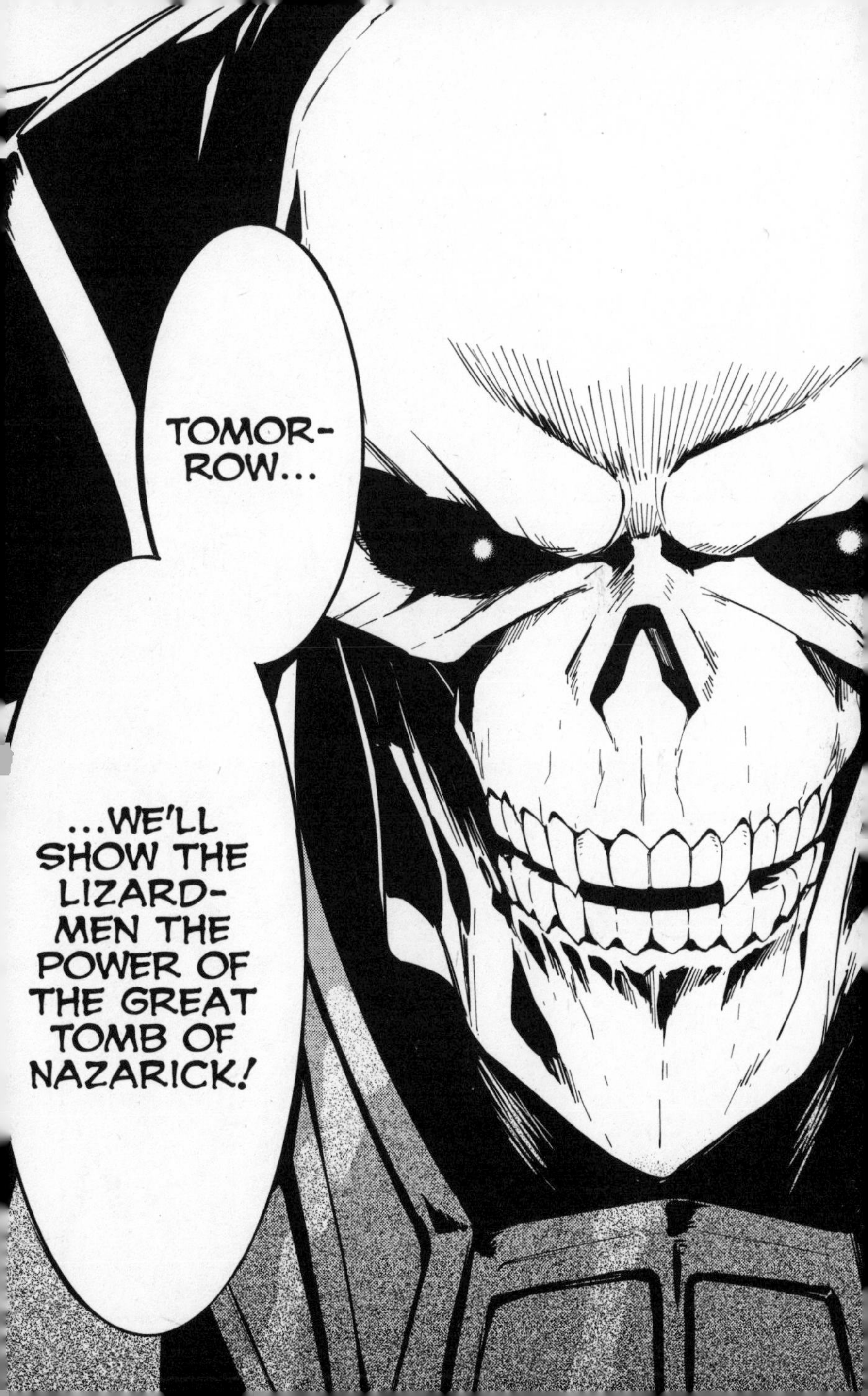
TOMORROW...
...WE'LL SHOW THE LIZARDMEN THE POWER OF THE GREAT TOMB OF NAZARICK!

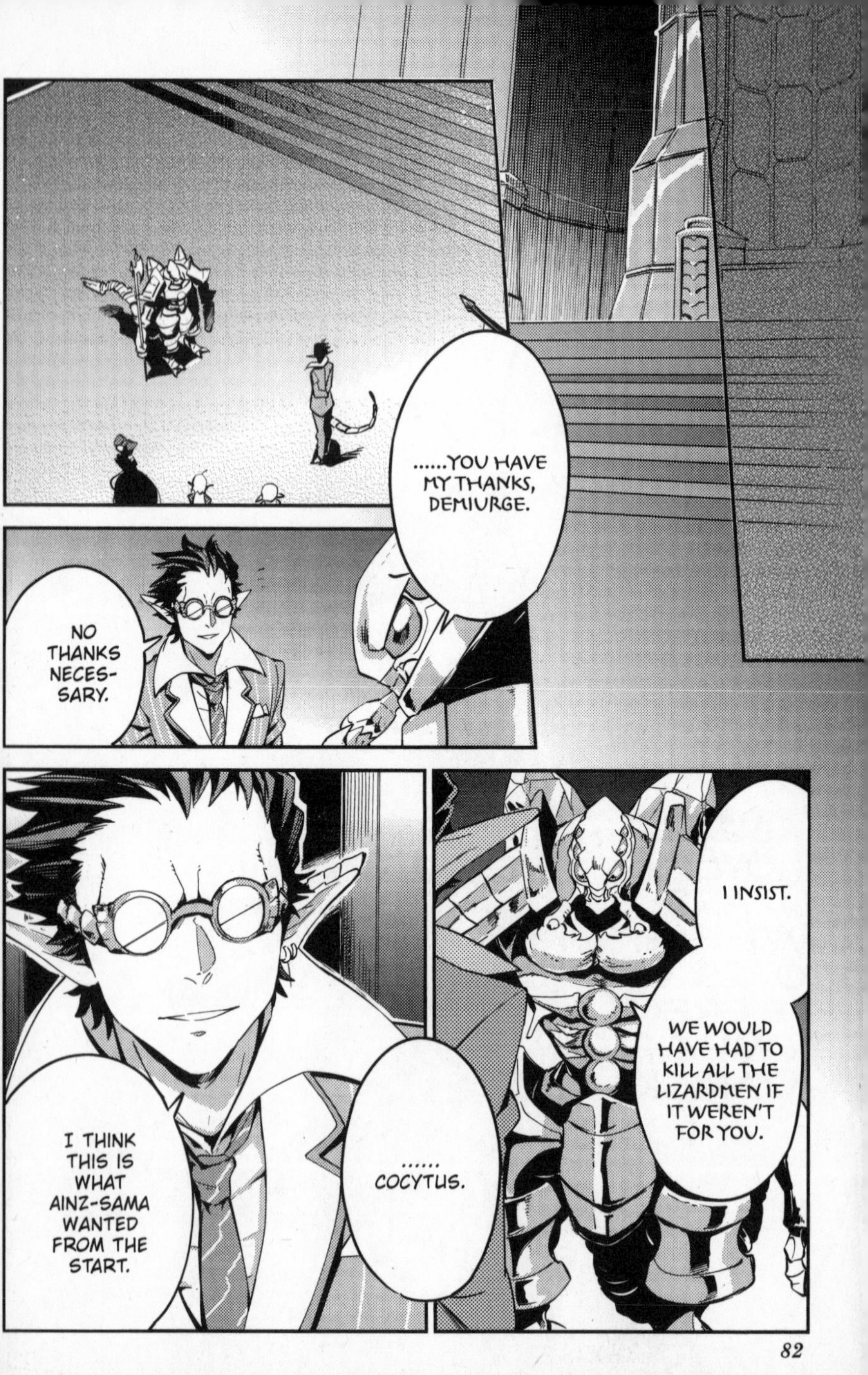
......YOU HAVE MY THANKS, DEMIURGE.
NO THANKS NECESSARY.
I INSIST.
WE WOULD HAVE HAD TO KILL ALL THE LIZARDMEN IF IT WEREN'T FOR YOU.
...... COCYTUS.
I THINK THIS IS WHAT AINZ-SAMA WANTED FROM THE START.

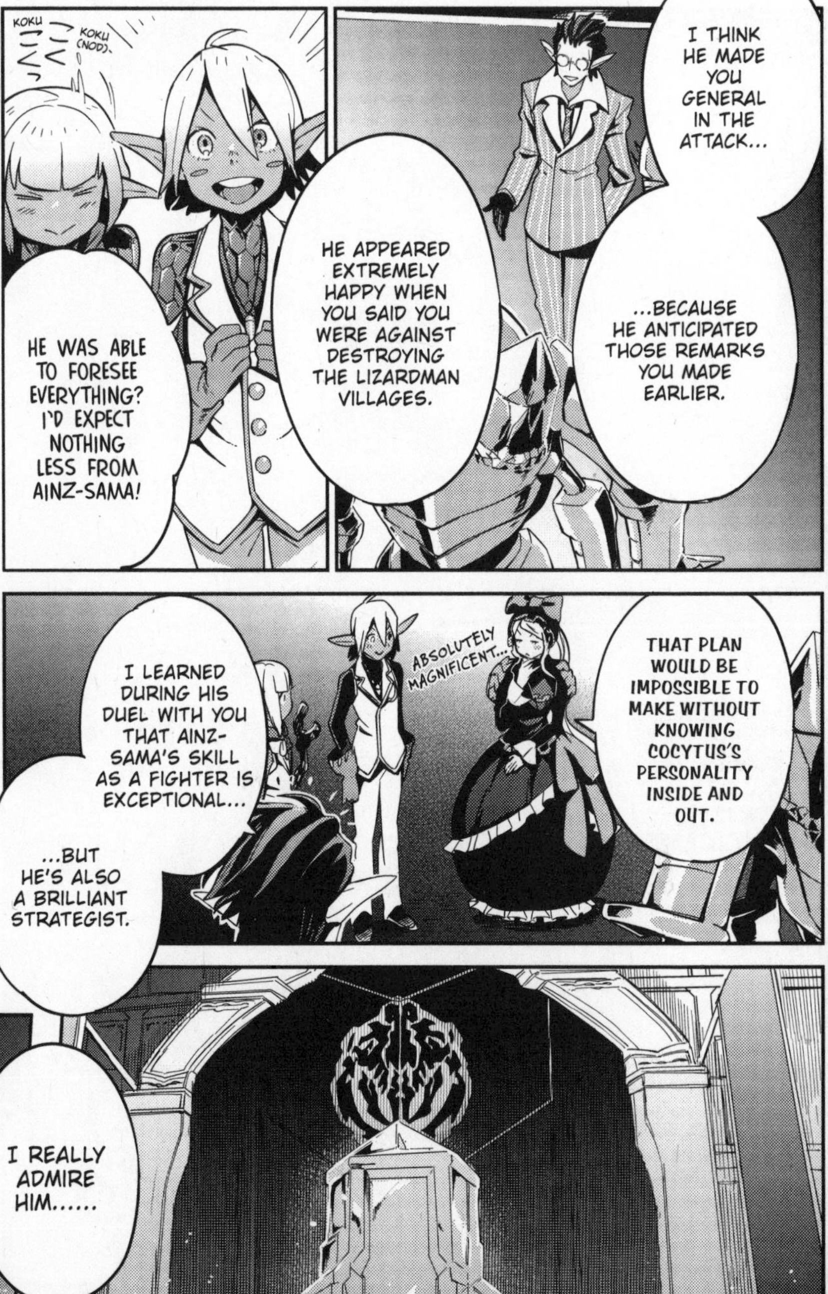
I THINK HE MADE YOU GENERAL IN THE ATTACK...
...BECAUSE HE ANTICIPATED THOSE REMARKS YOU MADE EARLIER.
HE APPEARED EXTREMELY HAPPY WHEN YOU SAID YOU WERE AGAINST DESTROYING THE LIZARDMAN VILLAGES.
KOKU
KOKU (NOD)
HE WAS ABLE TO FORESEE EVERYTHING? I'D EXPECT NOTHING LESS FROM AINZ-SAMA!
THAT PLAN WOULD BE IMPOSSIBLE TO MAKE WITHOUT KNOWING COCYTUS'S PERSONALITY INSIDE AND OUT.
ABSOLUTELY MAGNIFICENT...
I LEARNED DURING HIS DUEL WITH YOU THAT AINZ-SAMA'S SKILL AS A FIGHTER IS EXCEPTIONAL...
...BUT HE'S ALSO A BRILLIANT STRATEGIST.
I REALLY ADMIRE HIM......

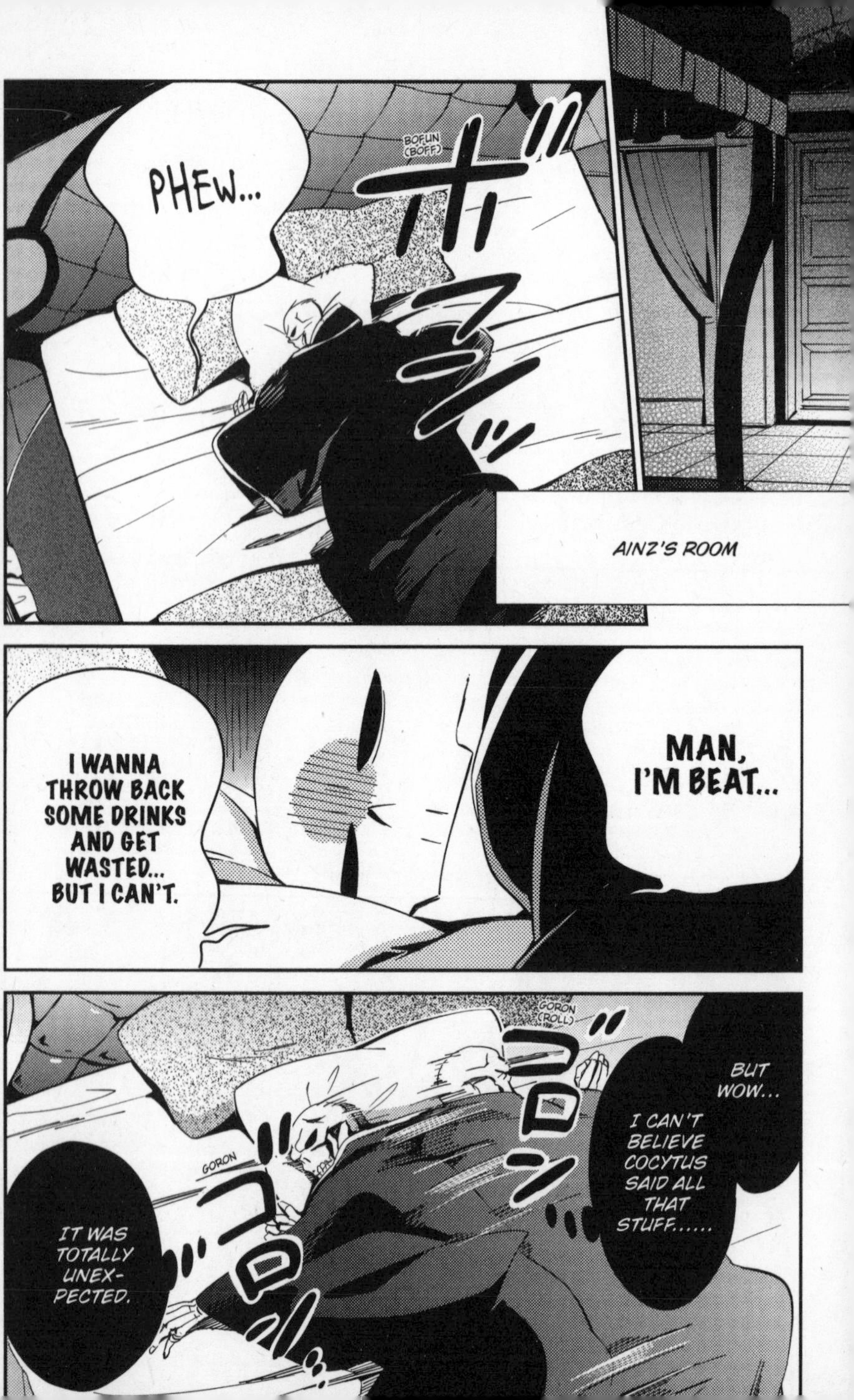
AINZ'S ROOM
BOFUN (BOFF)
PHEW...
MAN, I'M BEAT...
I WANNA THROW BACK SOME DRINKS AND GET WASTED... BUT I CAN'T.
GORON (ROLL)
BUT WOW...
I CAN'T BELIEVE COCYTUS SAID ALL THAT STUFF......
GORON
IT WAS TOTALLY UNEX-PECTED.

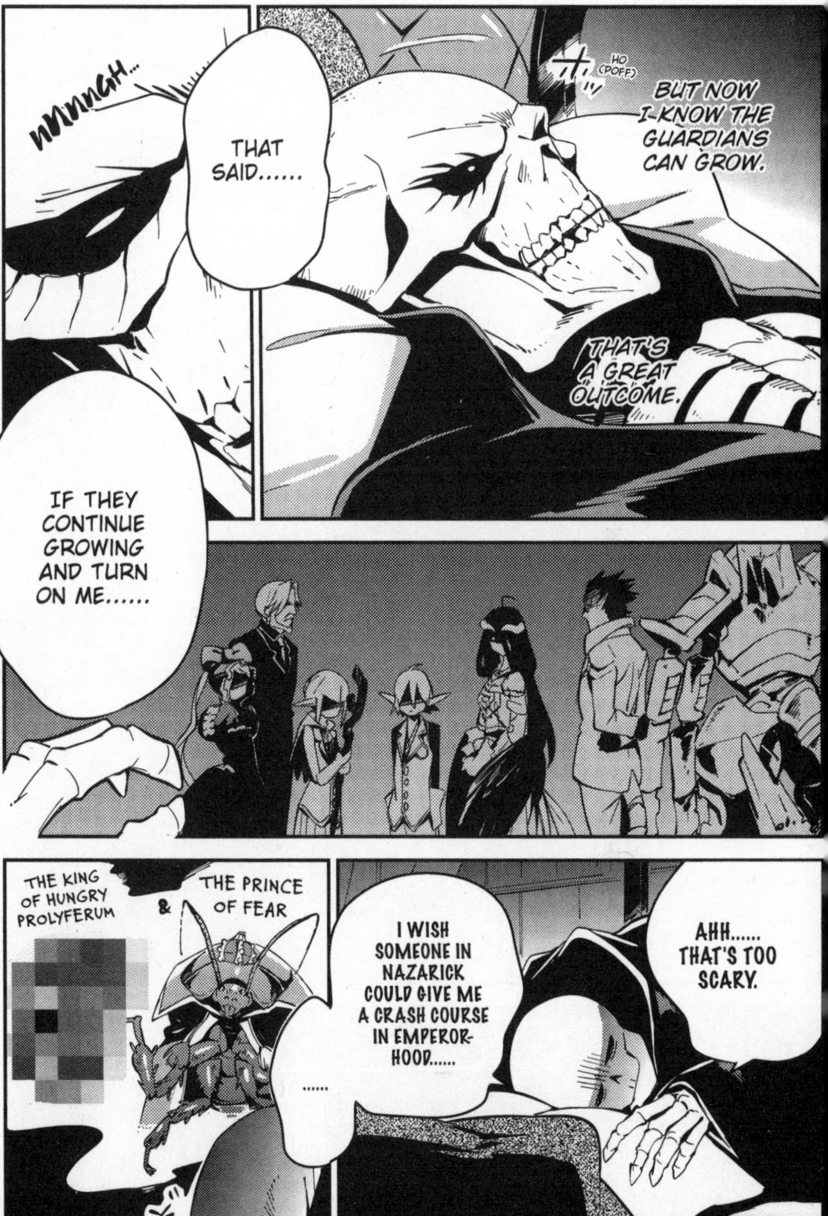
HO (POFF)
BUT NOW I KNOW THE GUARDIANS CAN GROW.
THAT'S A GREAT OUTCOME.
NNNNGH...
THAT SAID......
IF THEY CONTINUE GROWING AND TURN ON ME......
AHH...... THAT'S TOO SCARY.
I WISH SOMEONE IN NAZARICK COULD GIVE ME A CRASH COURSE IN EMPEROR-HOOD......
......
THE KING OF HUNGRY PROLYFERUM
&
THE PRINCE OF FEAR
ZO (SHUDDER)

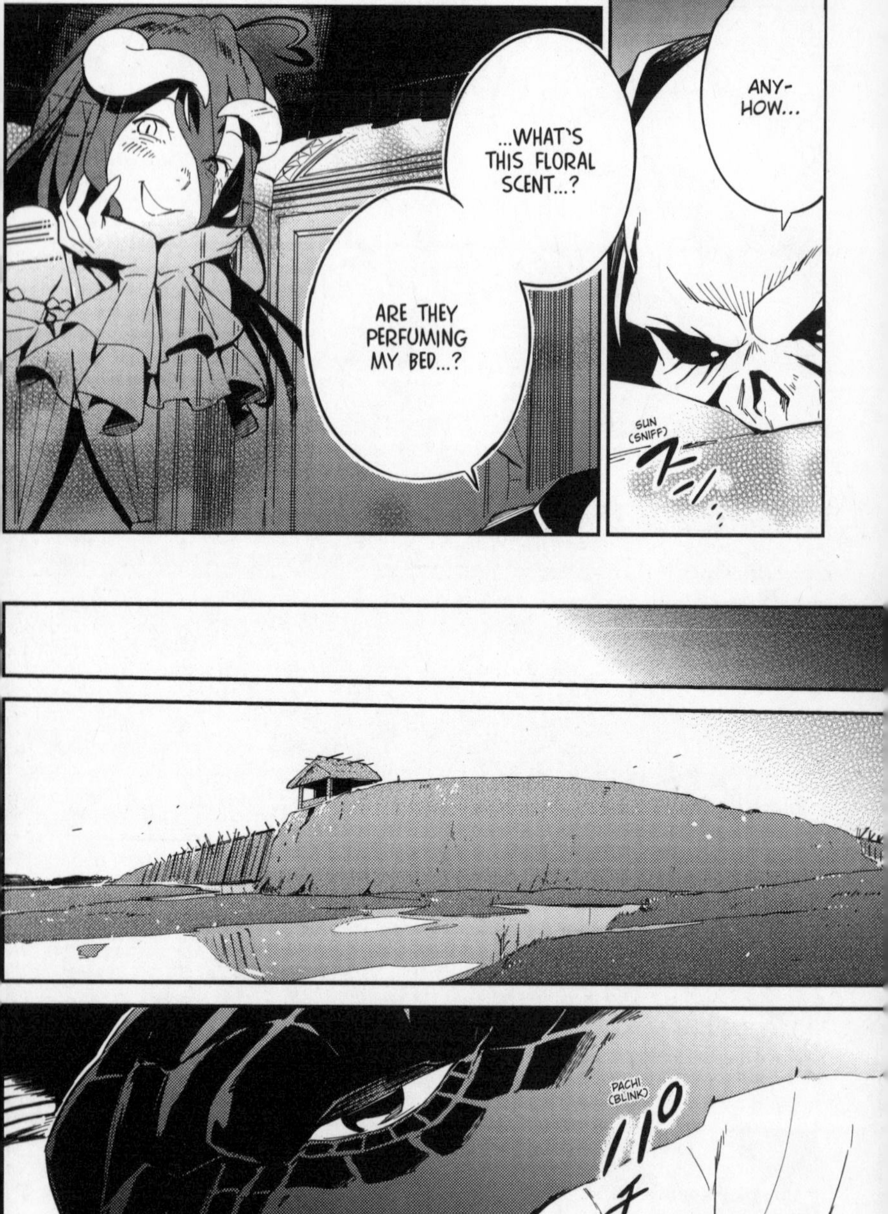
ANY-HOW...
SUN (SNIFF)
...WHAT'S THIS FLORAL SCENT...?
ARE THEY PERFUMING MY BED...?
PACHI (BLINK)

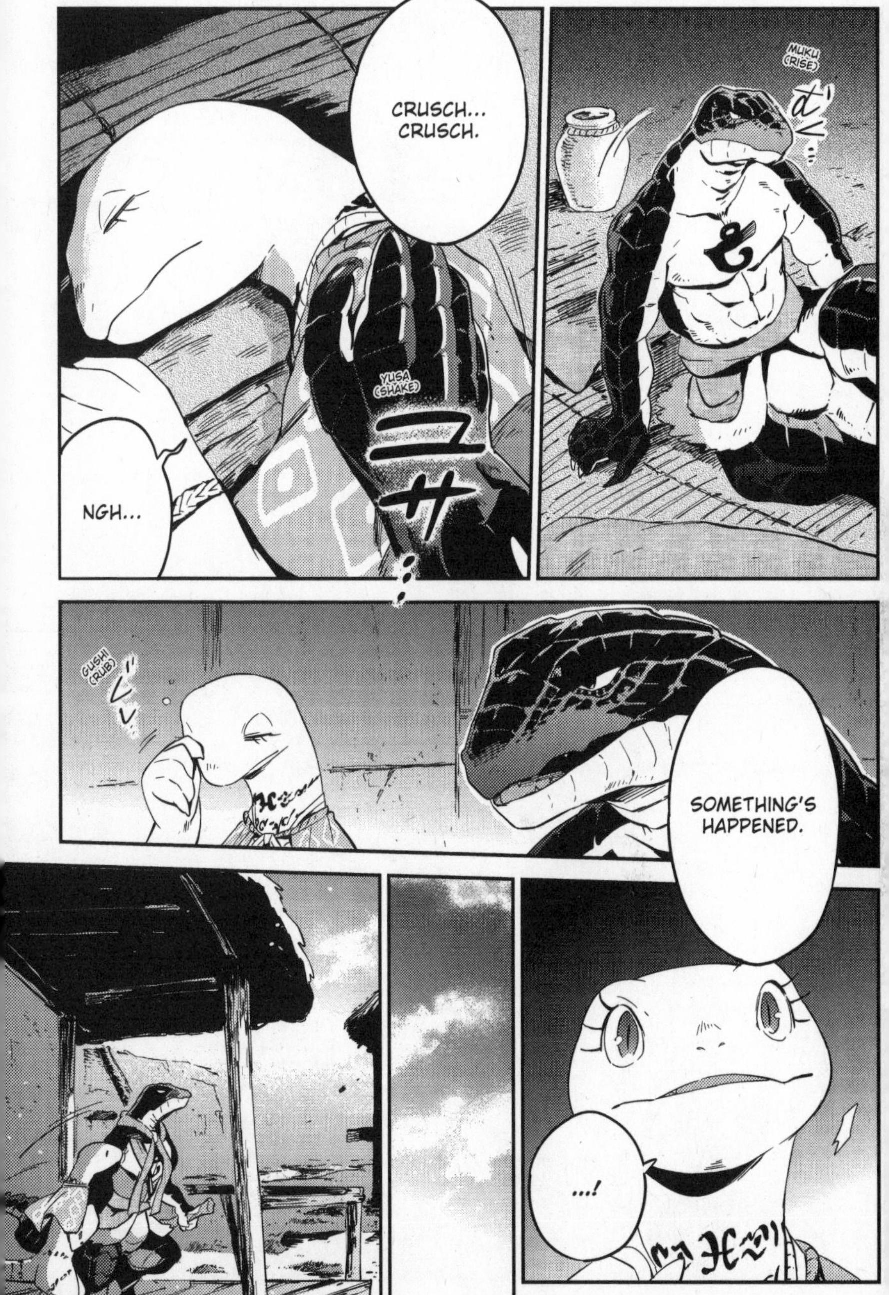
MUKU (RISE)
CRUSCH... CRUSCH.
YUSA (SHAKE)
NGH...
SOMETHING'S HAPPENED.
GUSHI (RUB)
...!

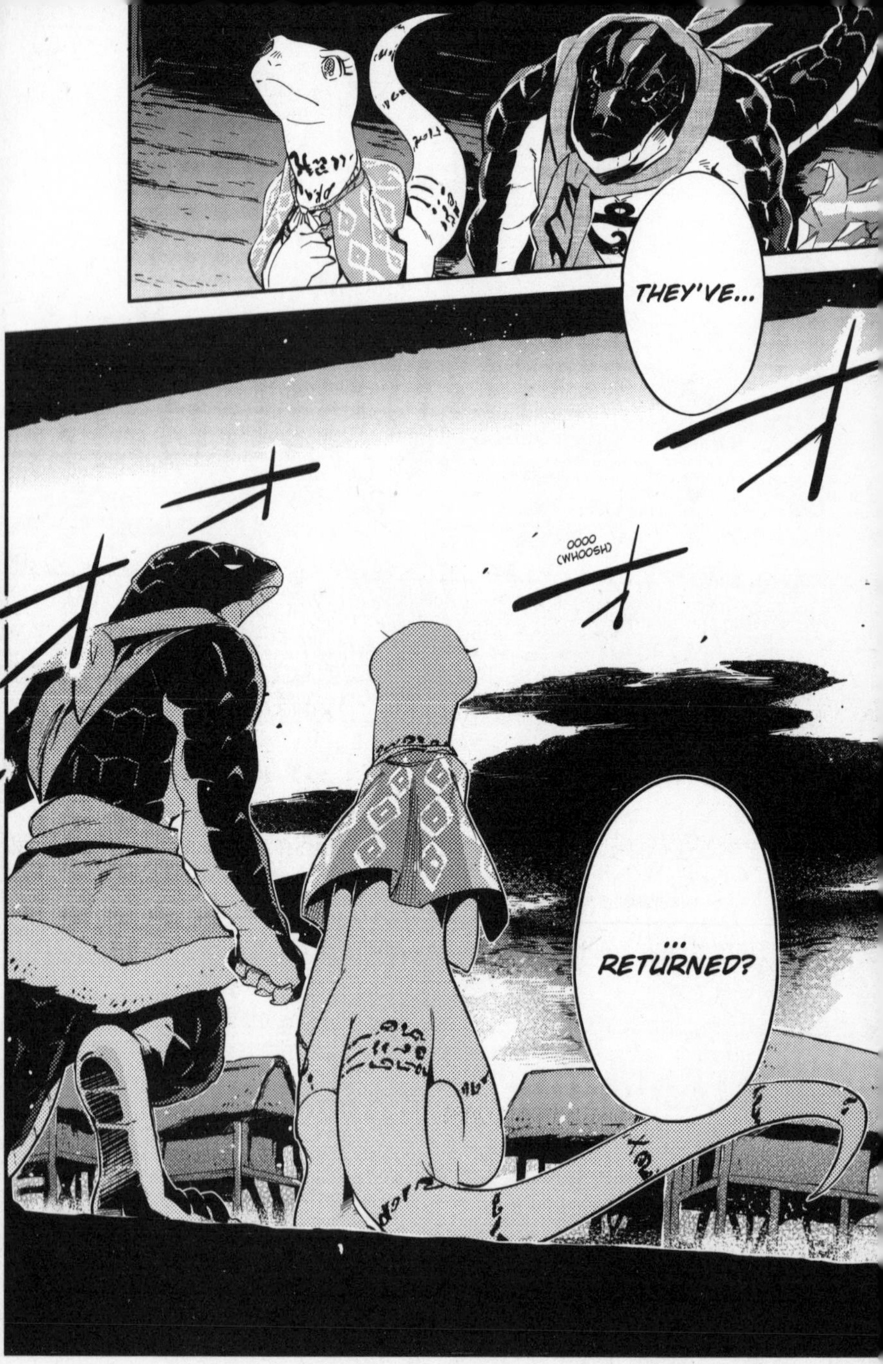
THEY'VE...
OOOO (WHOOSH)
...RETURNED?

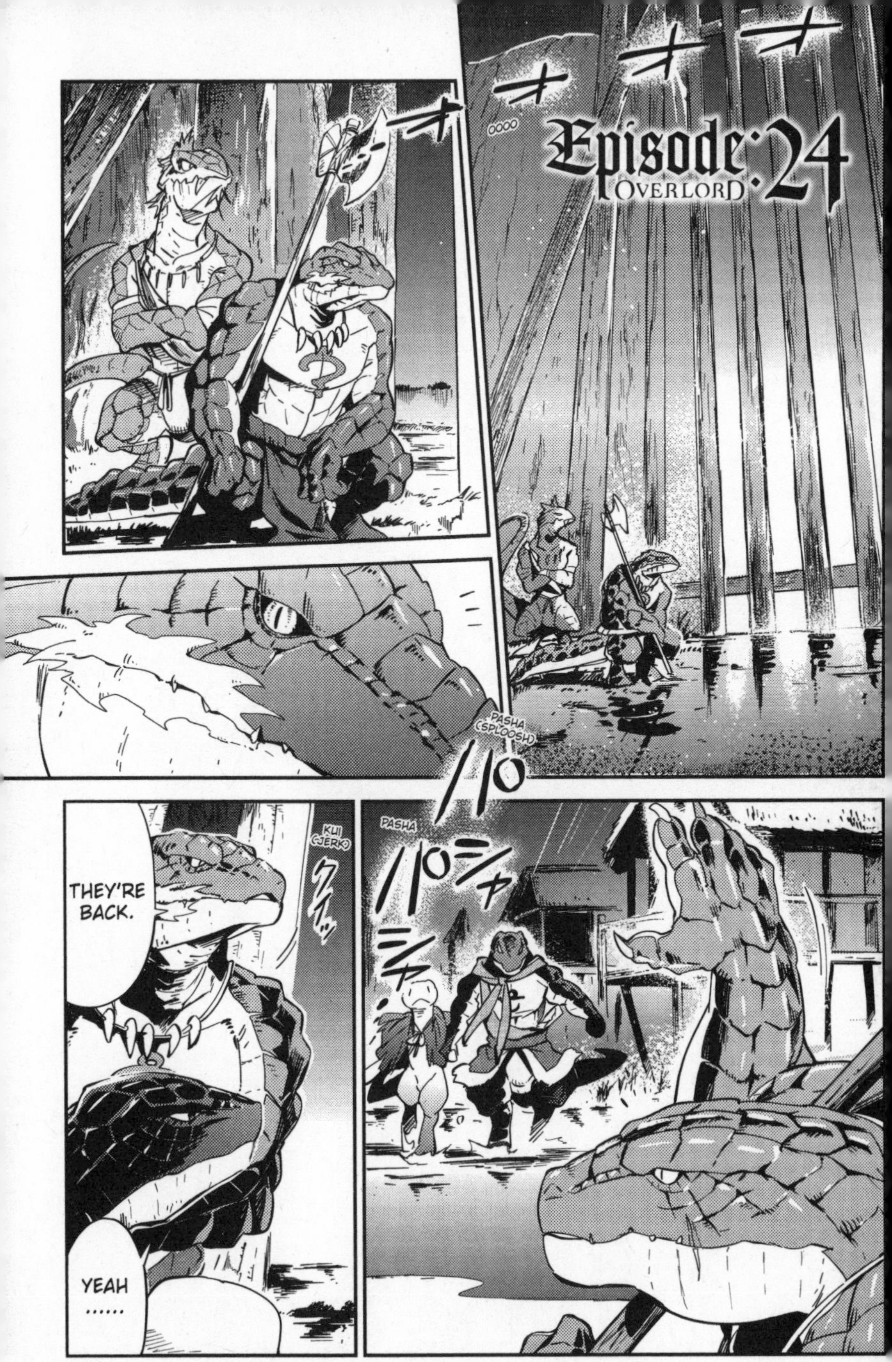
oooo
Episode: 24
OVERLORD
PASHA (SPLOOSH)
PASHA
KUI (JERK)
THEY'RE BACK.
YEAH ......

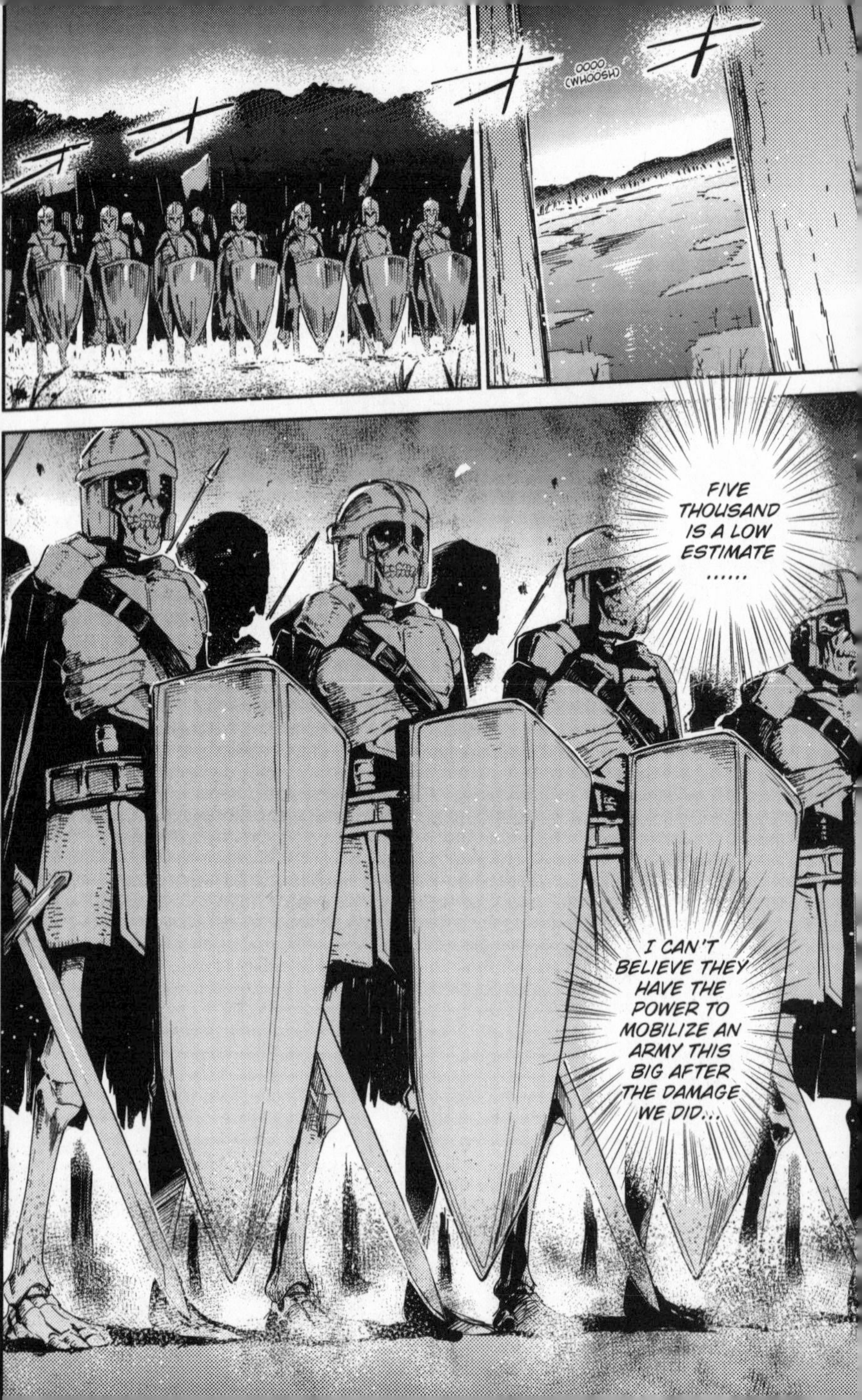
OOOO (WHOOSH)
FIVE THOUSAND IS A LOW ESTIMATE ......
I CAN'T BELIEVE THEY HAVE THE POWER TO MOBILIZE AN ARMY THIS BIG AFTER THE DAMAGE WE DID...

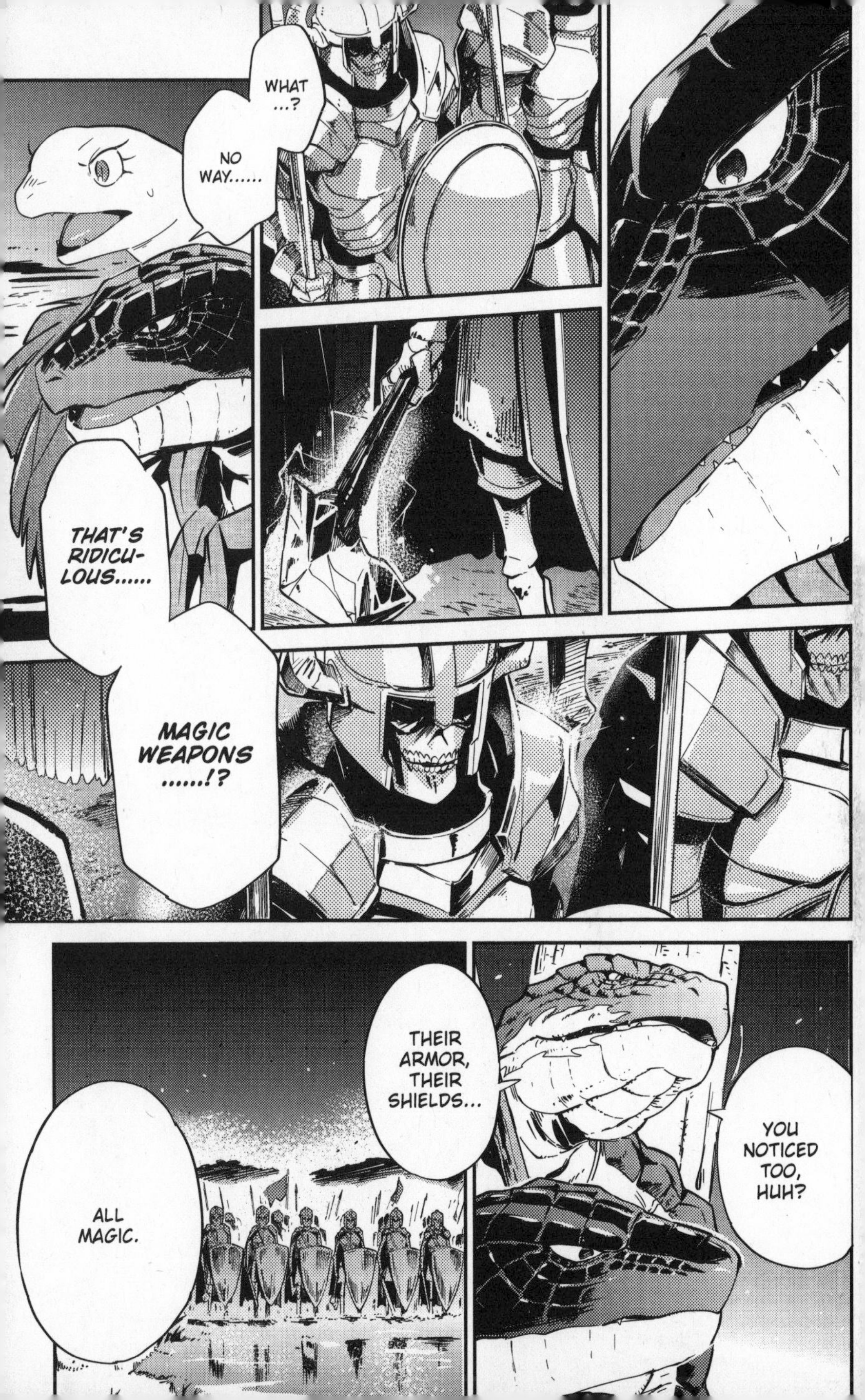
WHAT ...?
NO WAY......
THAT'S RIDICU-LOUS......
MAGIC WEAPONS ......!?
YOU NOTICED TOO, HUH?
THEIR ARMOR, THEIR SHIELDS...
ALL MAGIC.

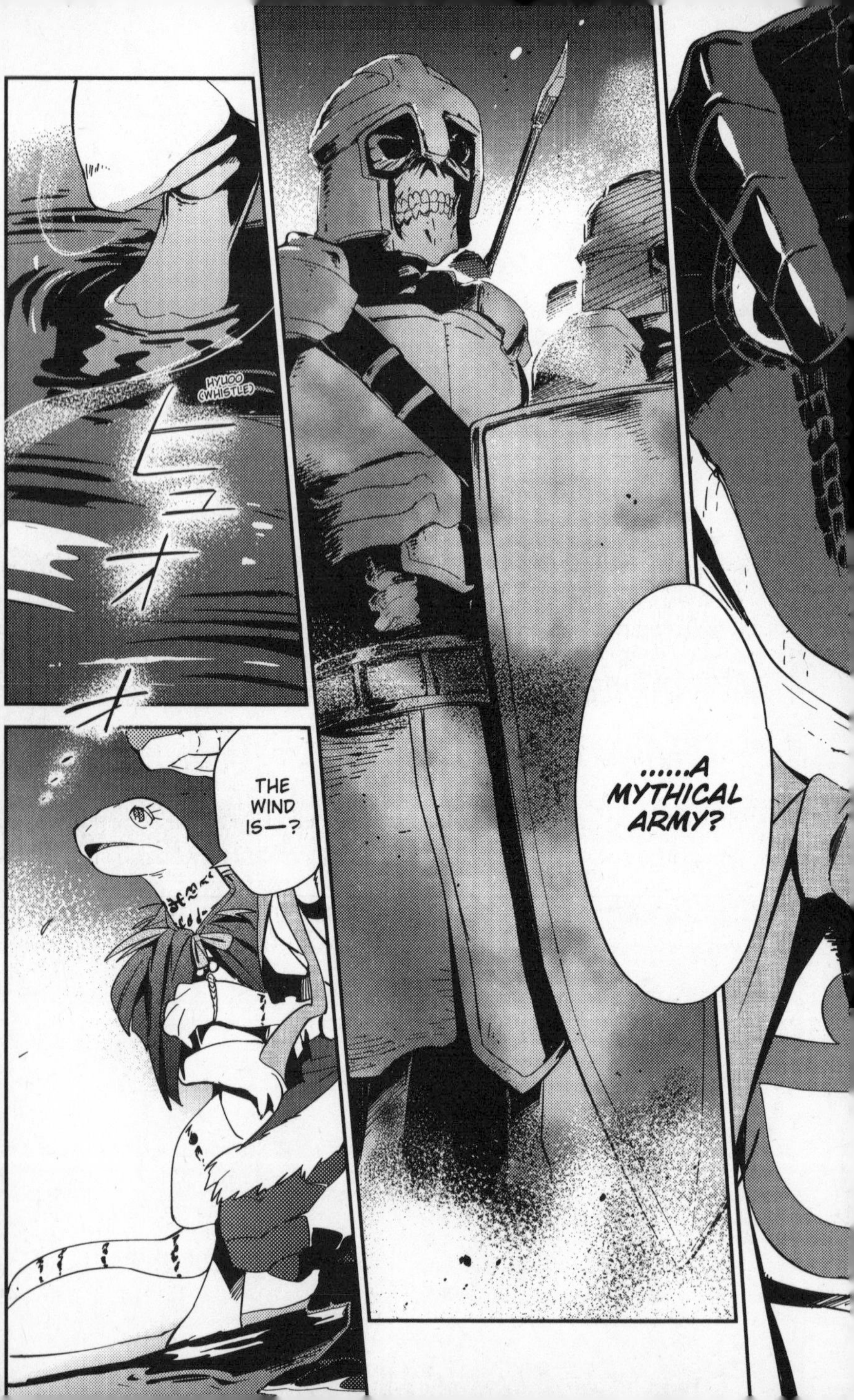
......A MYTHICAL ARMY?
HYUOO (WHISTLE)
THE WIND IS—?

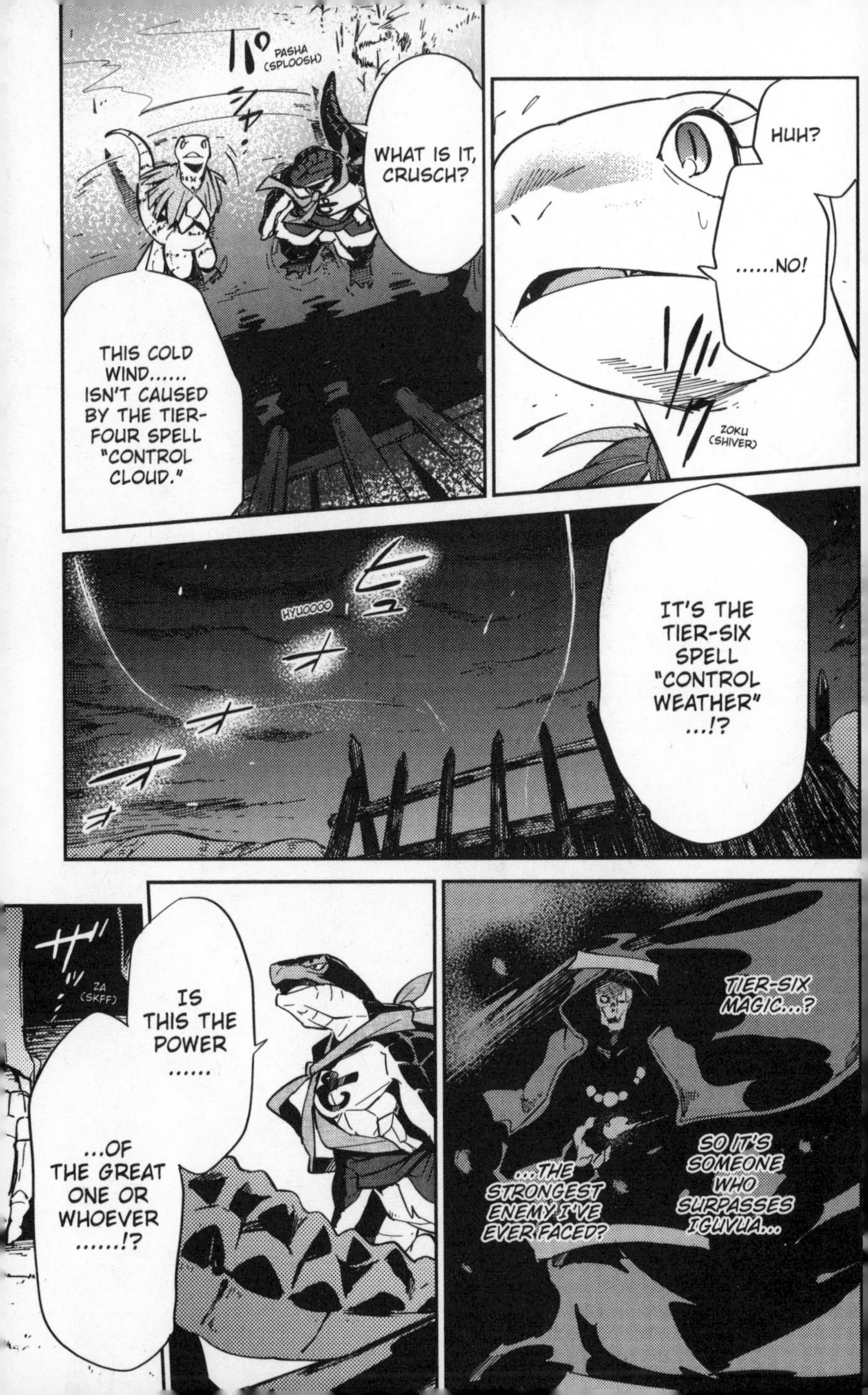
HUH?
......NO!
ZOKU (SHIVER)
PASHA (SPLOOSH)
WHAT IS IT, CRUSCH?
THIS COLD WIND...... ISN'T CAUSED BY THE TIER-FOUR SPELL "CONTROL CLOUD."
HYUOOOO
IT'S THE TIER-SIX SPELL "CONTROL WEATHER" ...!?
TIER-SIX MAGIC...?
SO IT'S SOMEONE WHO SURPASSES IGUVUA...
...THE STRONGEST ENEMY I'VE EVER FACED?
ZA (SKFF)
IS THIS THE POWER ......
...OF THE GREAT ONE OR WHOEVER ......!?

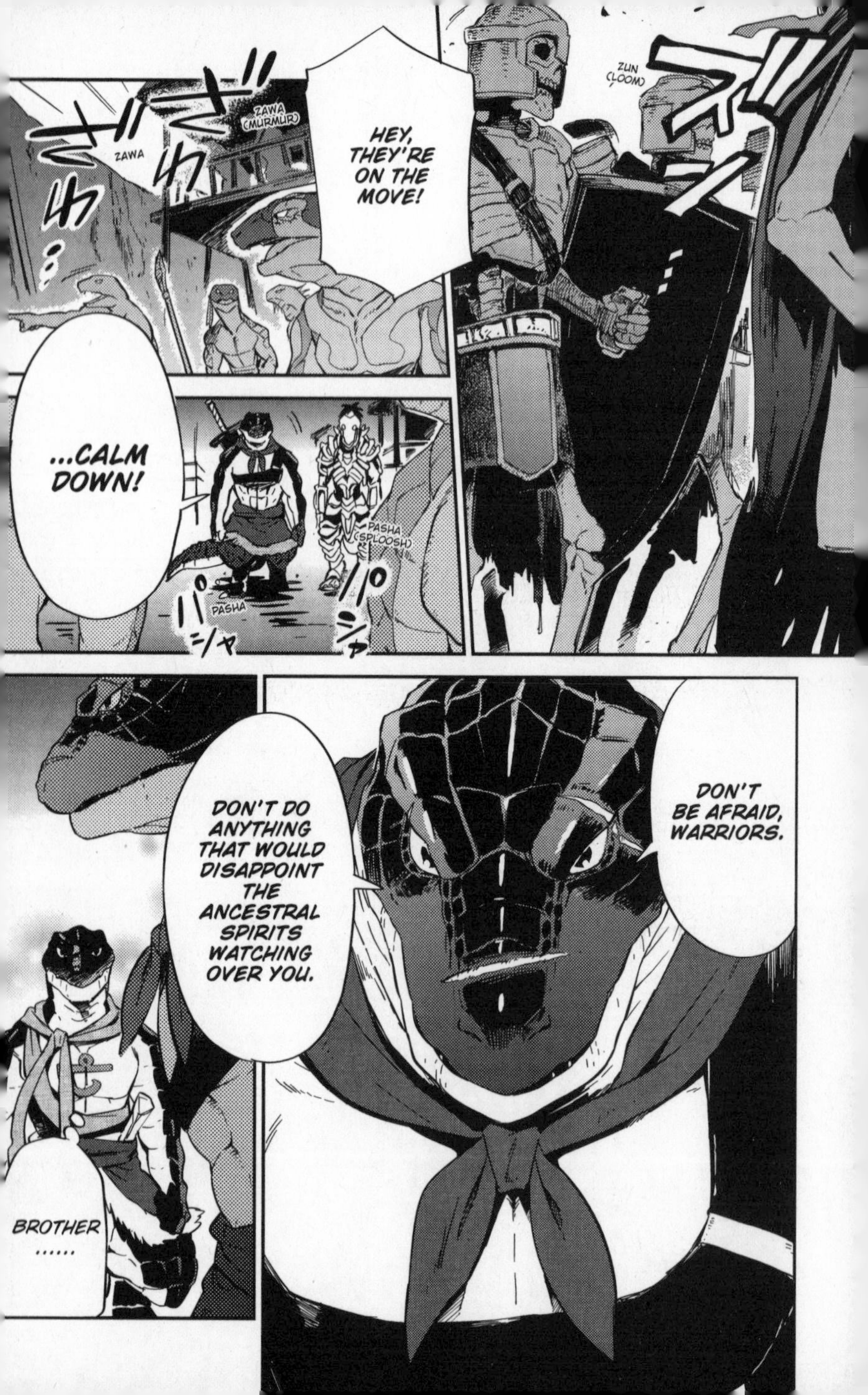
ZUN (LOOM)
HEY, THEY'RE ON THE MOVE!
ZAWA (MURMUR)
ZAWA
...CALM DOWN!
PASHA (SPLOOSH)
PASHA
DON'T BE AFRAID, WARRIORS.
DON'T DO ANYTHING THAT WOULD DISAPPOINT THE ANCESTRAL SPIRITS WATCHING OVER YOU.
BROTHER ......

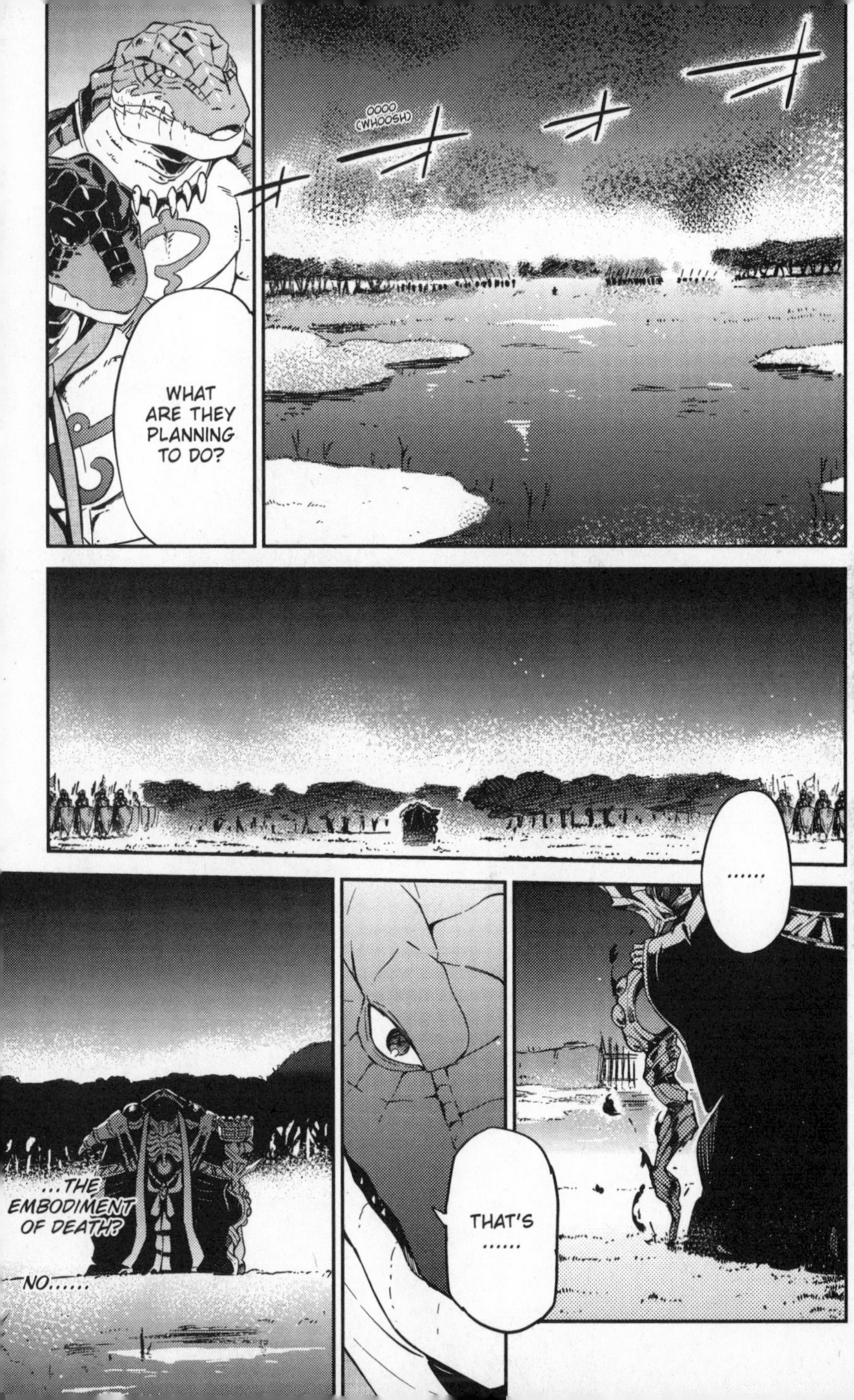
OOOO
(WHOOSH)
WHAT ARE THEY PLANNING TO DO?
......
THAT'S ......
...THE EMBODIMENT OF DEATH?
NO......

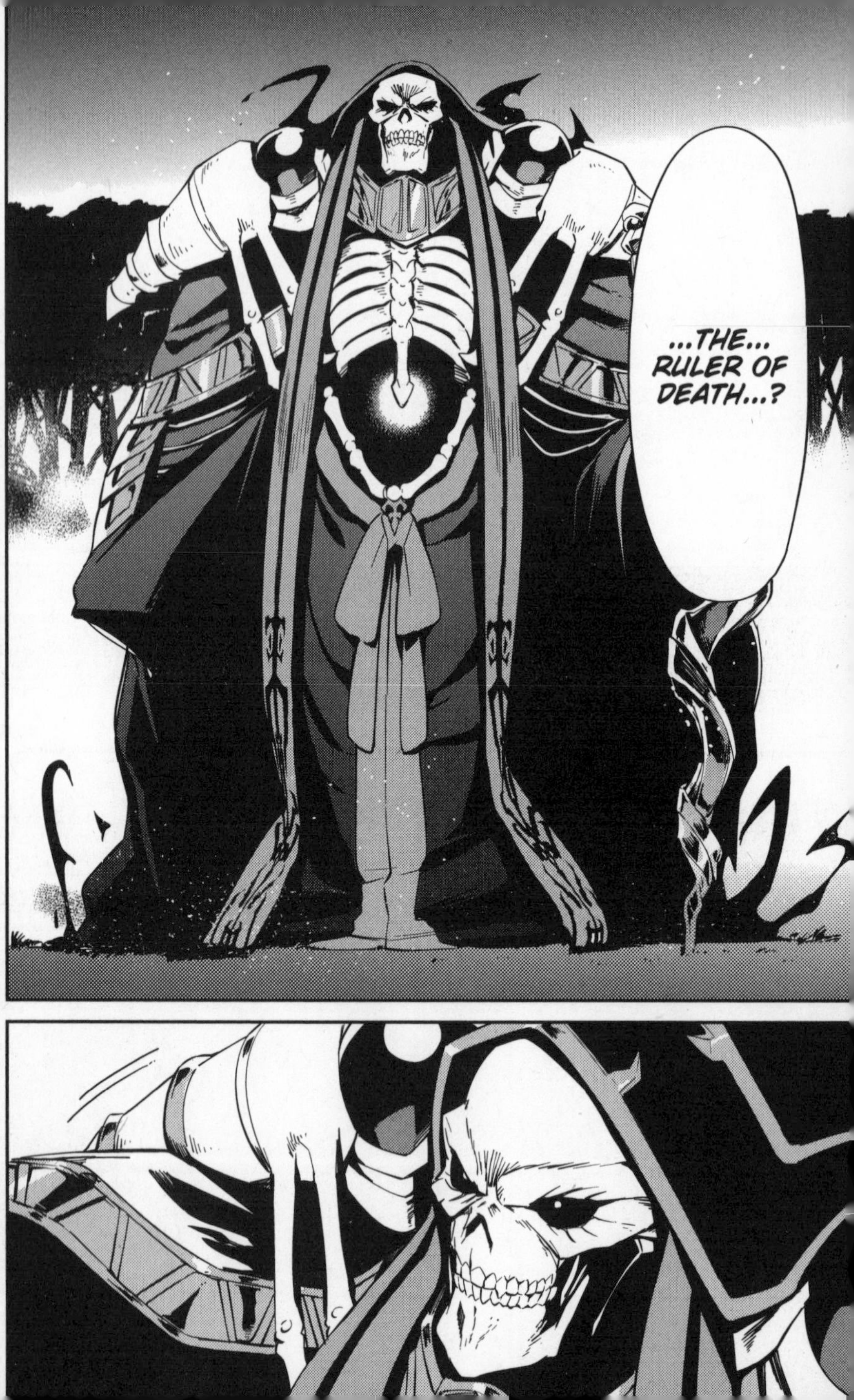
...THE... RULER OF DEATH...?

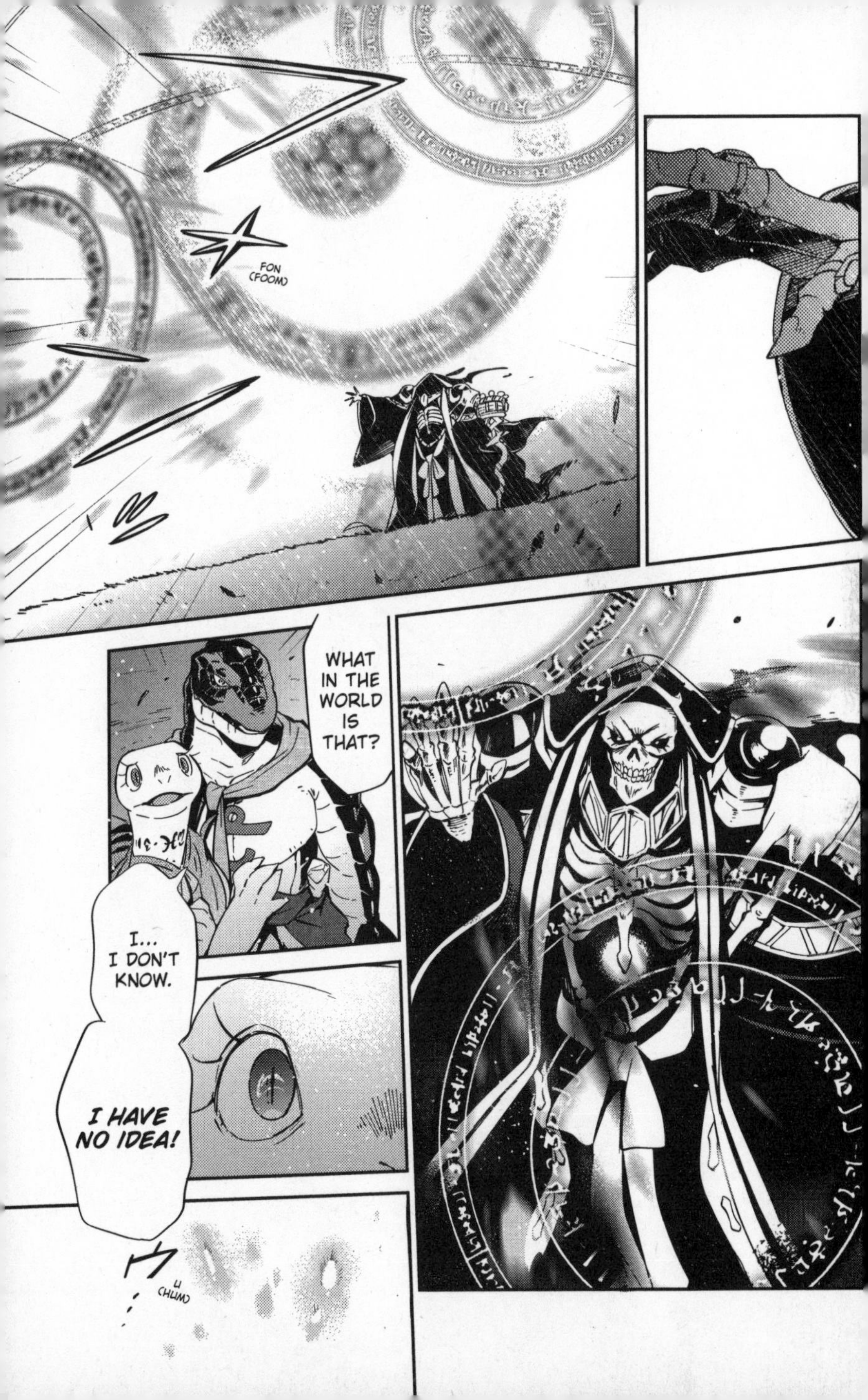
FON (FOOM)
WHAT IN THE WORLD IS THAT?
I... I DON'T KNOW.
I HAVE NO IDEA!
N (HUM)

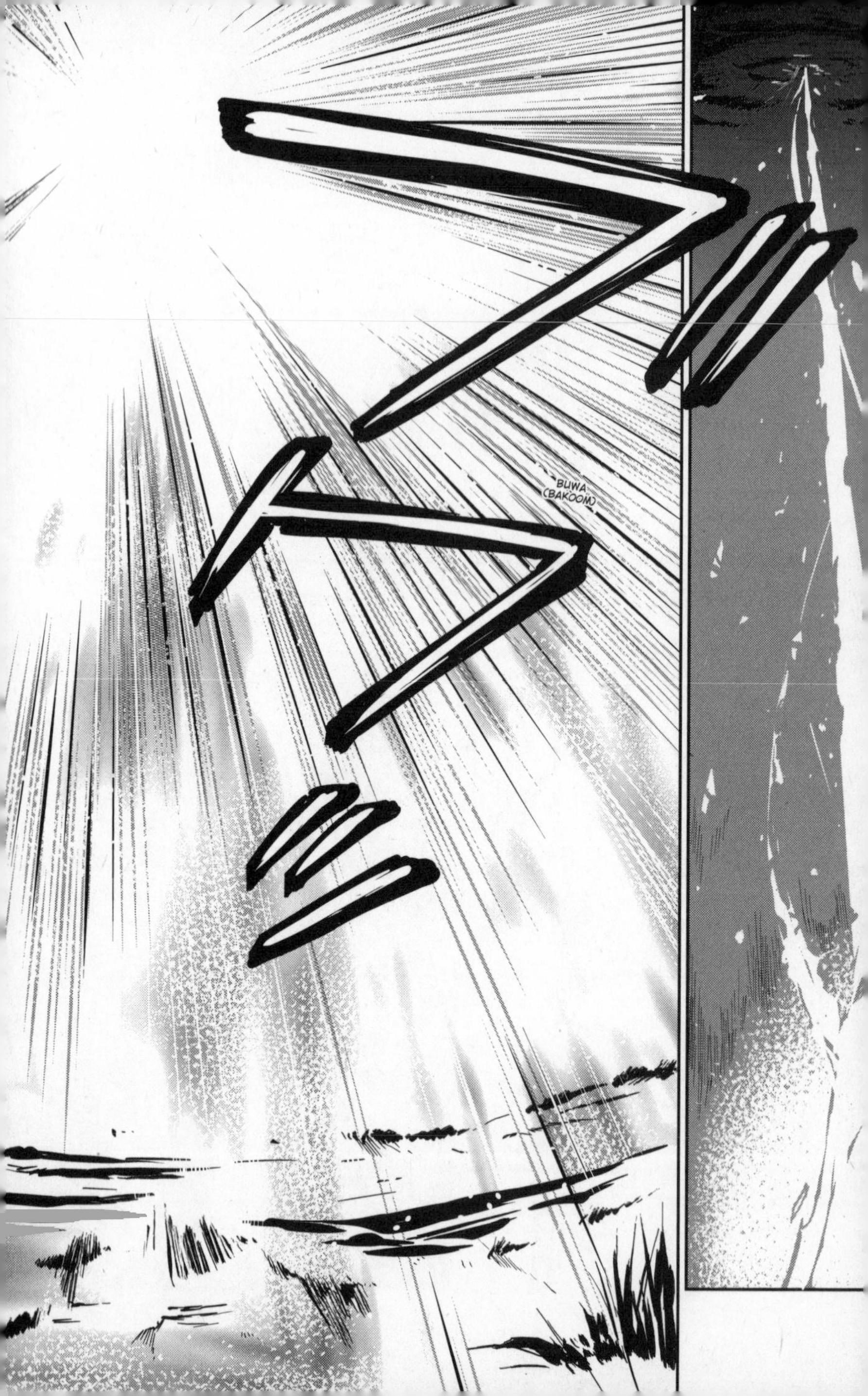
BUWA
(BAKOOM)

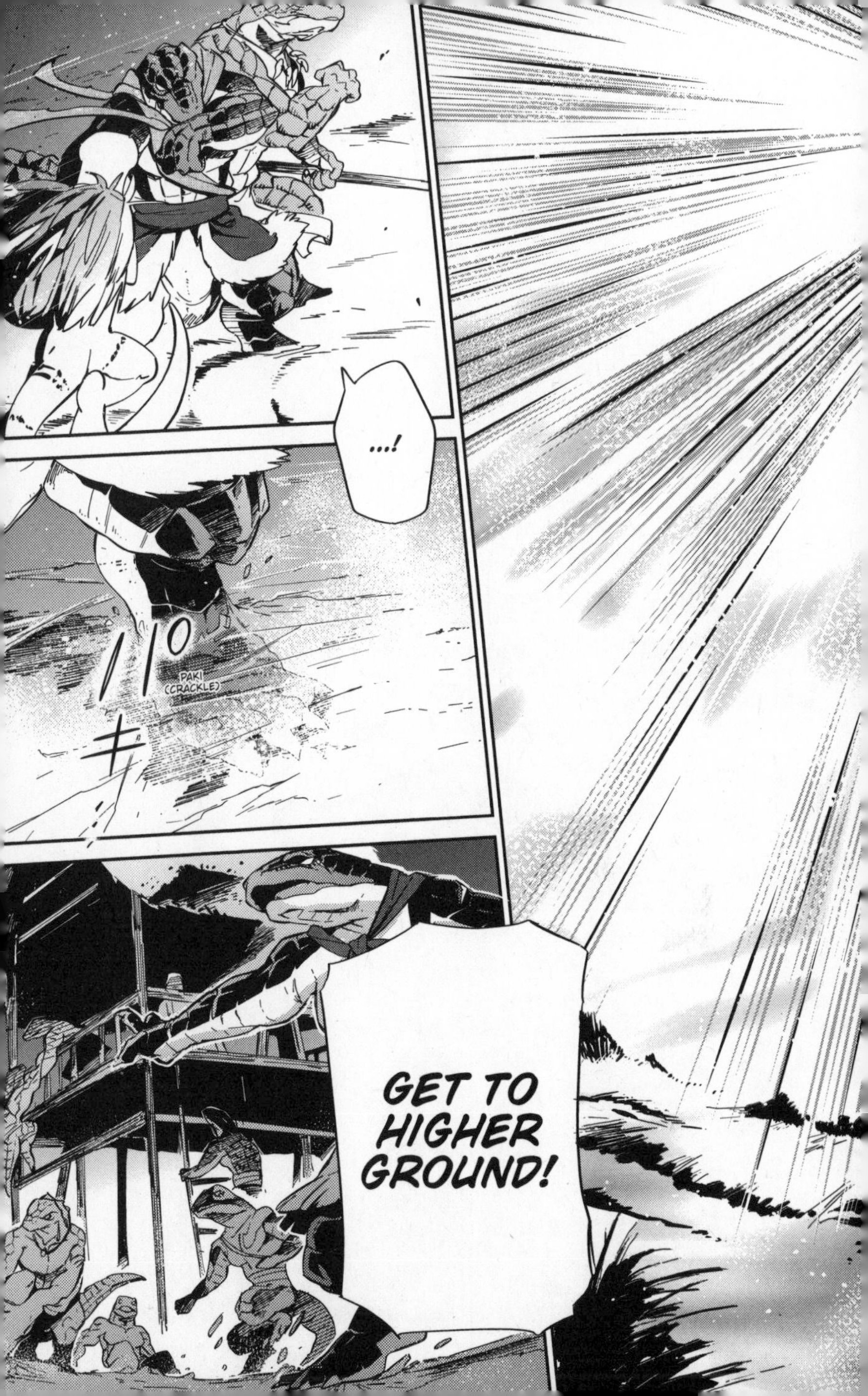
...!
PAKI (CRACKLE)
GET TO HIGHER GROUND!

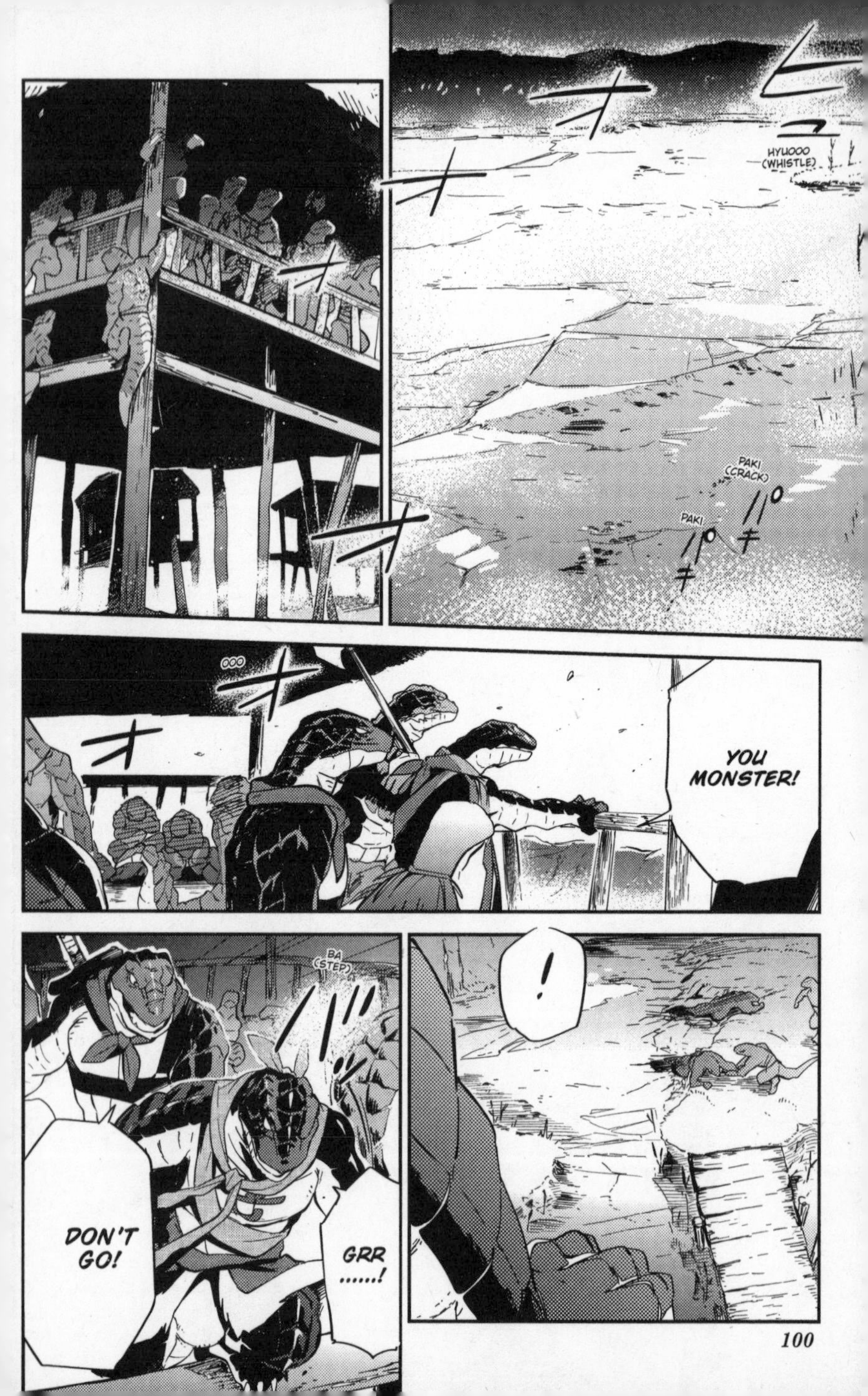
HYUOOO (WHISTLE)
PAKI (CRACK)
PAKI
OOO
YOU MONSTER!
!
BA (STEP)
GRR ......!
DON'T GO!

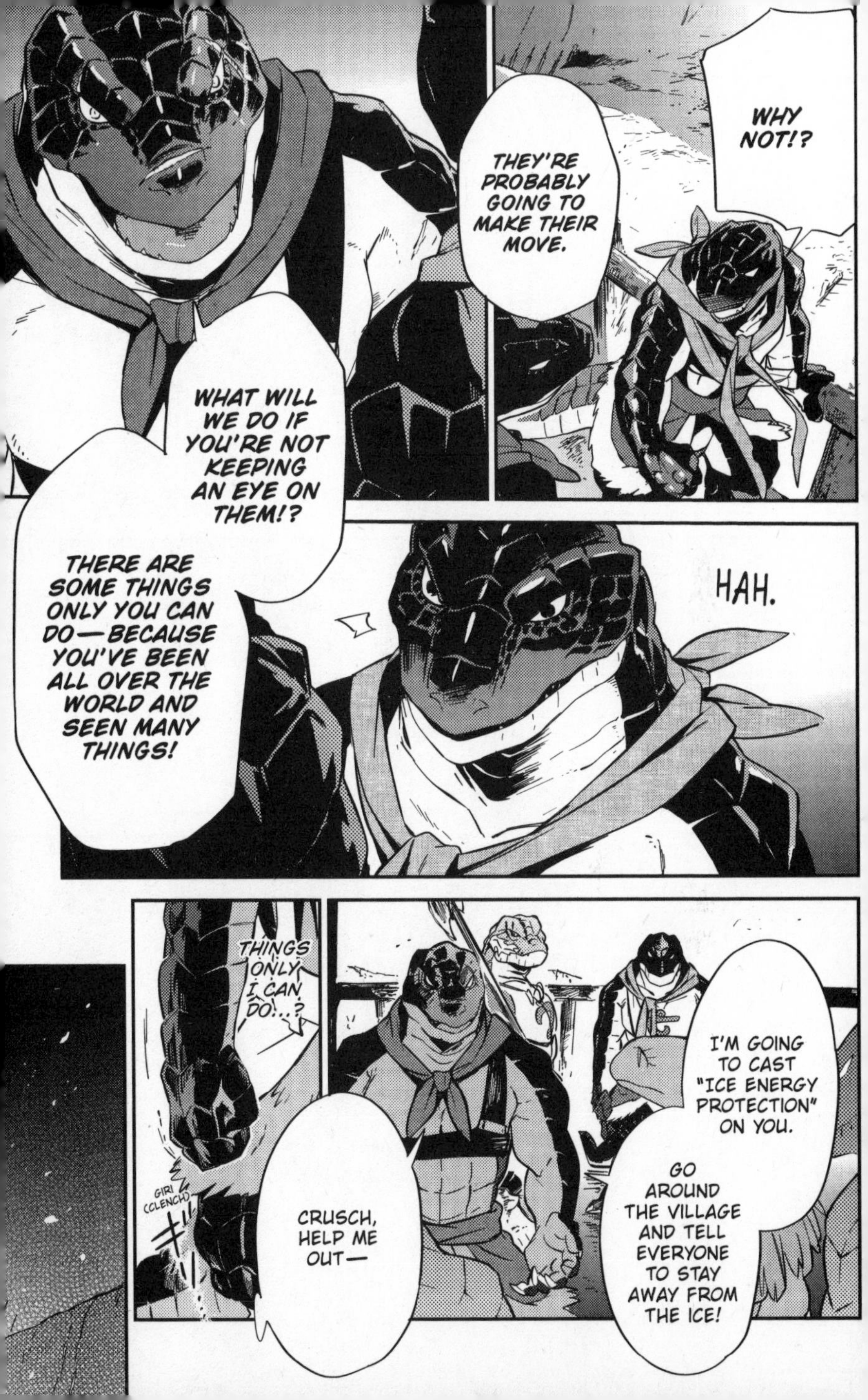
WHY NOT!?
THEY'RE PROBABLY GOING TO MAKE THEIR MOVE.
WHAT WILL WE DO IF YOU'RE NOT KEEPING AN EYE ON THEM!?
HAH.
THERE ARE SOME THINGS ONLY YOU CAN DO—BECAUSE YOU'VE BEEN ALL OVER THE WORLD AND SEEN MANY THINGS!
I'M GOING TO CAST "ICE ENERGY PROTECTION" ON YOU.
GO AROUND THE VILLAGE AND TELL EVERYONE TO STAY AWAY FROM THE ICE!
CRUSCH, HELP ME OUT—
THINGS ONLY I CAN DO...?
GIRI (CLENCH)

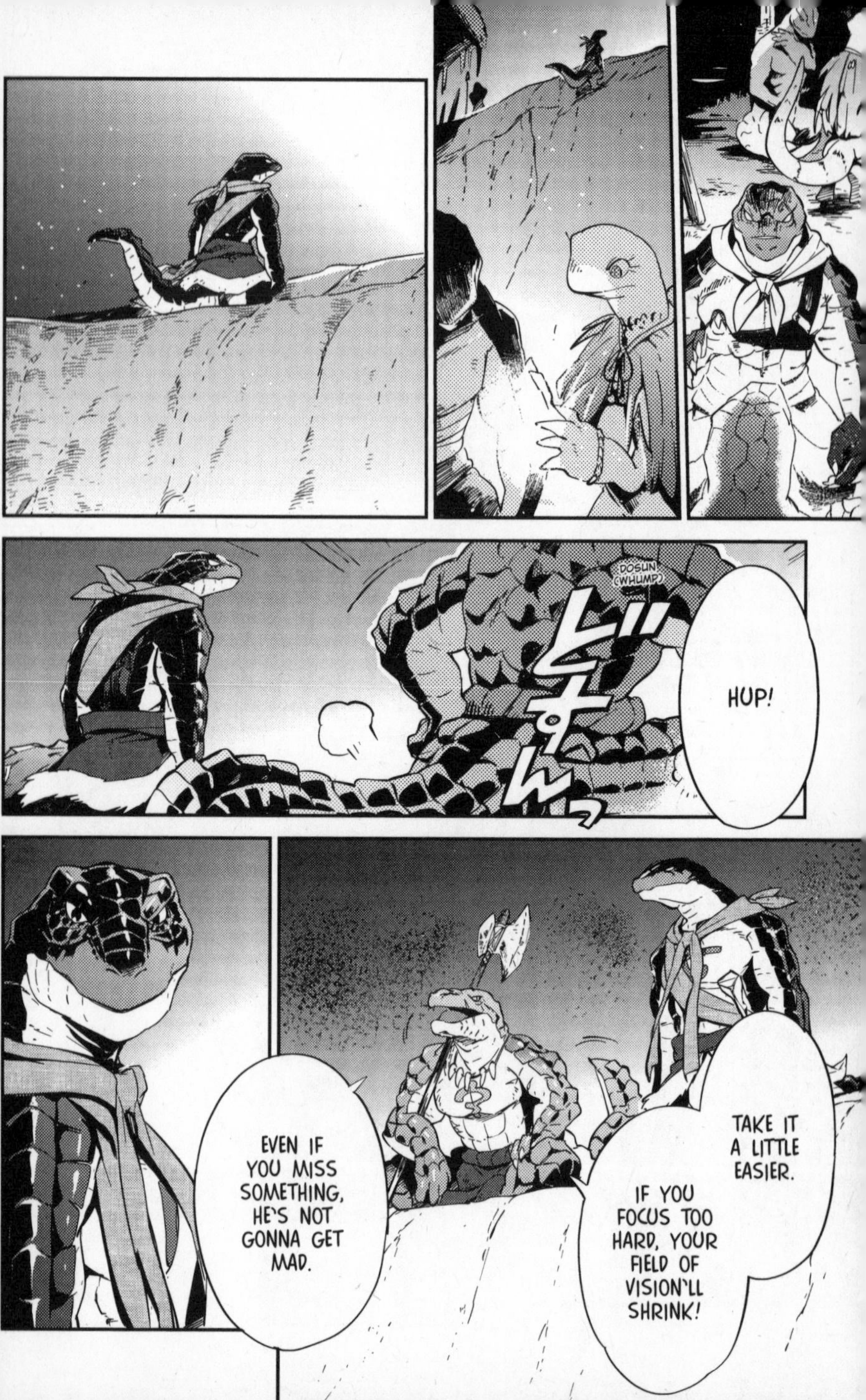
HUP!
DOSUN (WHUMP)
どすんっ
TAKE IT A LITTLE EASIER.
IF YOU FOCUS TOO HARD, YOUR FIELD OF VISION'LL SHRINK!
EVEN IF YOU MISS SOMETHING, HE'S NOT GONNA GET MAD.

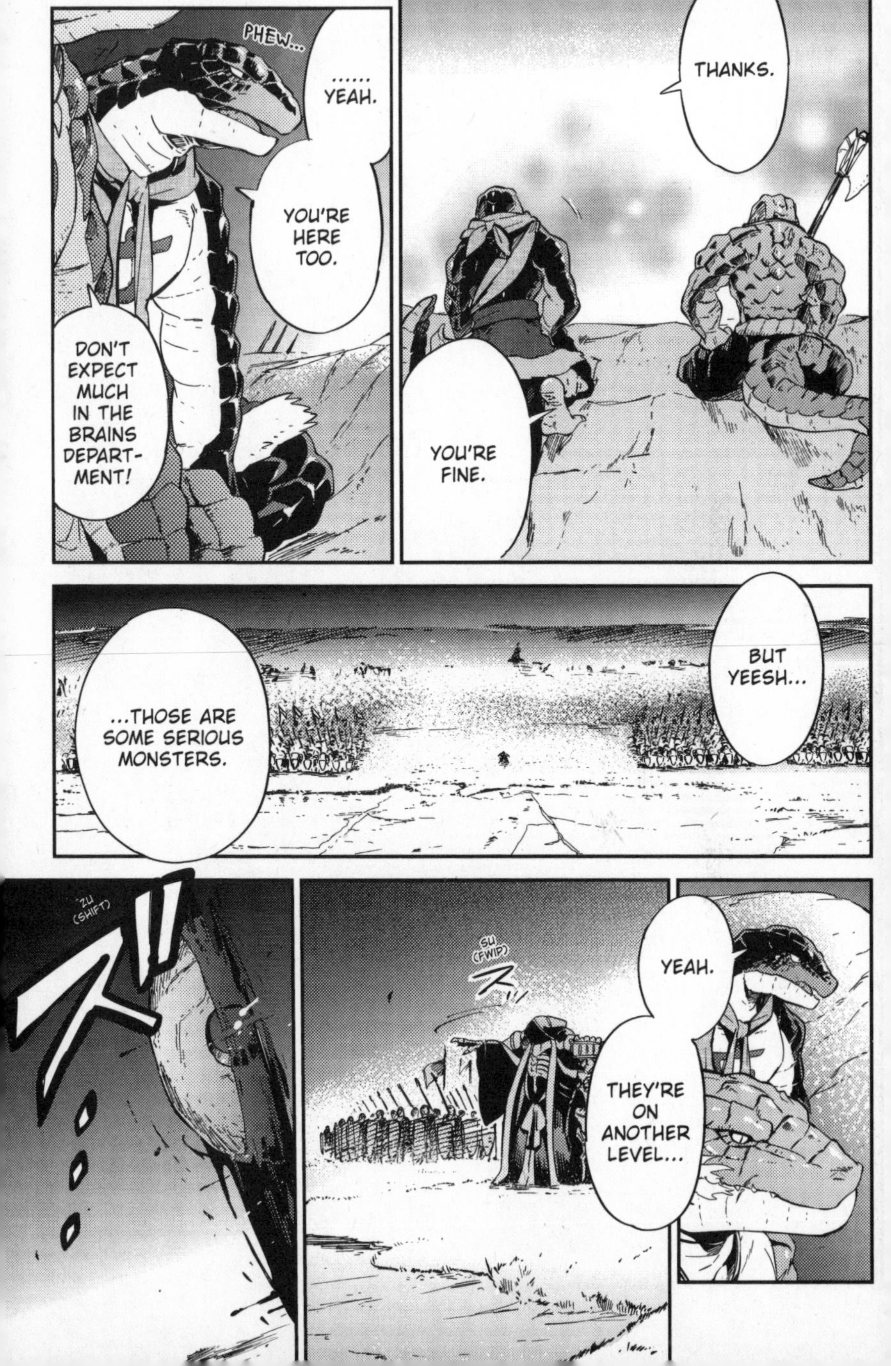
THANKS.
YOU'RE FINE.
PHEW...
......YEAH.
YOU'RE HERE TOO.
DON'T EXPECT MUCH IN THE BRAINS DEPARTMENT!
BUT YEESH...
...THOSE ARE SOME SERIOUS MONSTERS.
YEAH.
THEY'RE ON ANOTHER LEVEL...
SU (FWIP)
ZU (SHIFT)

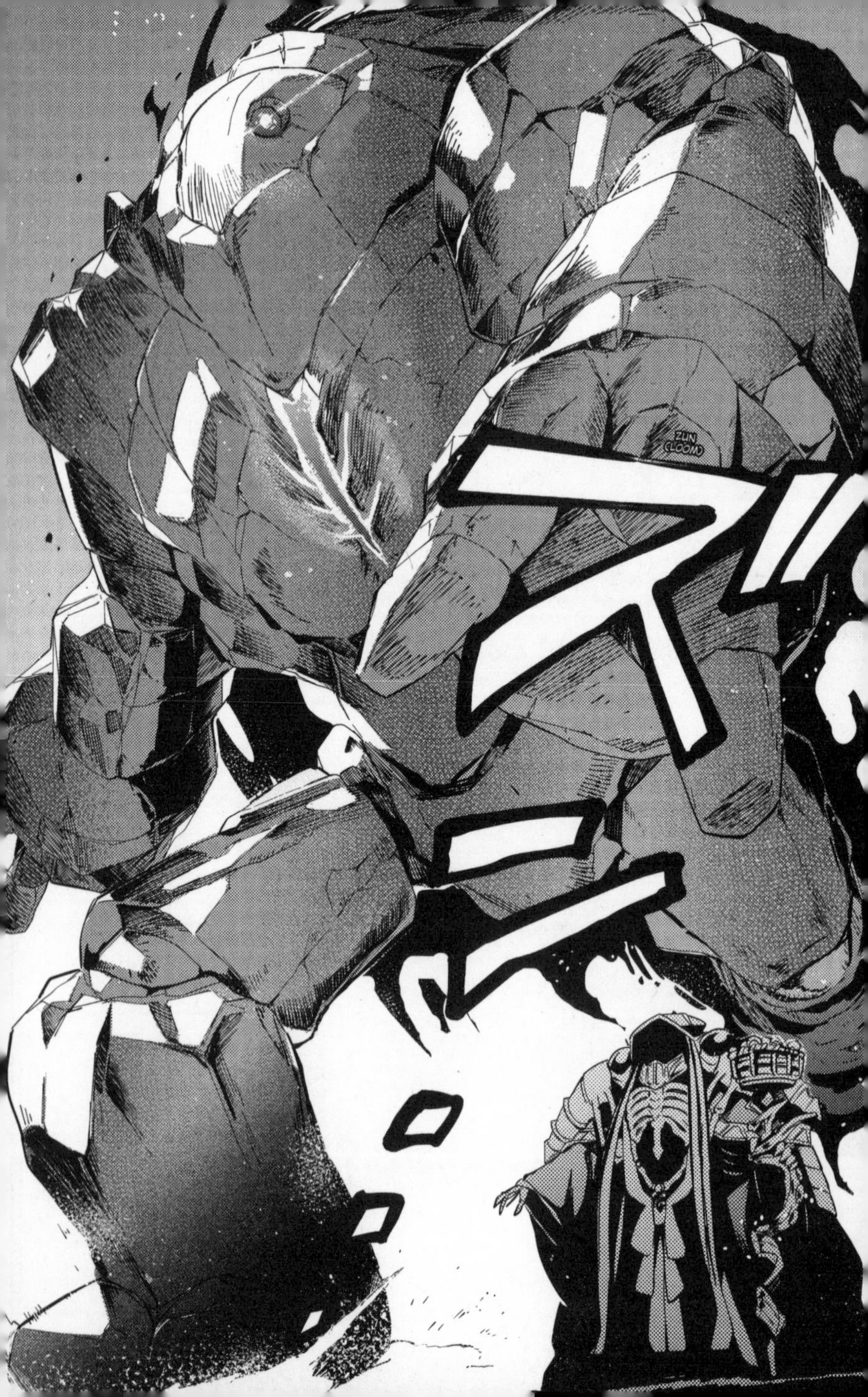
ZUN (LOOM)

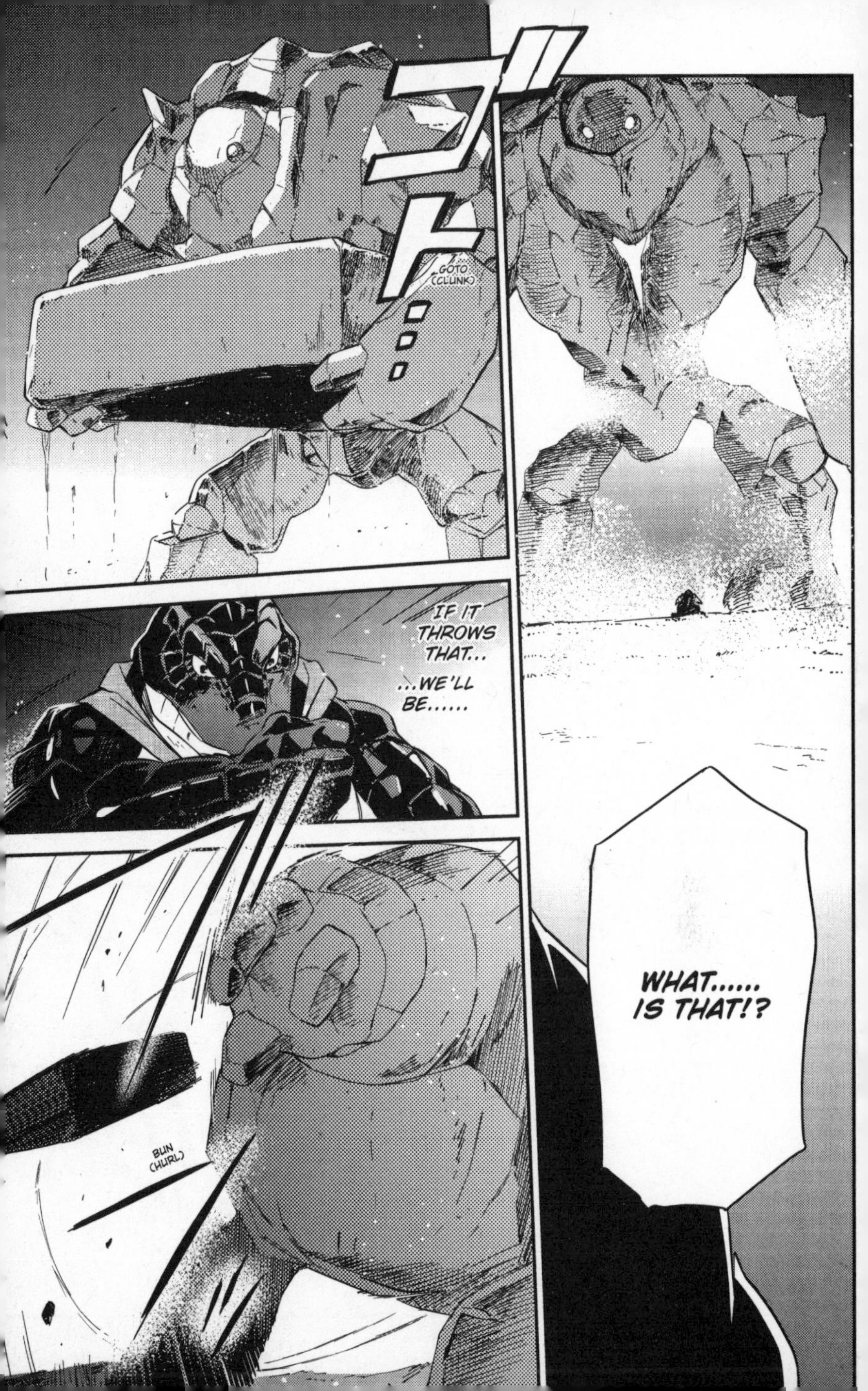
WHAT...... IS THAT!?
ゴト
GOTO (CLUNK)
IF IT THROWS THAT...
...WE'LL BE......
BUN (HURL)

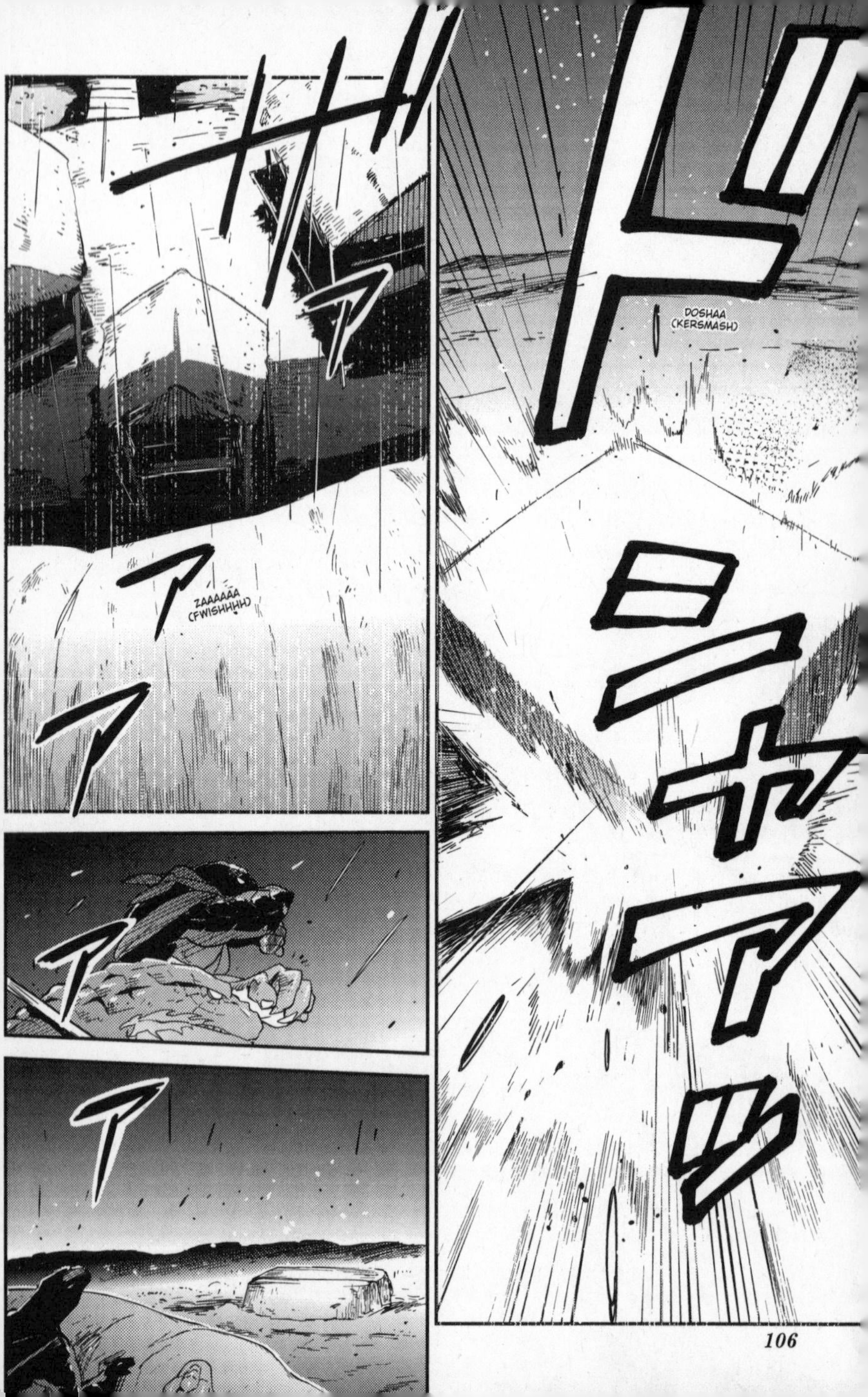
ドシャアッ
DOSHAA
(KERSMASH)
ザァァァァ
ZAAAAAA
(FWISHHHH)
ァァ
ァ

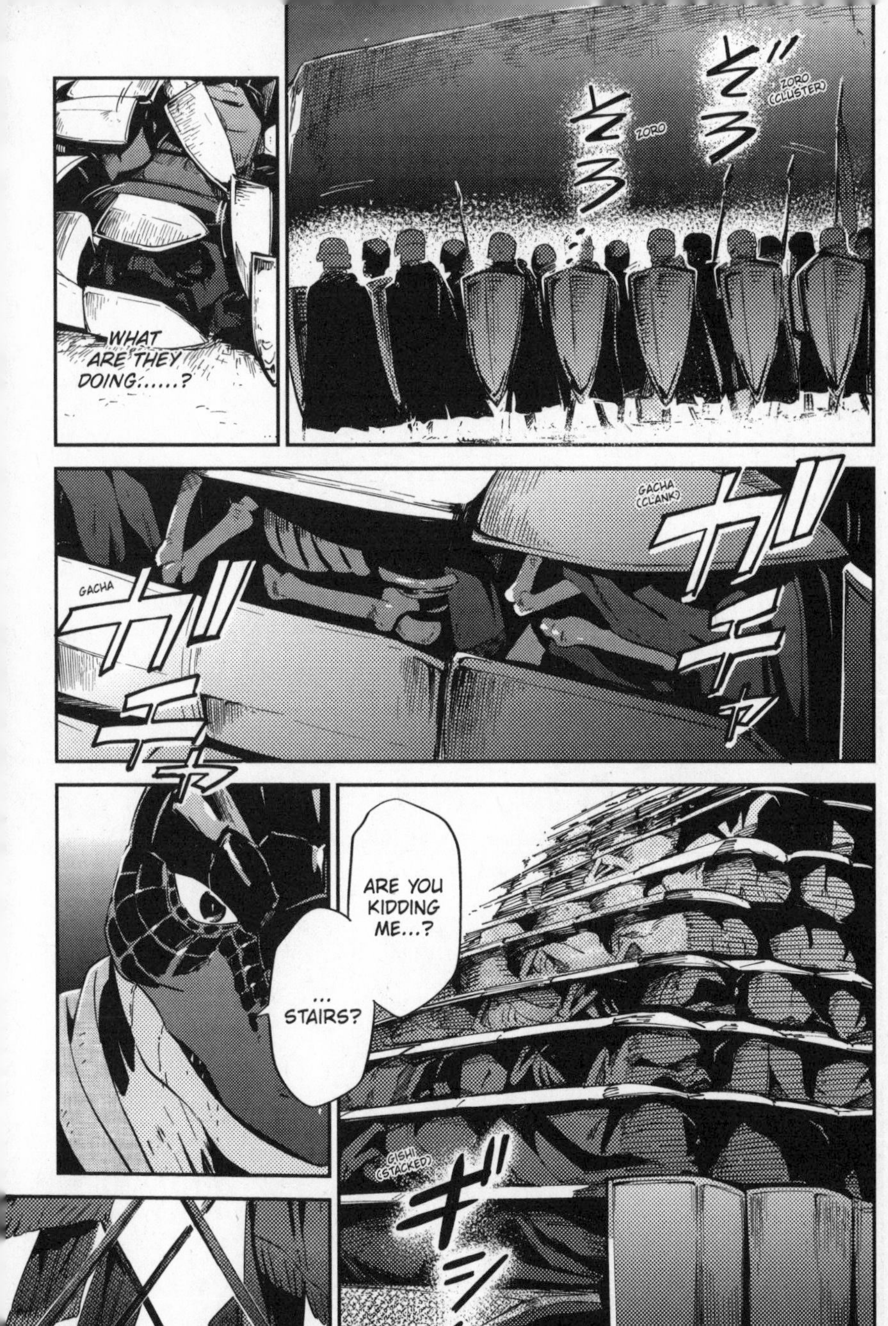
ZORO (CLUSTER)
ZORO
WHAT ARE THEY DOING......?
GACHA (CLANK)
GACHA
GISHI (STACKED)
ARE YOU KIDDING ME...?
... STAIRS?

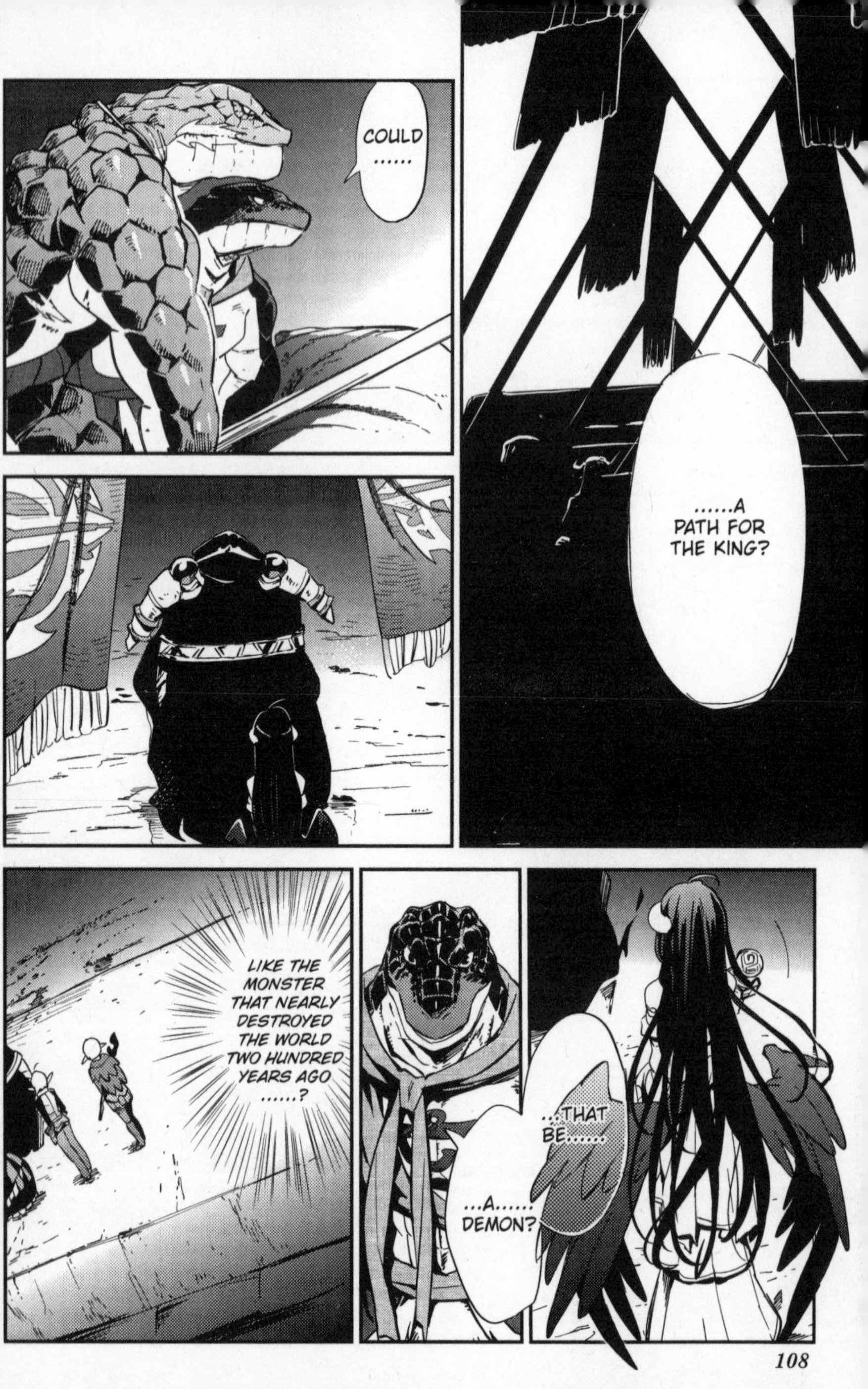
......A PATH FOR THE KING?
COULD ......
...THAT BE......
...A...... DEMON?
LIKE THE MONSTER THAT NEARLY DESTROYED THE WORLD TWO HUNDRED YEARS AGO ......?

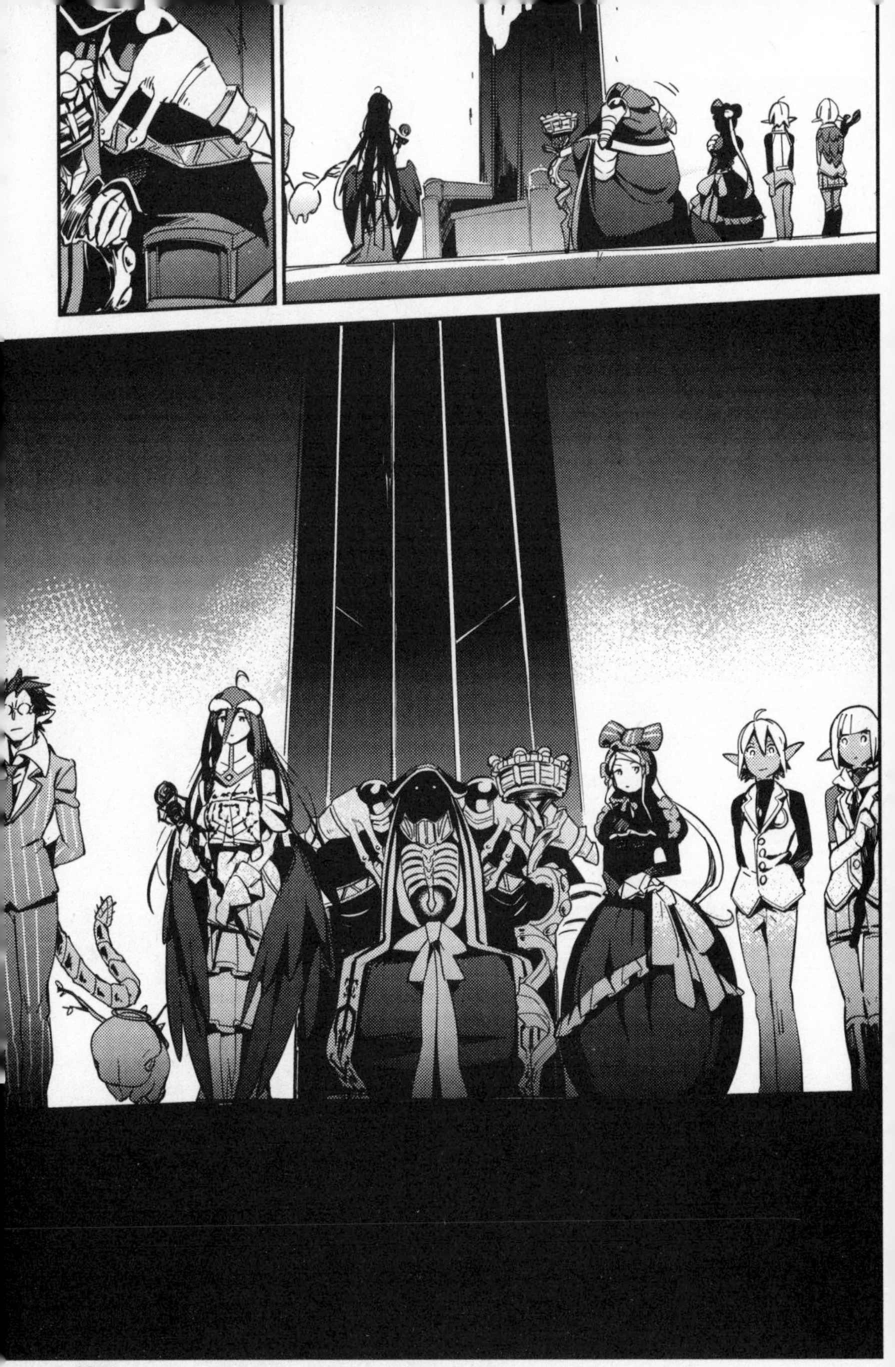

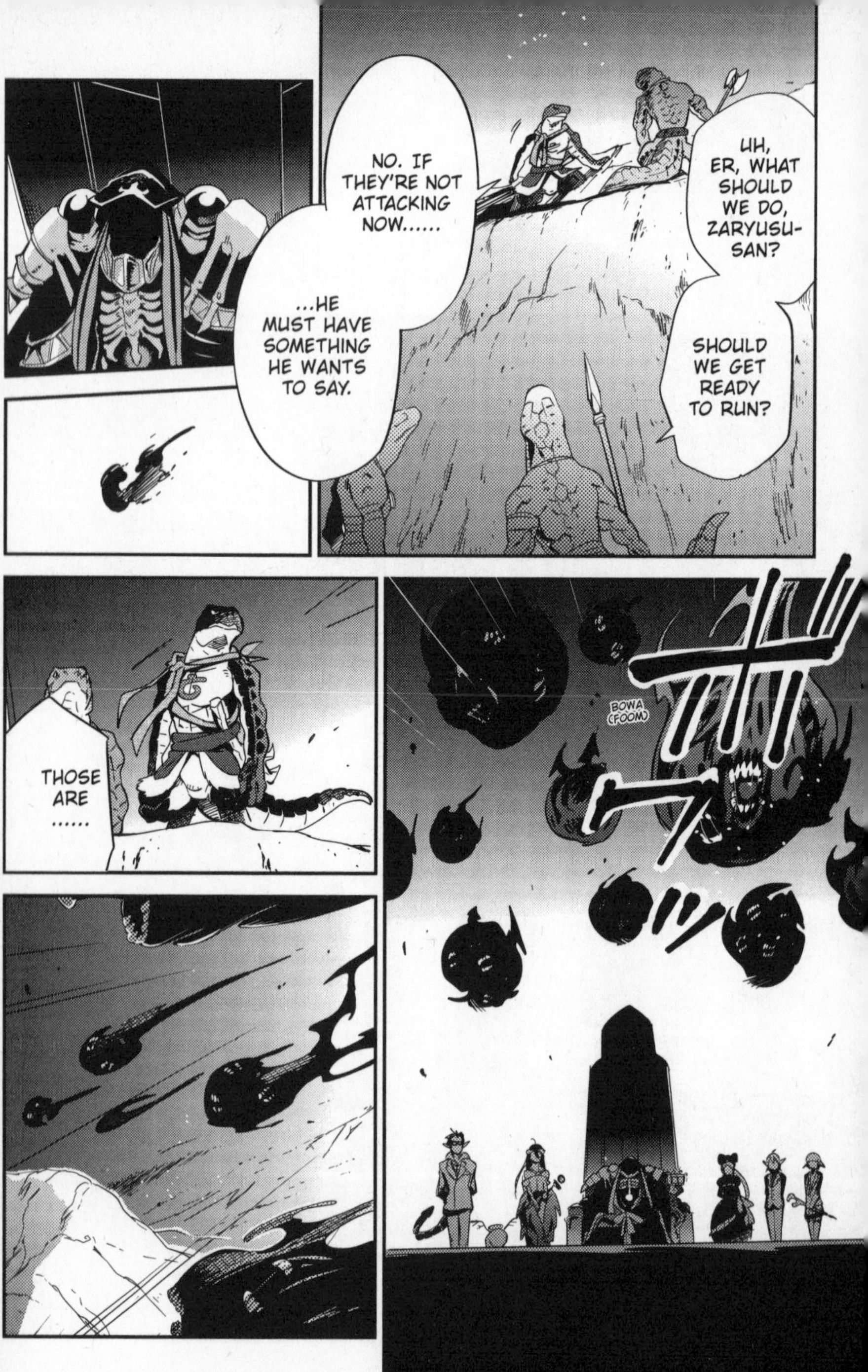
UH, ER, WHAT SHOULD WE DO, ZARYUSU-SAN?
SHOULD WE GET READY TO RUN?
NO. IF THEY'RE NOT ATTACKING NOW......
...HE MUST HAVE SOMETHING HE WANTS TO SAY.
BOWA (FOOM)
THOSE ARE ......

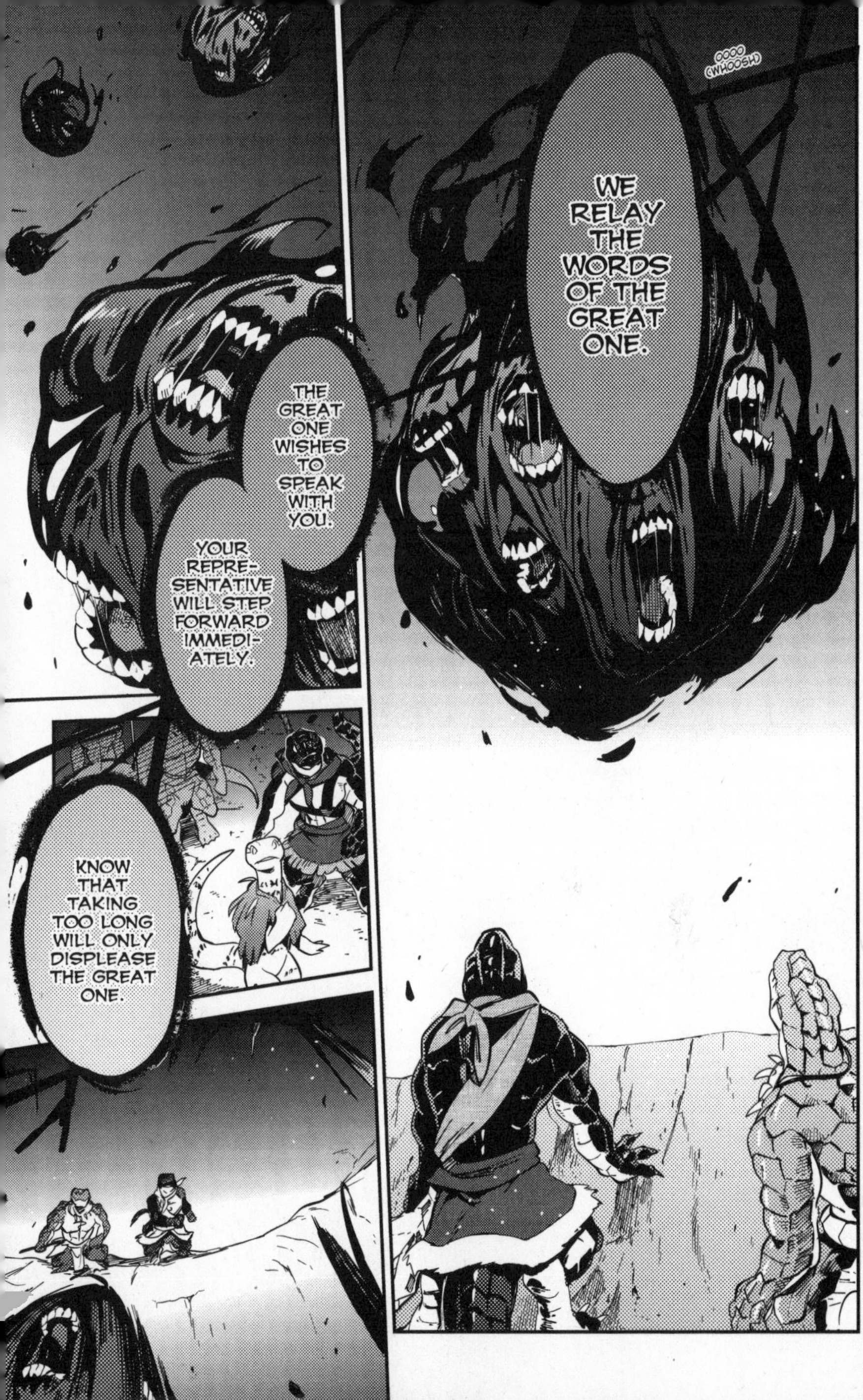
OOOO (WHOOSH)
WE RELAY THE WORDS OF THE GREAT ONE.
THE GREAT ONE WISHES TO SPEAK WITH YOU.
YOUR REPRESENTATIVE WILL STEP FORWARD IMMEDIATELY.
KNOW THAT TAKING TOO LONG WILL ONLY DISPLEASE THE GREAT ONE.

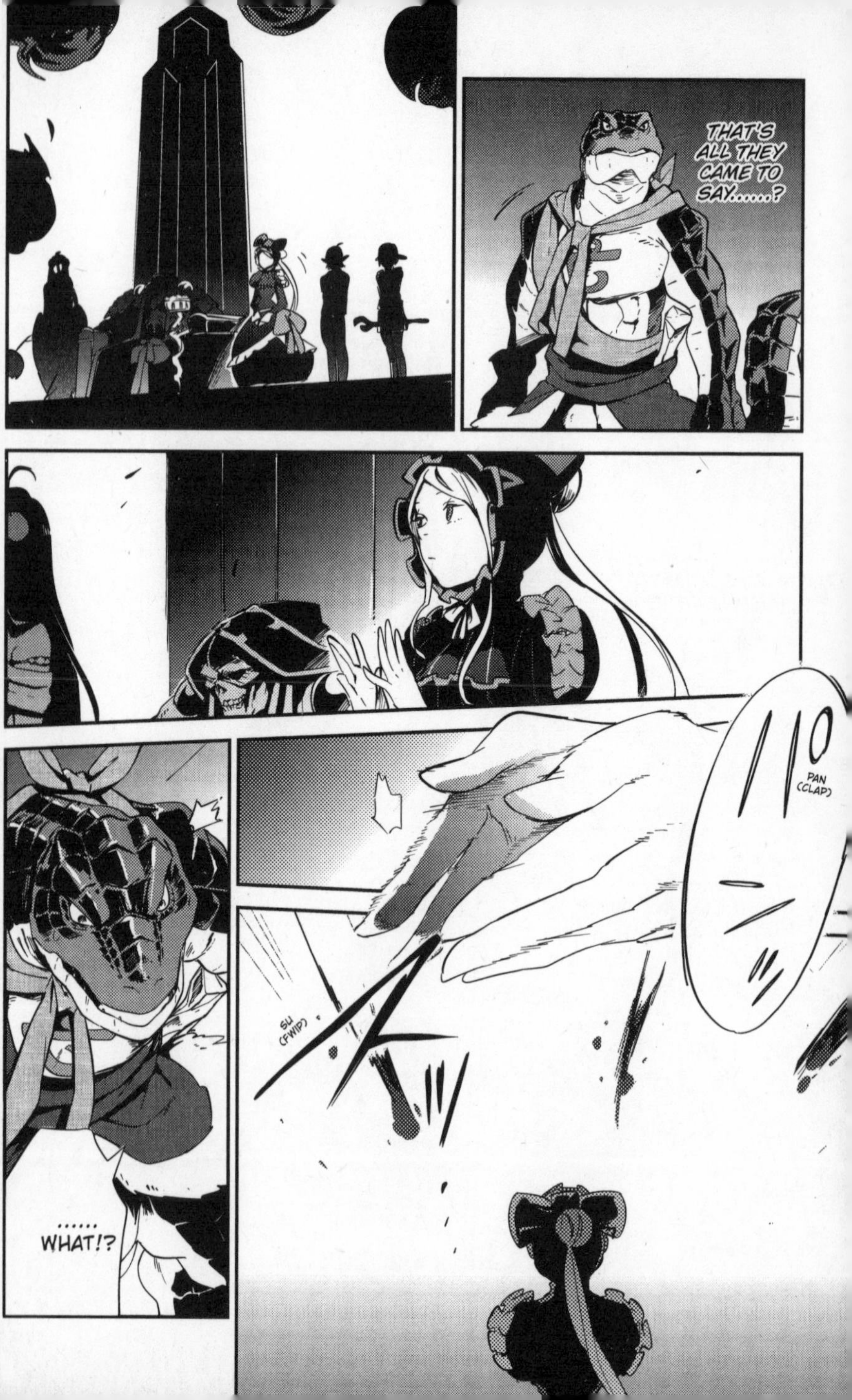

THAT'S ALL THEY CAME TO SAY......?
PAN (CLAP)
SU (FWIP)
...... WHAT!?

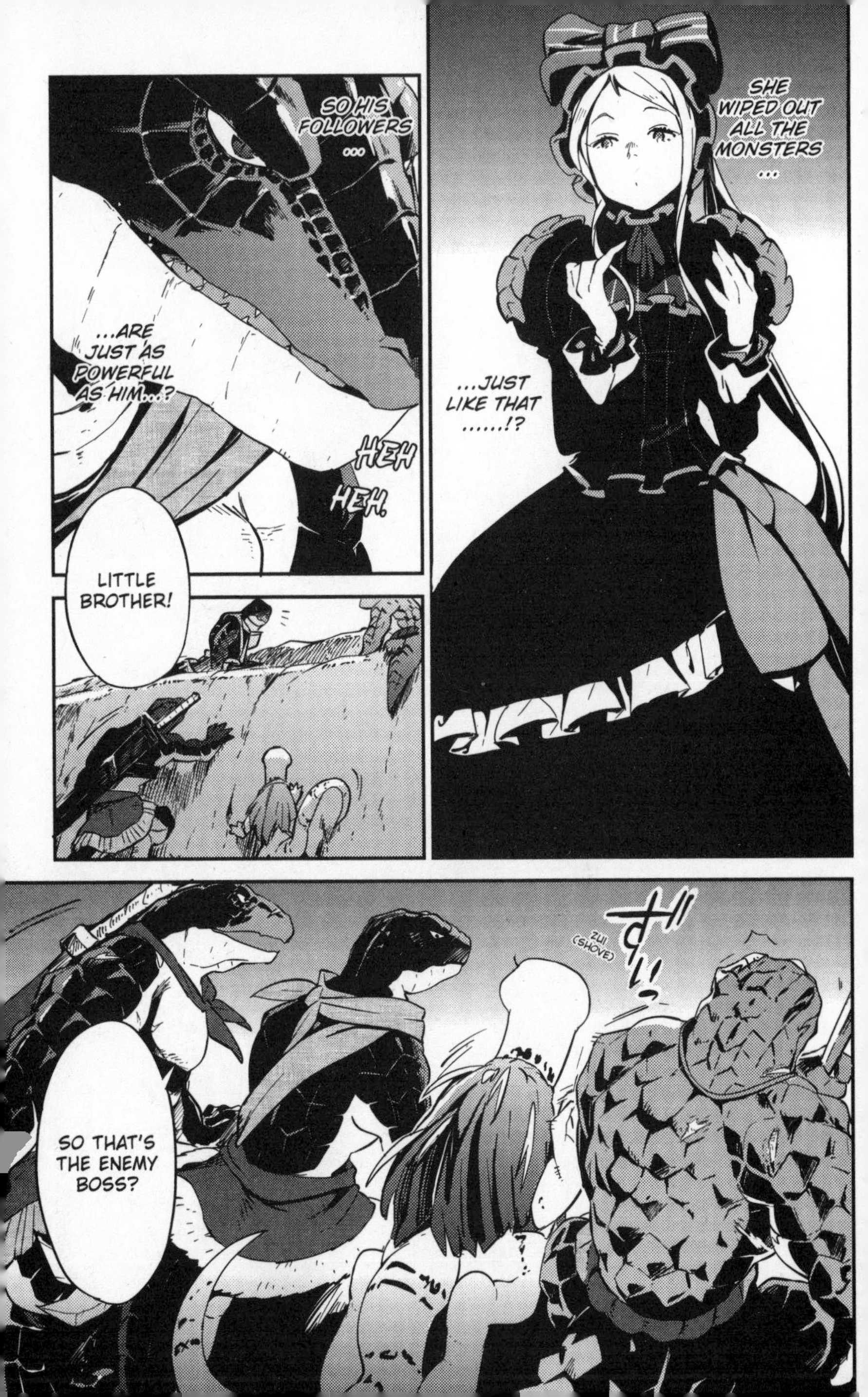
SHE WIPED OUT ALL THE MONSTERS ...
...JUST LIKE THAT ......!?
SO HIS FOLLOWERS ...
...ARE JUST AS POWERFUL AS HIM...?
HEH HEH.
LITTLE BROTHER!
ZUI (SHOVE)
SO THAT'S THE ENEMY BOSS?

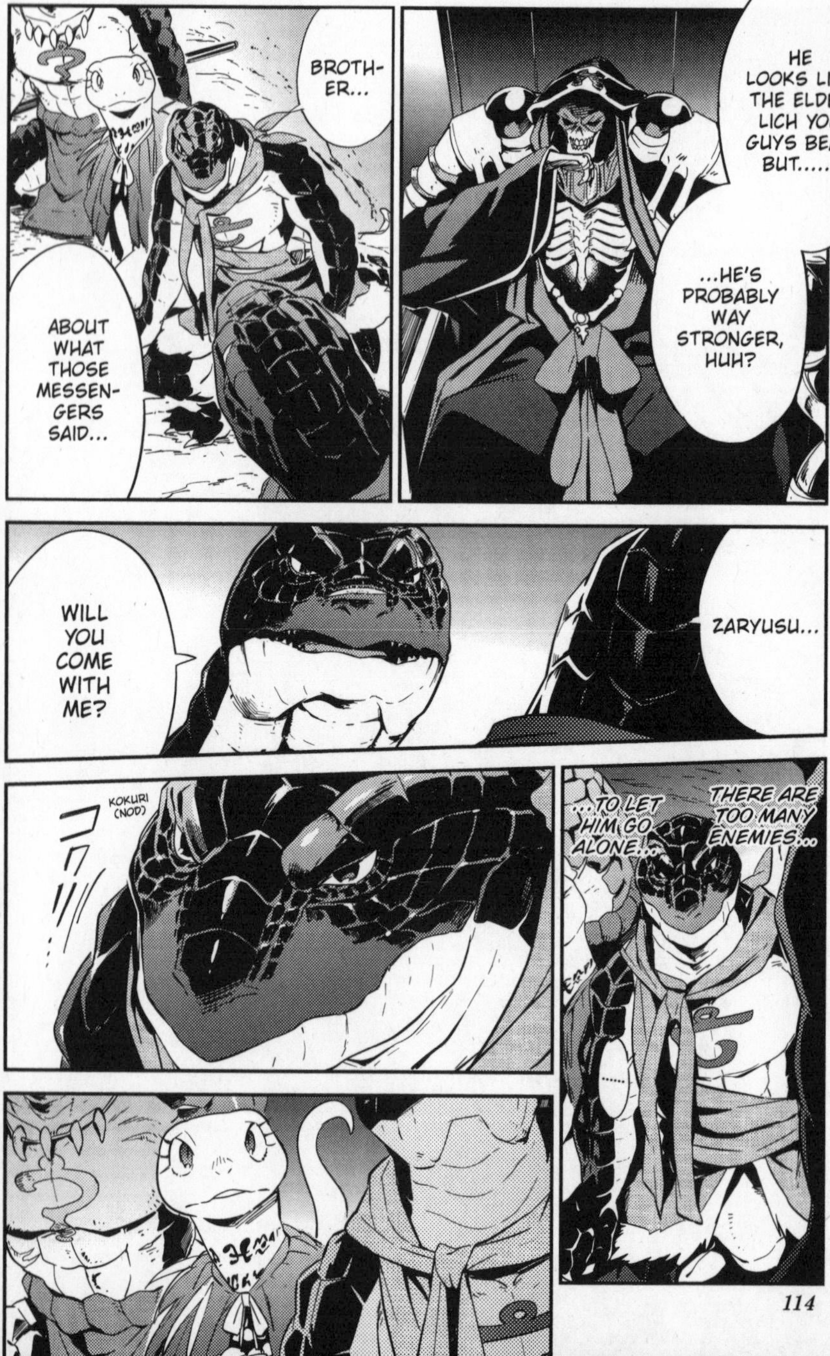
HE LOOKS LIKE THE ELDER LICH YOU GUYS BEAT, BUT......
...HE'S PROBABLY WAY STRONGER, HUH?
BROTH-ER...
ABOUT WHAT THOSE MESSEN-GERS SAID...
ZARYUSU...
WILL YOU COME WITH ME?
THERE ARE TOO MANY ENEMIES...
...TO LET HIM GO ALONE...
......
KOKURI (NOD)

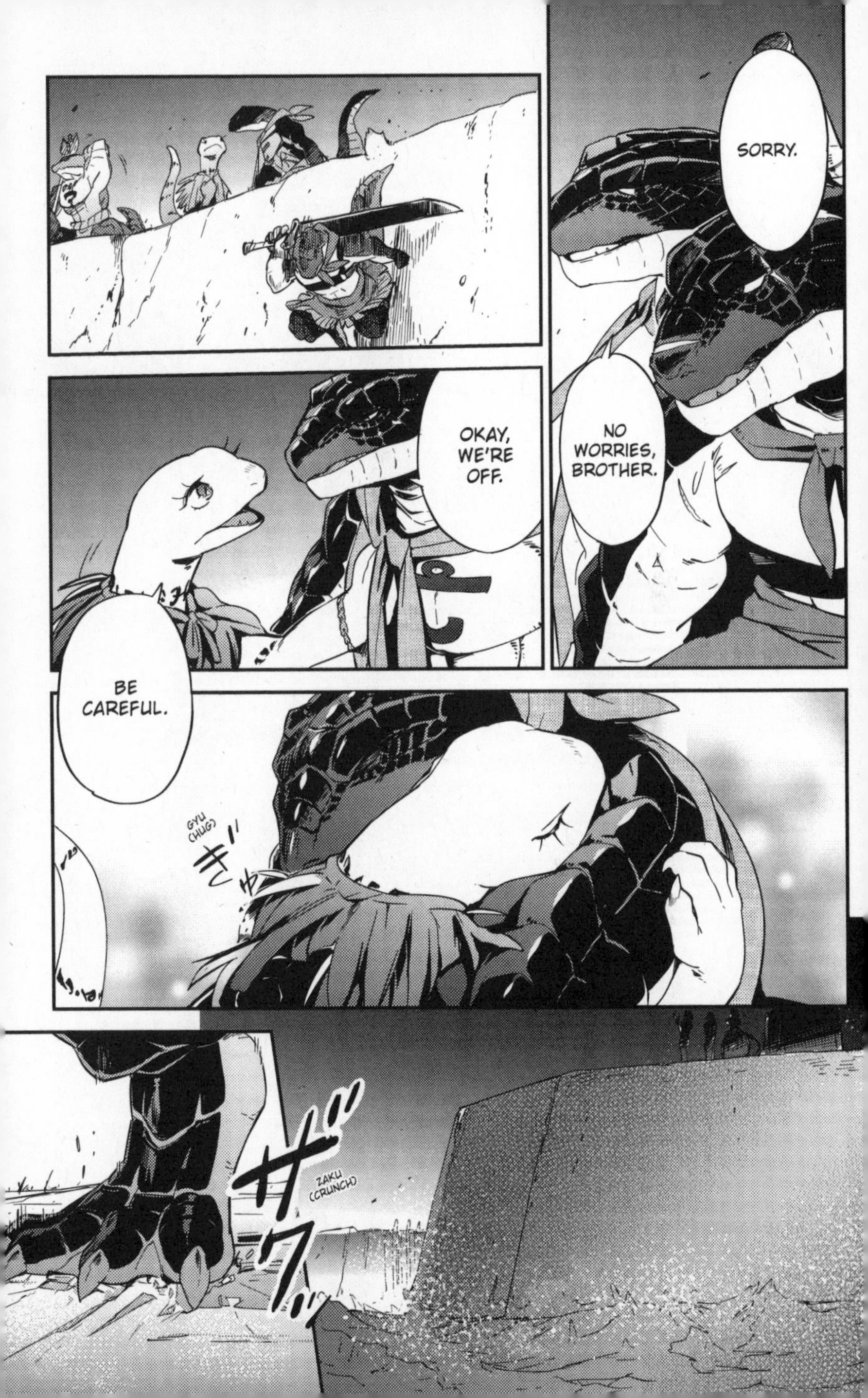
SORRY.
NO WORRIES, BROTHER.
OKAY, WE'RE OFF.
BE CAREFUL.
GYU (HUG)
ZAKU (CRUNCH)

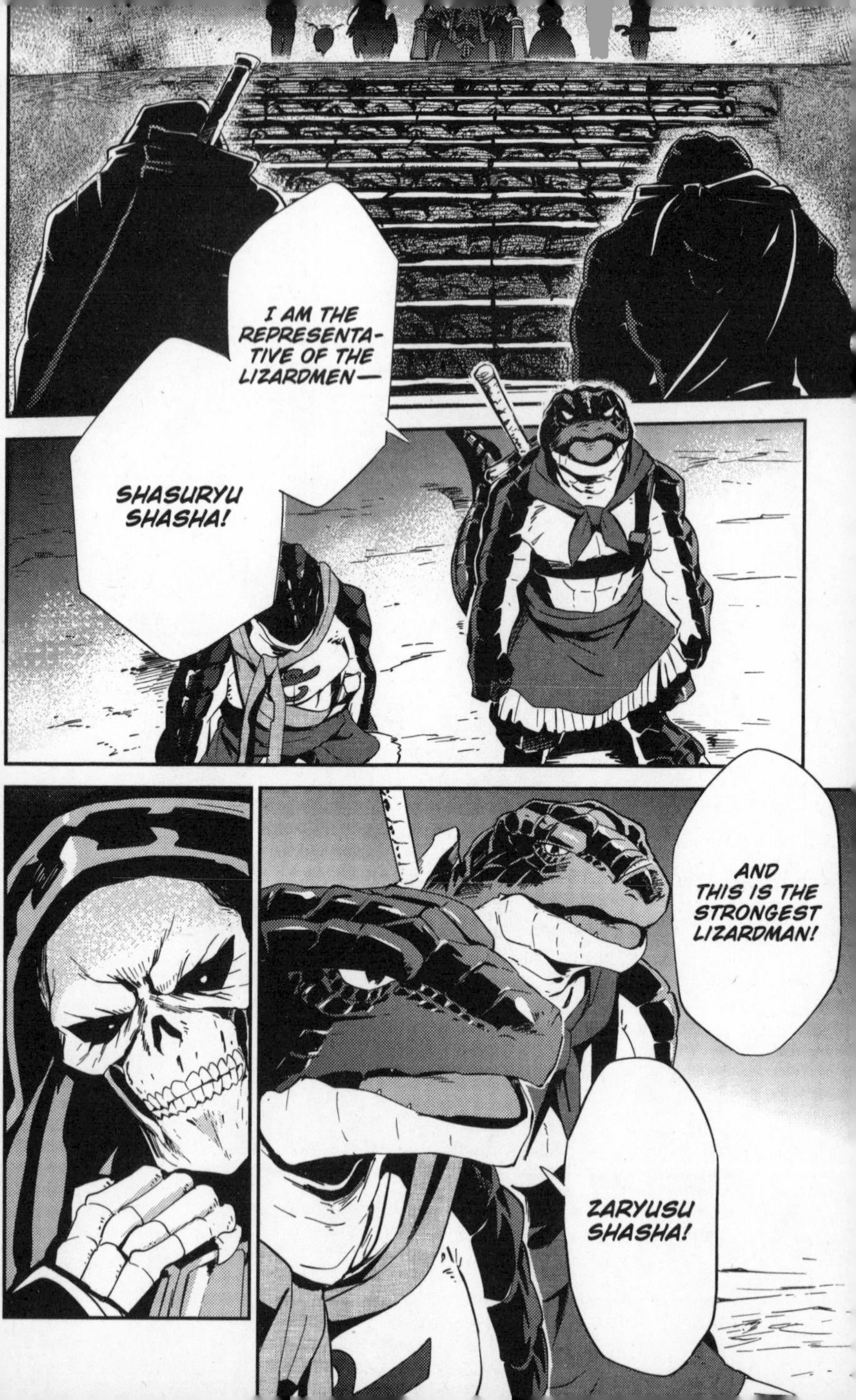
I AM THE REPRESENTATIVE OF THE LIZARDMEN—
SHASURYU SHASHA!
AND THIS IS THE STRONGEST LIZARDMAN!
ZARYUSU SHASHA!

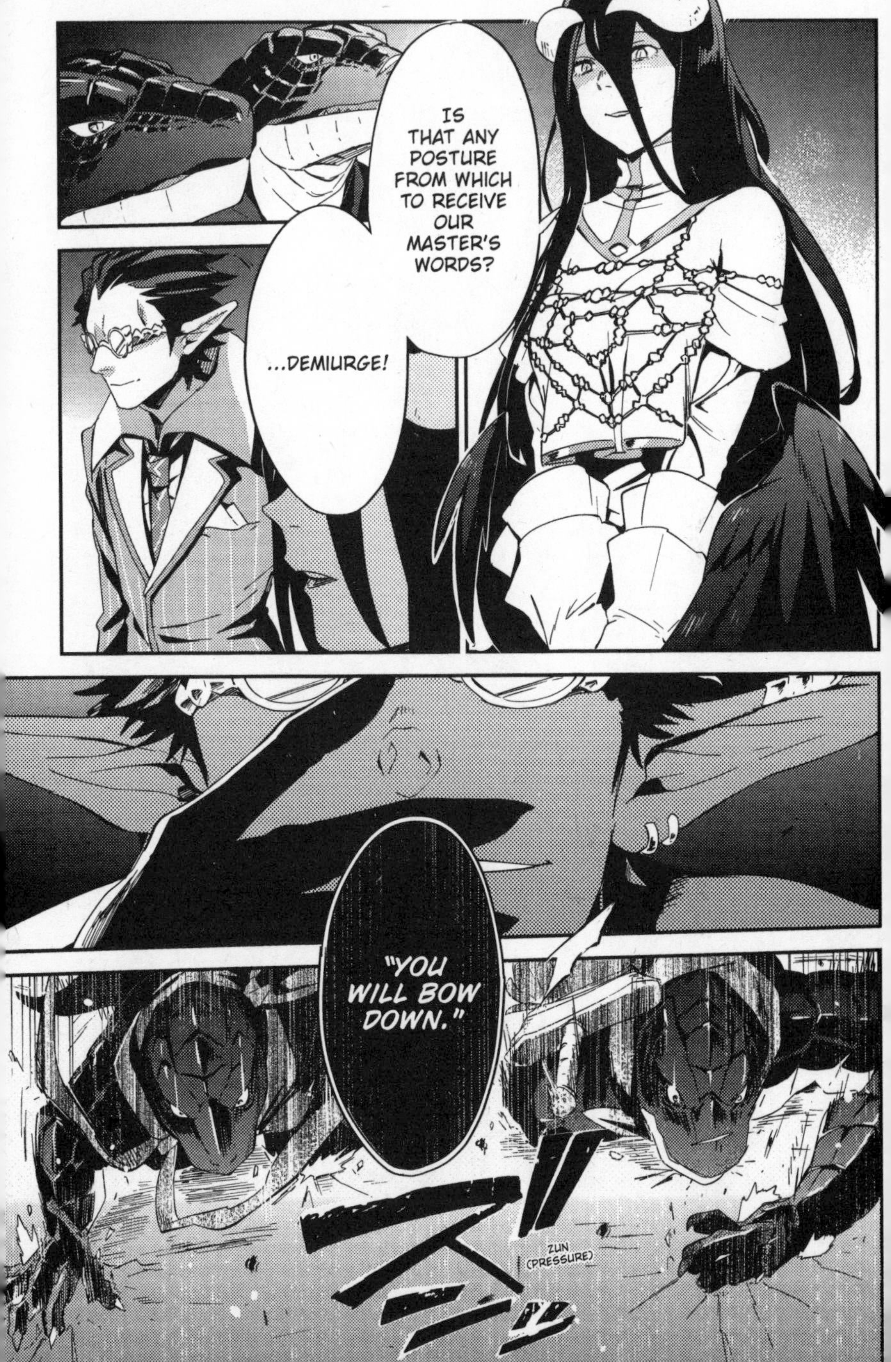
IS THAT ANY POSTURE FROM WHICH TO RECEIVE OUR MASTER'S WORDS?
...DEMIURGE!
"YOU WILL BOW DOWN."
ZUN (PRESSURE)

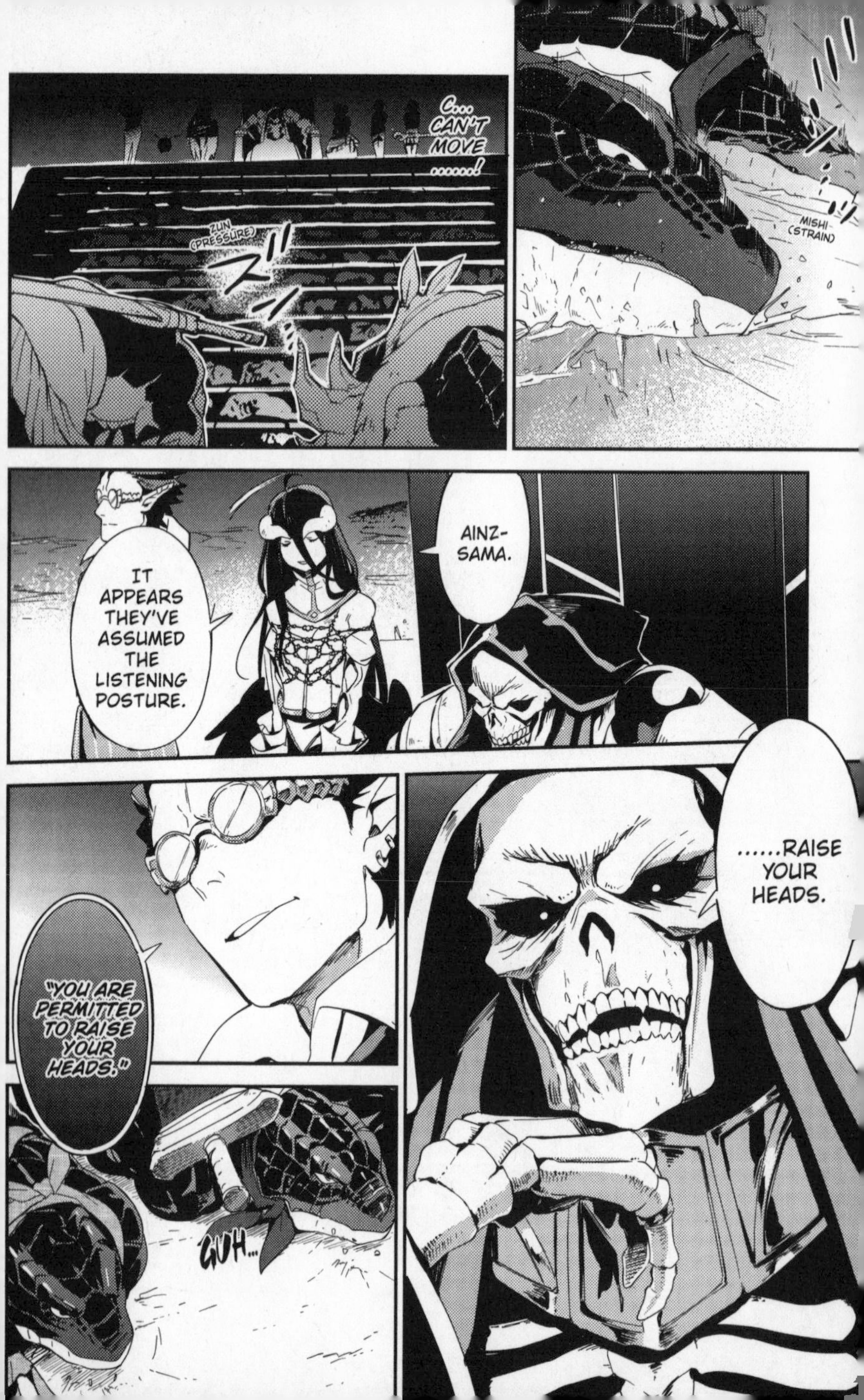
MISHI (STRAIN)
C... CAN'T MOVE ......!
ZUN (PRESSURE)
AINZ-SAMA.
IT APPEARS THEY'VE ASSUMED THE LISTENING POSTURE.
......RAISE YOUR HEADS.
"YOU ARE PERMITTED TO RAISE YOUR HEADS."
GUH...

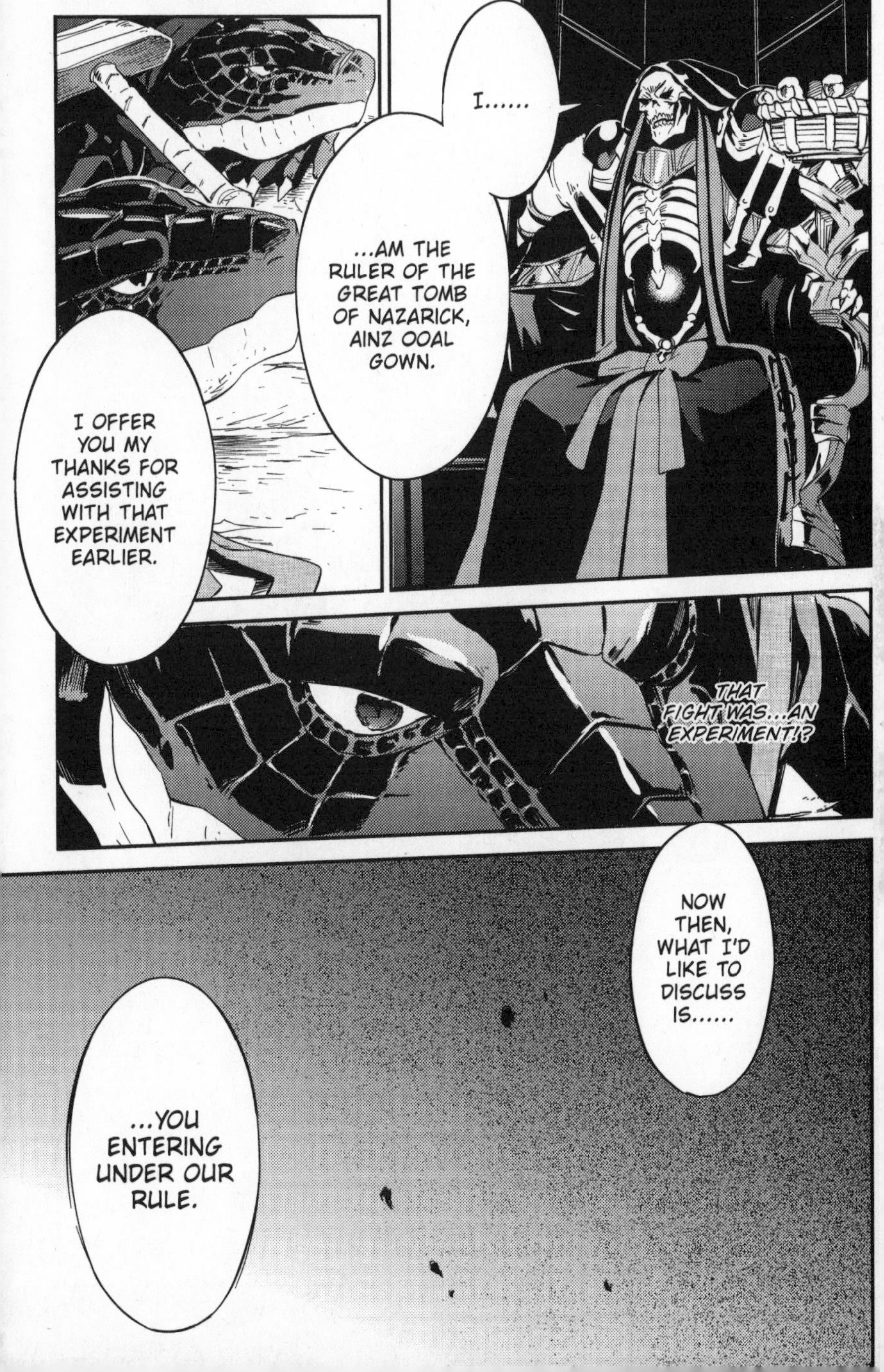
I......
...AM THE RULER OF THE GREAT TOMB OF NAZARICK, AINZ OOAL GOWN.
I OFFER YOU MY THANKS FOR ASSISTING WITH THAT EXPERIMENT EARLIER.
THAT FIGHT WAS...AN EXPERIMENT!?
NOW THEN, WHAT I'D LIKE TO DISCUSS IS......
...YOU ENTERING UNDER OUR RULE.

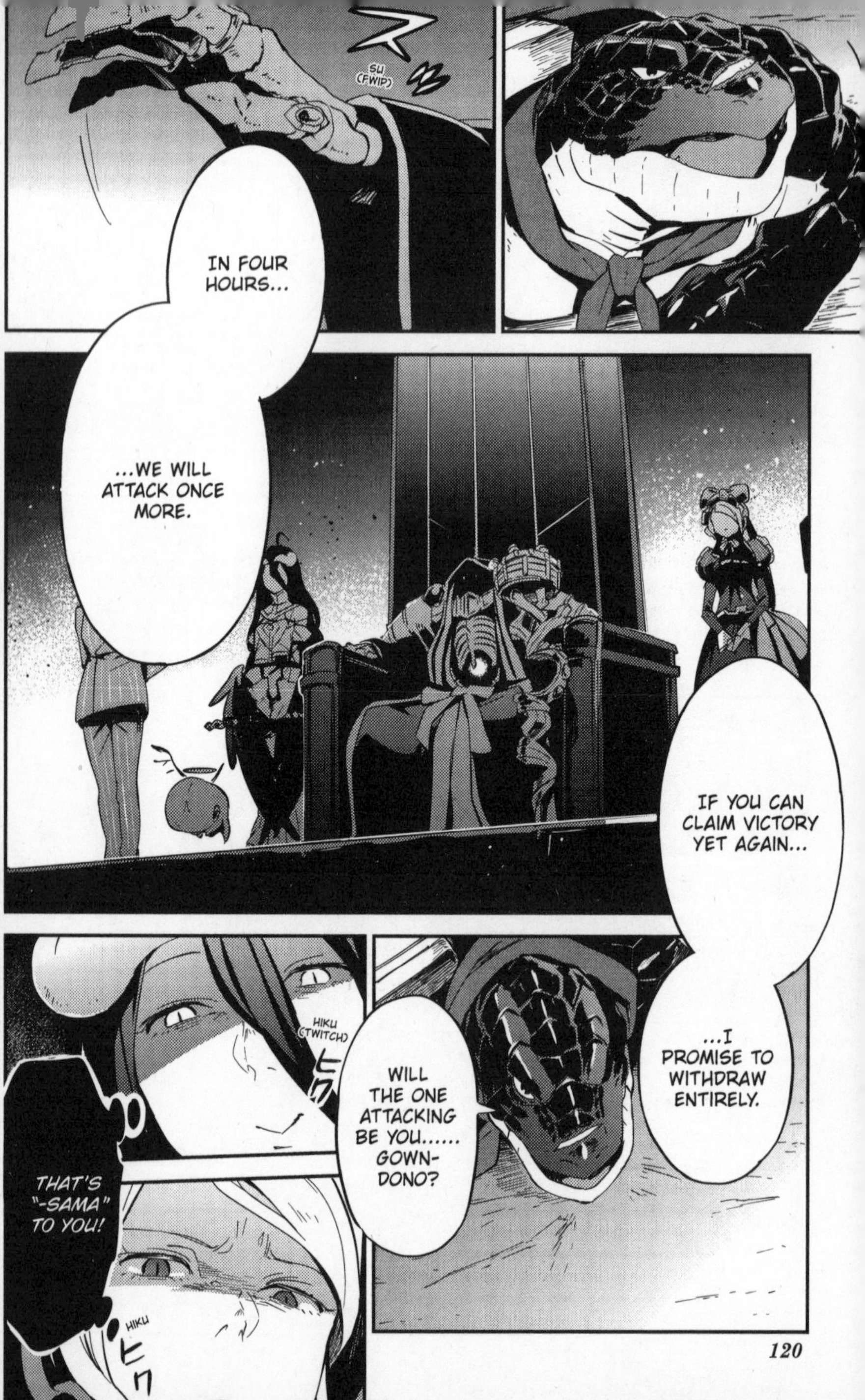
SU (FWIP)
IN FOUR HOURS...
...WE WILL ATTACK ONCE MORE.
IF YOU CAN CLAIM VICTORY YET AGAIN...
...I PROMISE TO WITHDRAW ENTIRELY.
WILL THE ONE ATTACKING BE YOU...... GOWN-DONO?
HIKU (TWITCH)
THAT'S "-SAMA" TO YOU!
HIKU

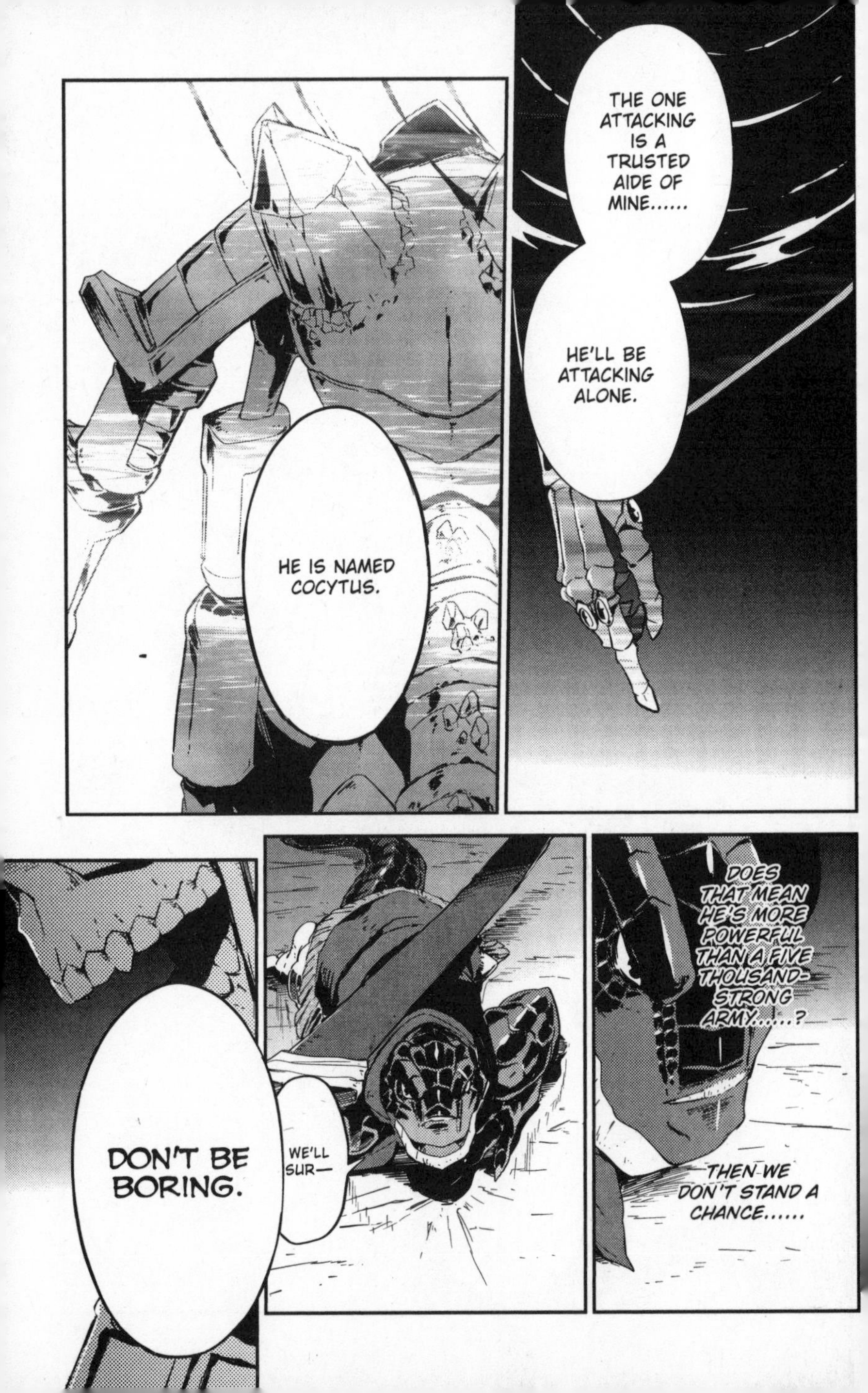
THE ONE ATTACKING IS A TRUSTED AIDE OF MINE......
HE'LL BE ATTACKING ALONE.
HE IS NAMED COCYTUS.
DOES THAT MEAN HE'S MORE POWERFUL THAN A FIVE THOUSAND-STRONG ARMY......?
THEN WE DON'T STAND A CHANCE......
WE'LL SUR—
DON'T BE BORING.

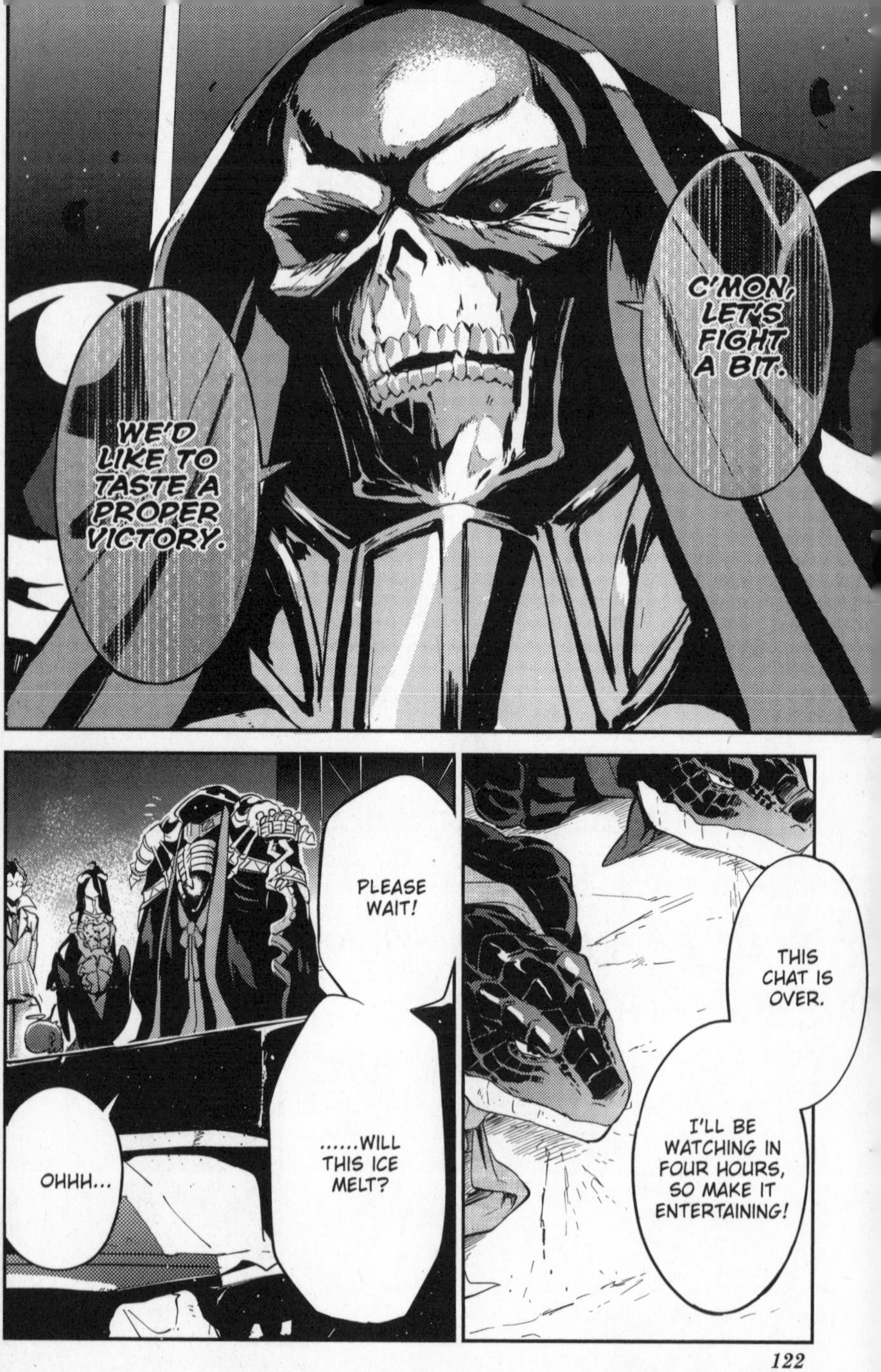
C'MON, LET'S FIGHT A BIT.
WE'D LIKE TO TASTE A PROPER VICTORY.
THIS CHAT IS OVER.
I'LL BE WATCHING IN FOUR HOURS, SO MAKE IT ENTERTAINING!
PLEASE WAIT!
......WILL THIS ICE MELT?
OHHH...

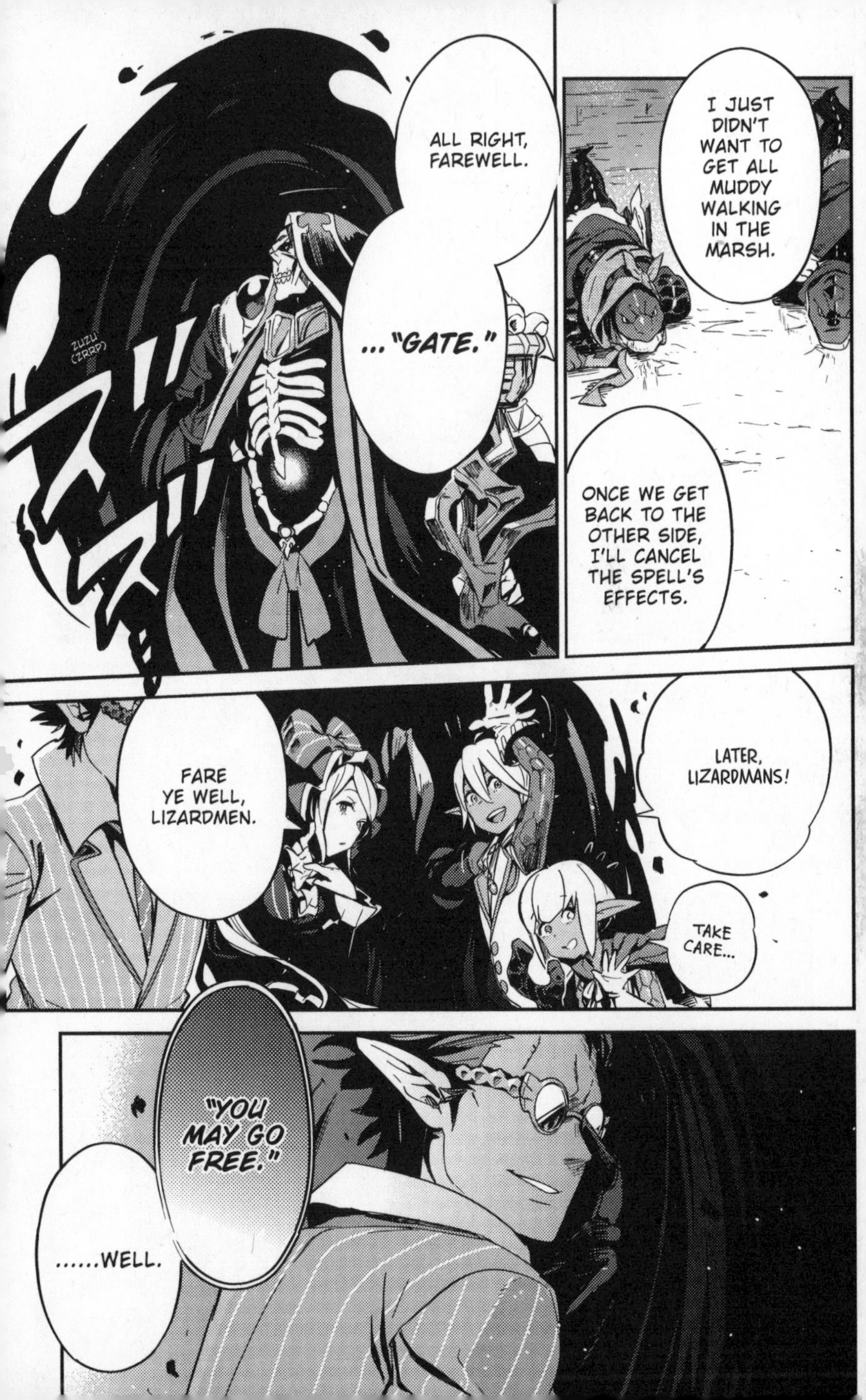
I JUST DIDN'T WANT TO GET ALL MUDDY WALKING IN THE MARSH.
ONCE WE GET BACK TO THE OTHER SIDE, I'LL CANCEL THE SPELL'S EFFECTS.
ALL RIGHT, FAREWELL.
..."GATE."
ZUZU' (ZRRP)
LATER, LIZARDMANS!
TAKE CARE...
FARE YE WELL, LIZARDMEN.
"YOU MAY GO FREE."
......WELL.

ZUZU
(ZRRP)

SHOW
US SOME
FUN...

...LIZARD-
MEN.

ZUZU

GIRI
(CLENCH)

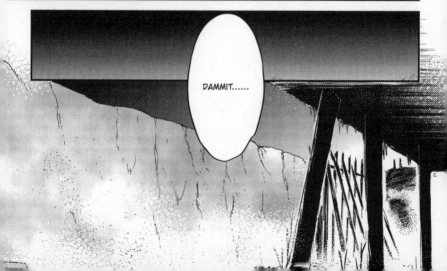

DAMMIT......

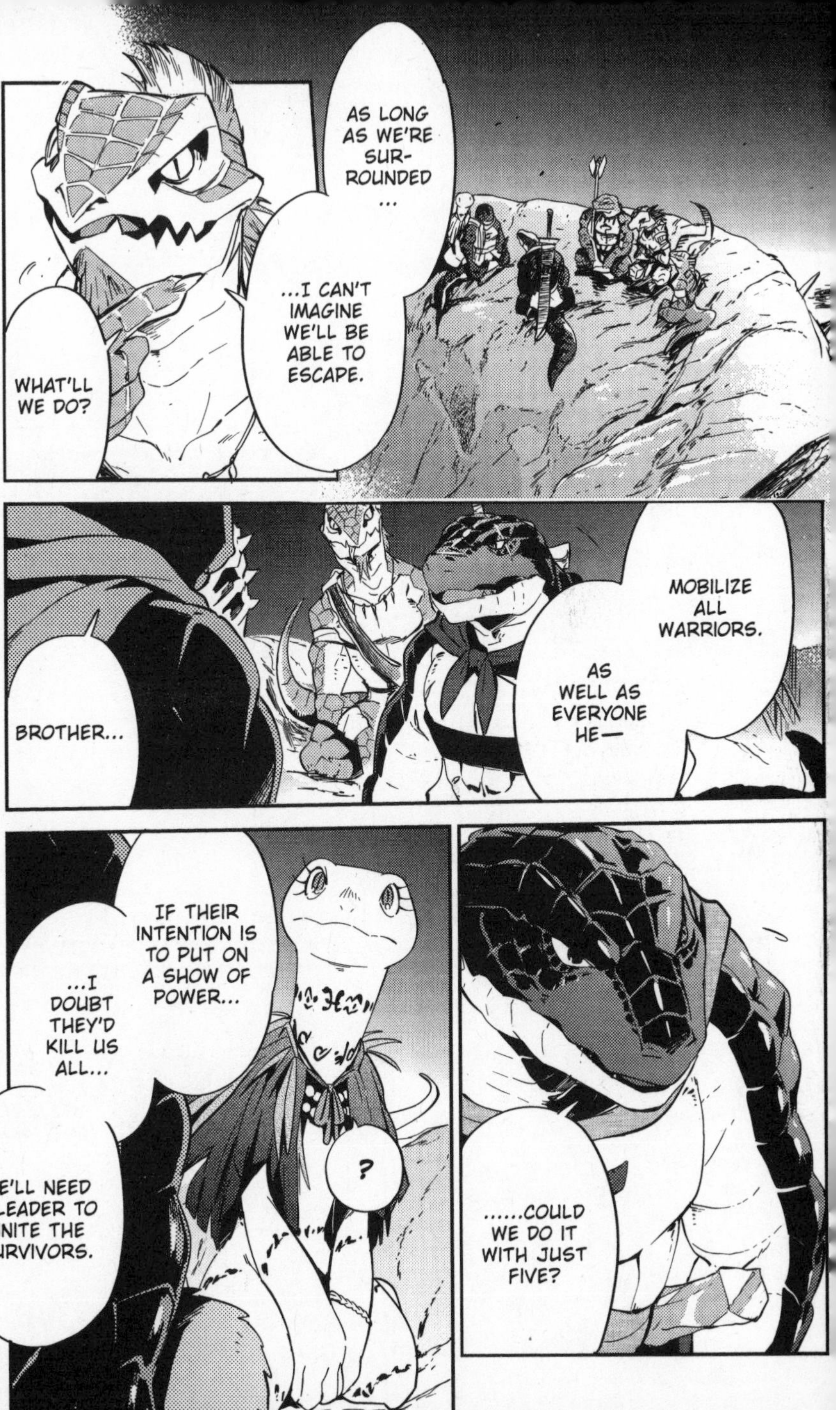
AS LONG AS WE'RE SUR-ROUNDED ...
...I CAN'T IMAGINE WE'LL BE ABLE TO ESCAPE.
WHAT'LL WE DO?
MOBILIZE ALL WARRIORS.
AS WELL AS EVERYONE HE—
BROTHER...
......COULD WE DO IT WITH JUST FIVE?
IF THEIR INTENTION IS TO PUT ON A SHOW OF POWER...
...I DOUBT THEY'D KILL US ALL...
?
WE'LL NEED A LEADER TO UNITE THE SURVIVORS.

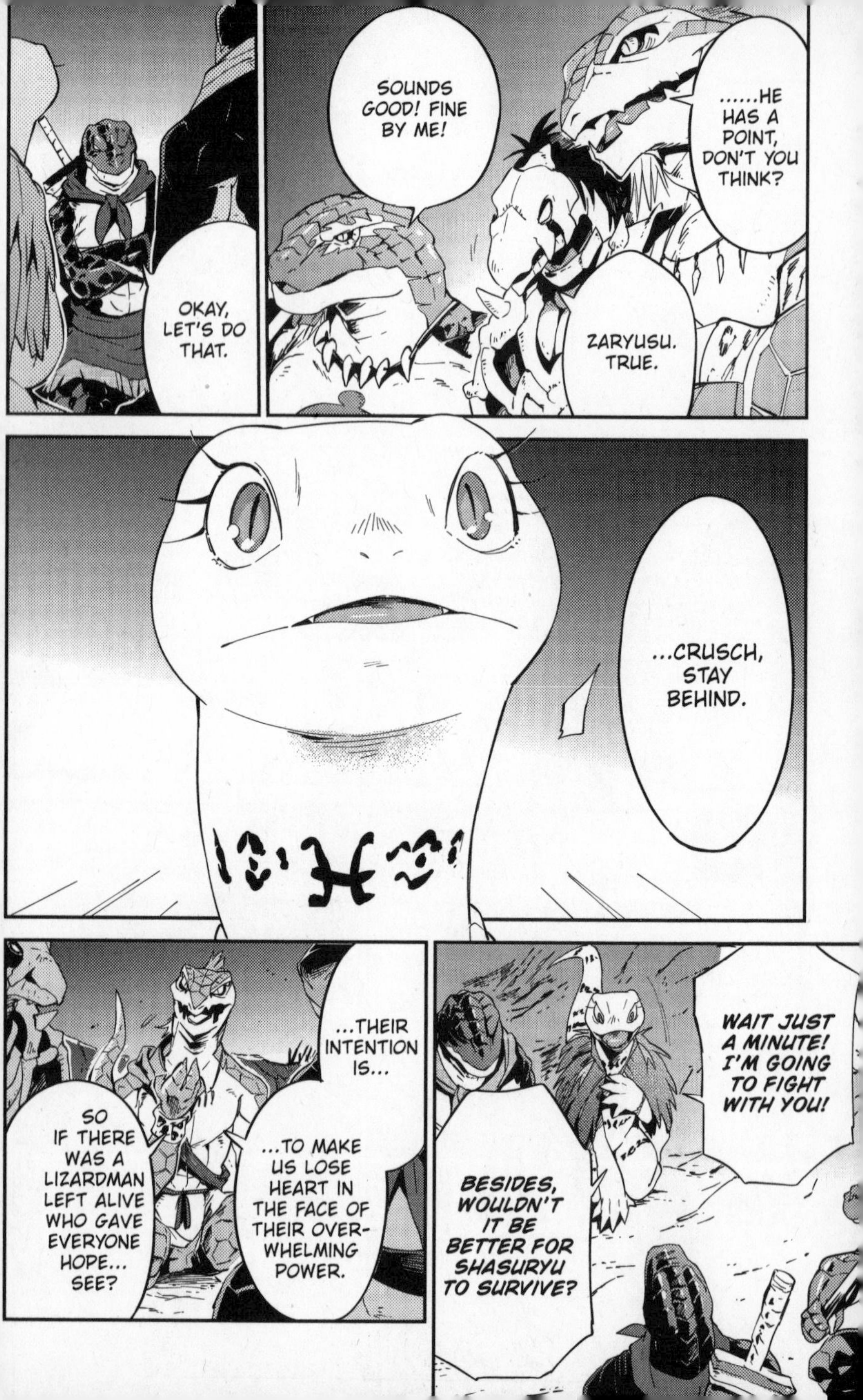
......HE HAS A POINT, DON'T YOU THINK?
SOUNDS GOOD! FINE BY ME!
ZARYUSU. TRUE.
OKAY, LET'S DO THAT.
...CRUSCH, STAY BEHIND.
WAIT JUST A MINUTE! I'M GOING TO FIGHT WITH YOU!
BESIDES, WOULDN'T IT BE BETTER FOR SHASURYU TO SURVIVE?
...THEIR INTENTION IS...
...TO MAKE US LOSE HEART IN THE FACE OF THEIR OVER-WHELMING POWER.
SO IF THERE WAS A LIZARDMAN LEFT ALIVE WHO GAVE EVERYONE HOPE... SEE?

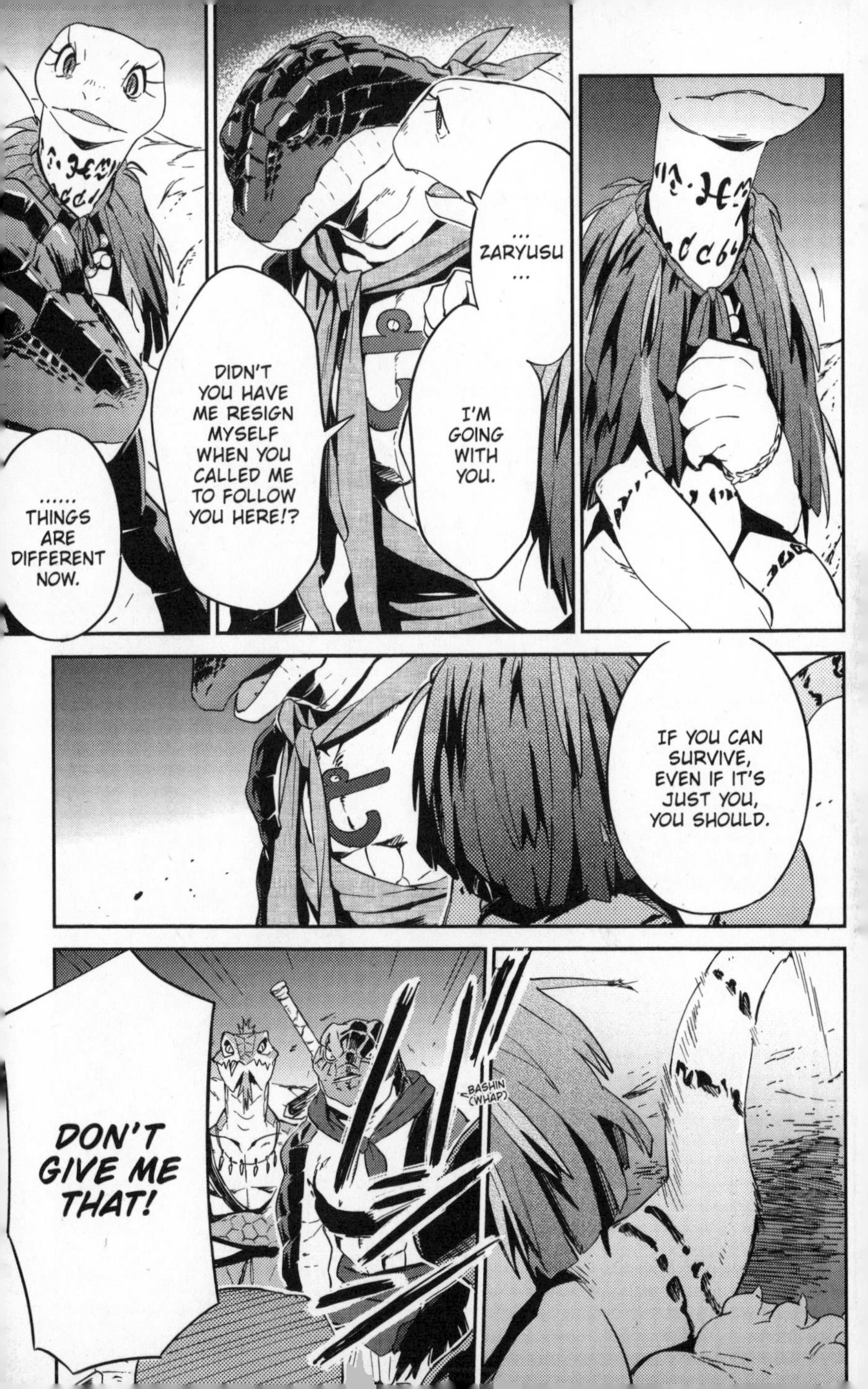

... ZARYUSU ...
I'M GOING WITH YOU.
DIDN'T YOU HAVE ME RESIGN MYSELF WHEN YOU CALLED ME TO FOLLOW YOU HERE!?
...... THINGS ARE DIFFERENT NOW.
IF YOU CAN SURVIVE, EVEN IF IT'S JUST YOU, YOU SHOULD.
BASHIN (WHAP)
DON'T GIVE ME THAT!

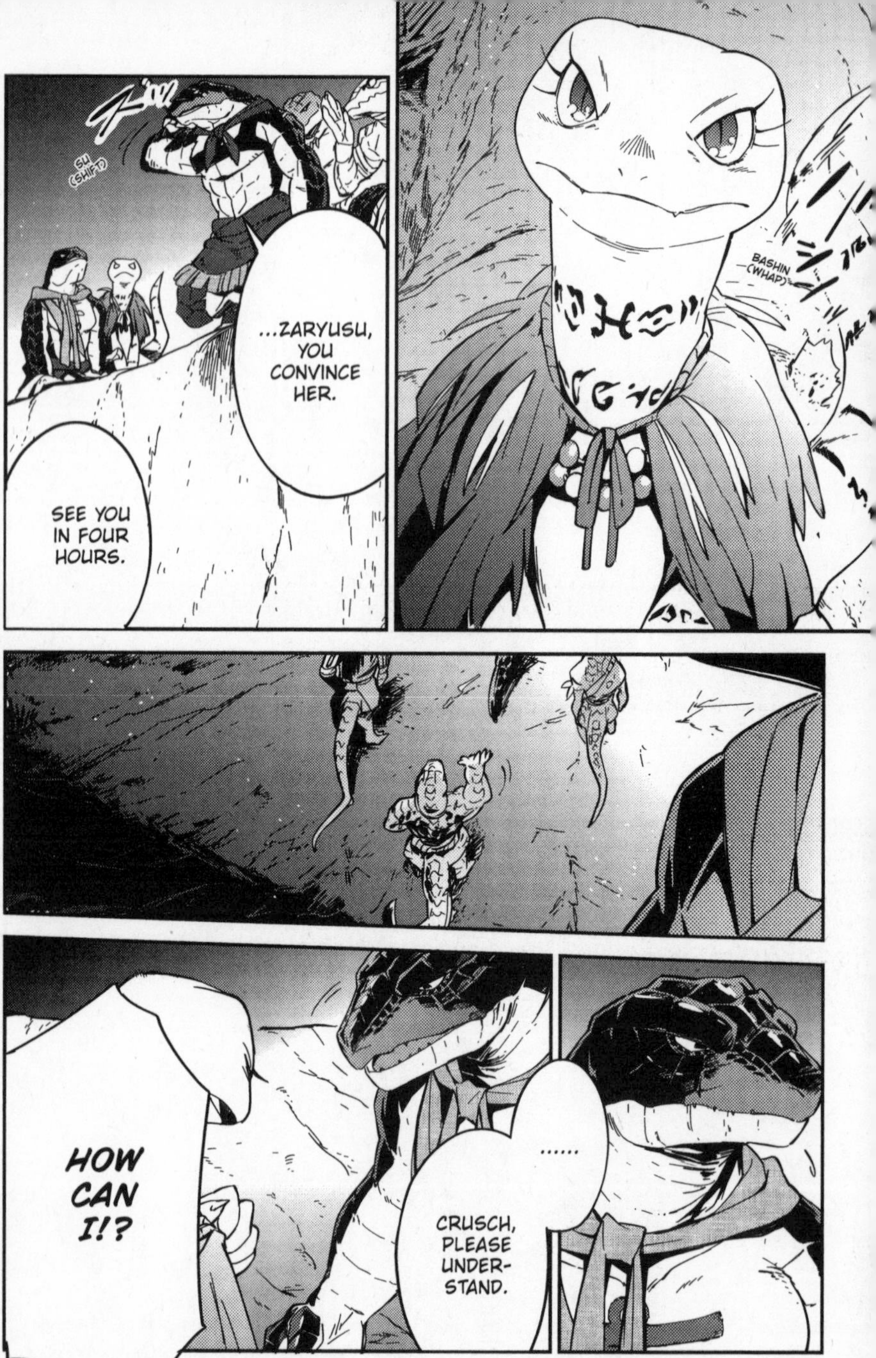
BASHIN (WHAP)
SU (SHIFT)
...ZARYUSU, YOU CONVINCE HER.
SEE YOU IN FOUR HOURS.
......
CRUSCH, PLEASE UNDER-STAND.
HOW CAN I!?

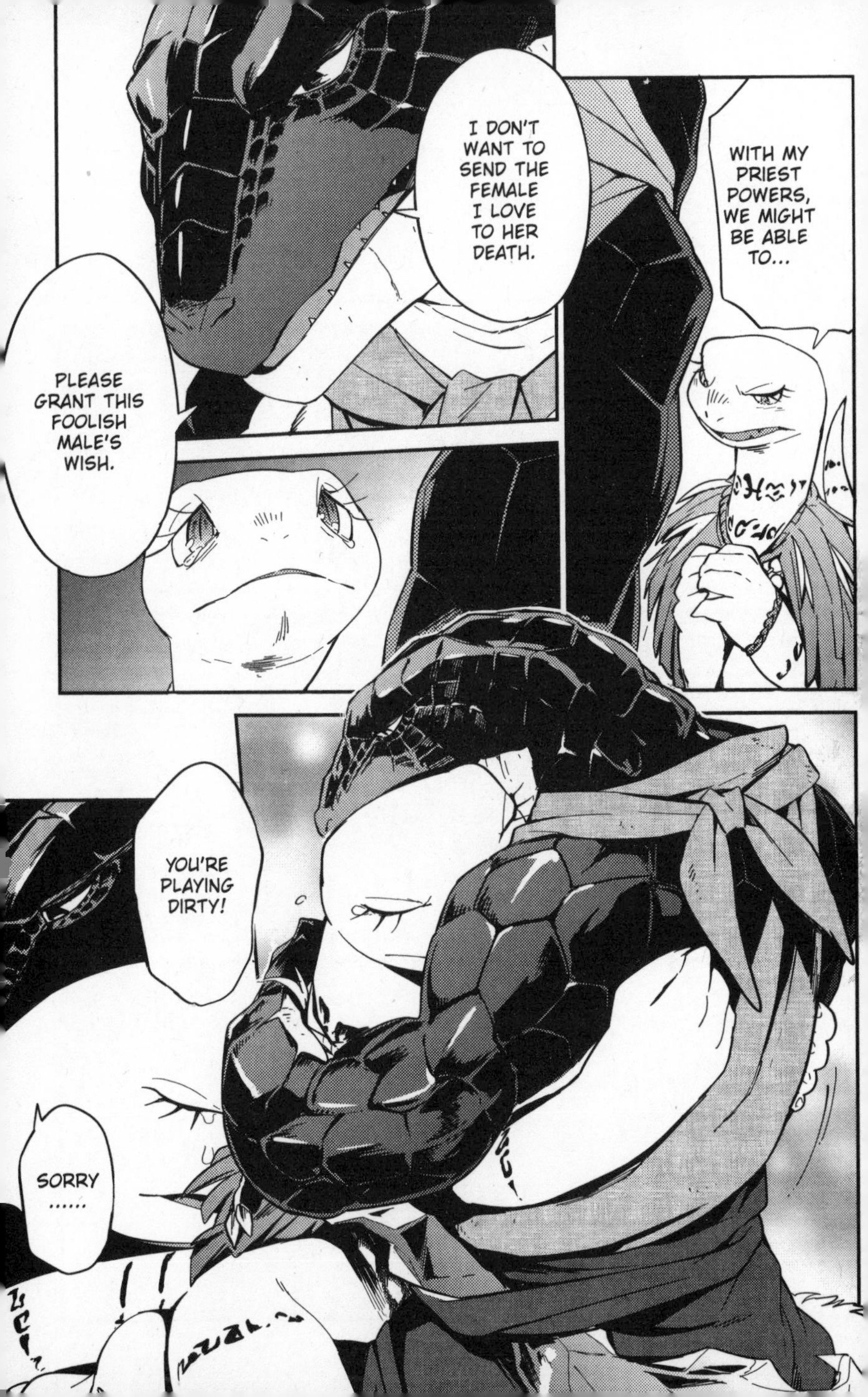
WITH MY PRIEST POWERS, WE MIGHT BE ABLE TO...
I DON'T WANT TO SEND THE FEMALE I LOVE TO HER DEATH.
PLEASE GRANT THIS FOOLISH MALE'S WISH.
YOU'RE PLAYING DIRTY!
SORRY ......

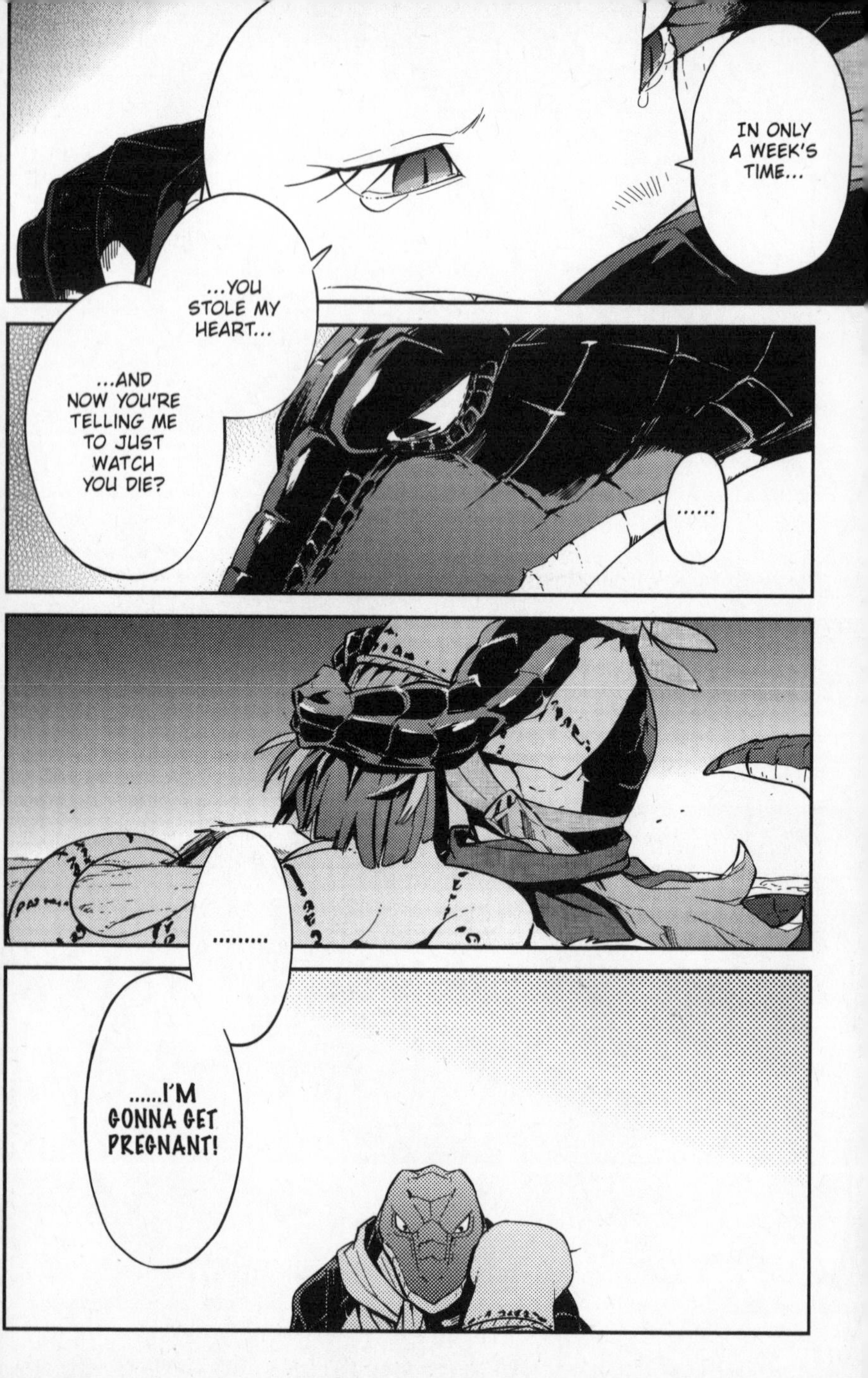
IN ONLY A WEEK'S TIME...
...YOU STOLE MY HEART...
...AND NOW YOU'RE TELLING ME TO JUST WATCH YOU DIE?
......
....
......I'M GONNA GET PREGNANT!

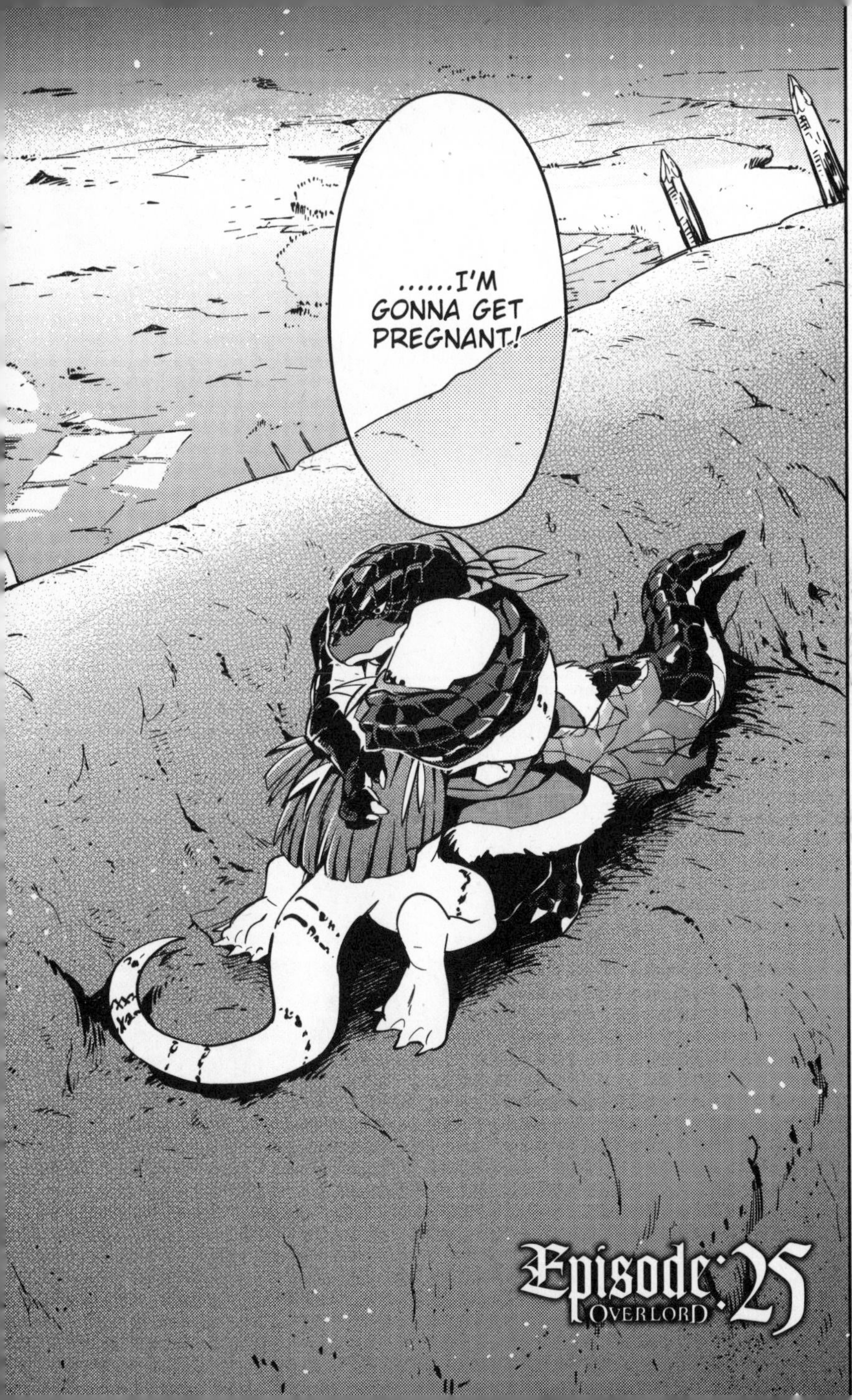
......I'M GONNA GET PREGNANT!
Episode: 25
OVERLORD

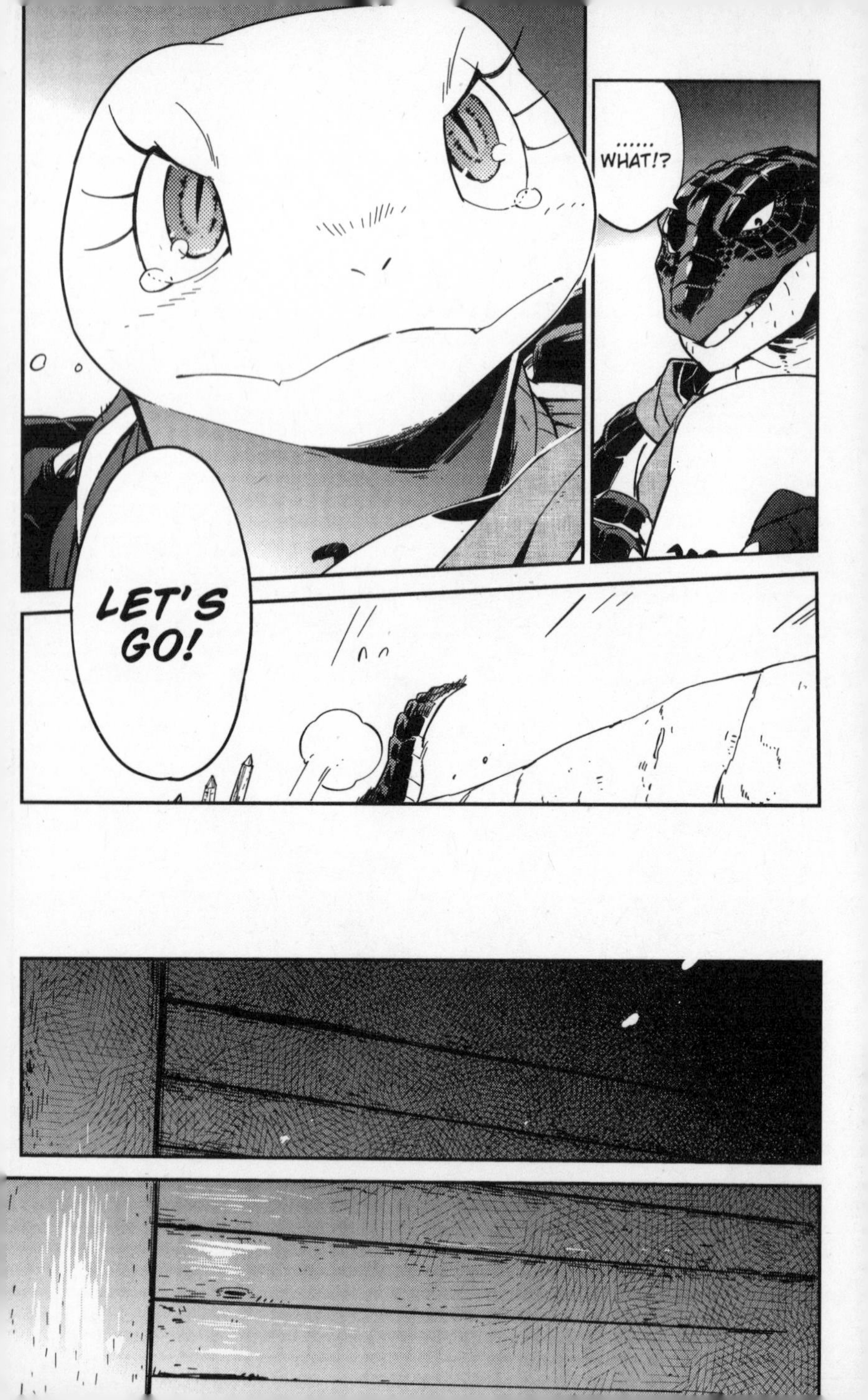

...... WHAT!?
LET'S GO!

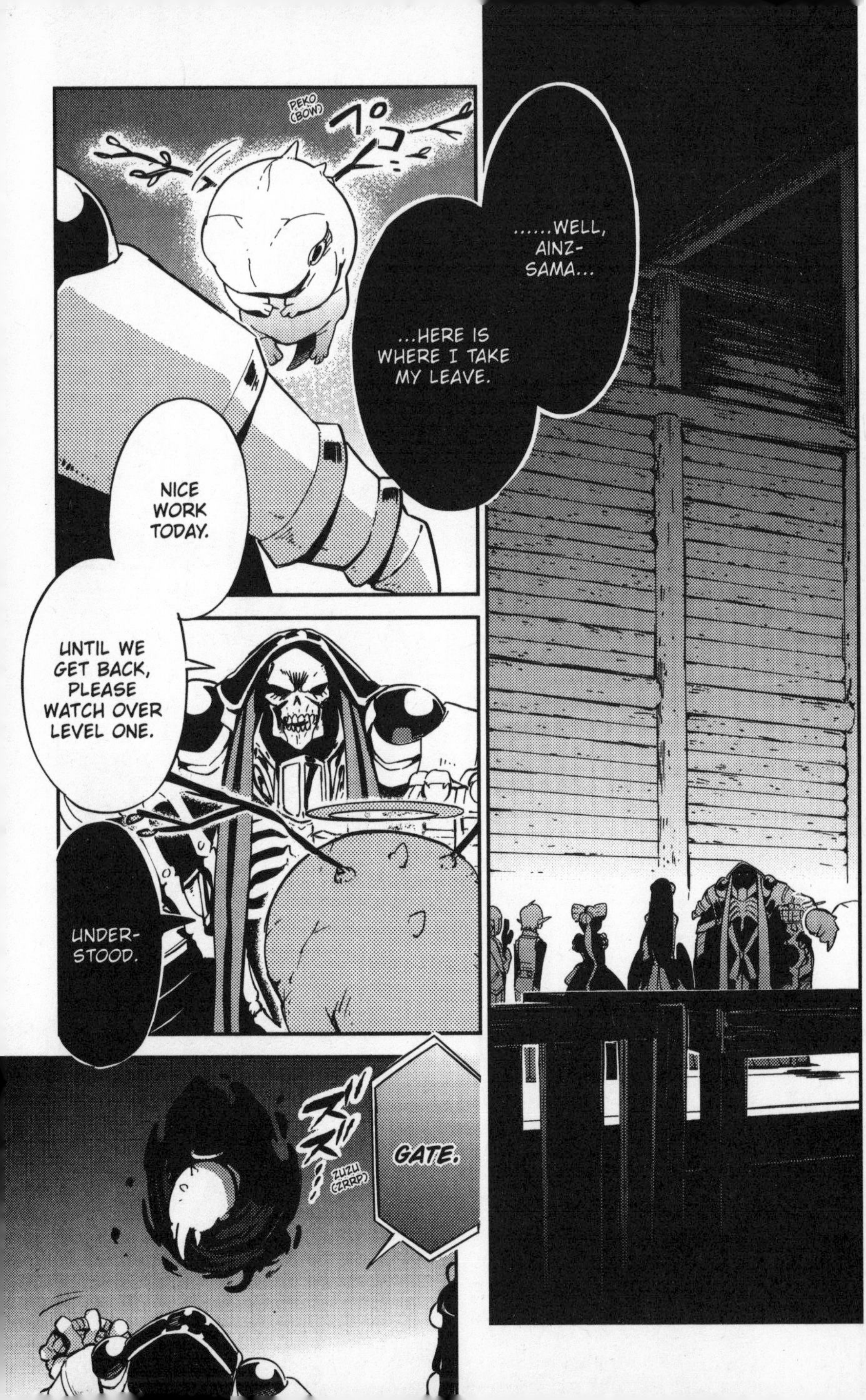
......WELL, AINZ-SAMA...
...HERE IS WHERE I TAKE MY LEAVE.
PEKO (BOW)
NICE WORK TODAY.
UNTIL WE GET BACK, PLEASE WATCH OVER LEVEL ONE.
UNDER-STOOD.
GATE.
ZUZU (ZRRP)

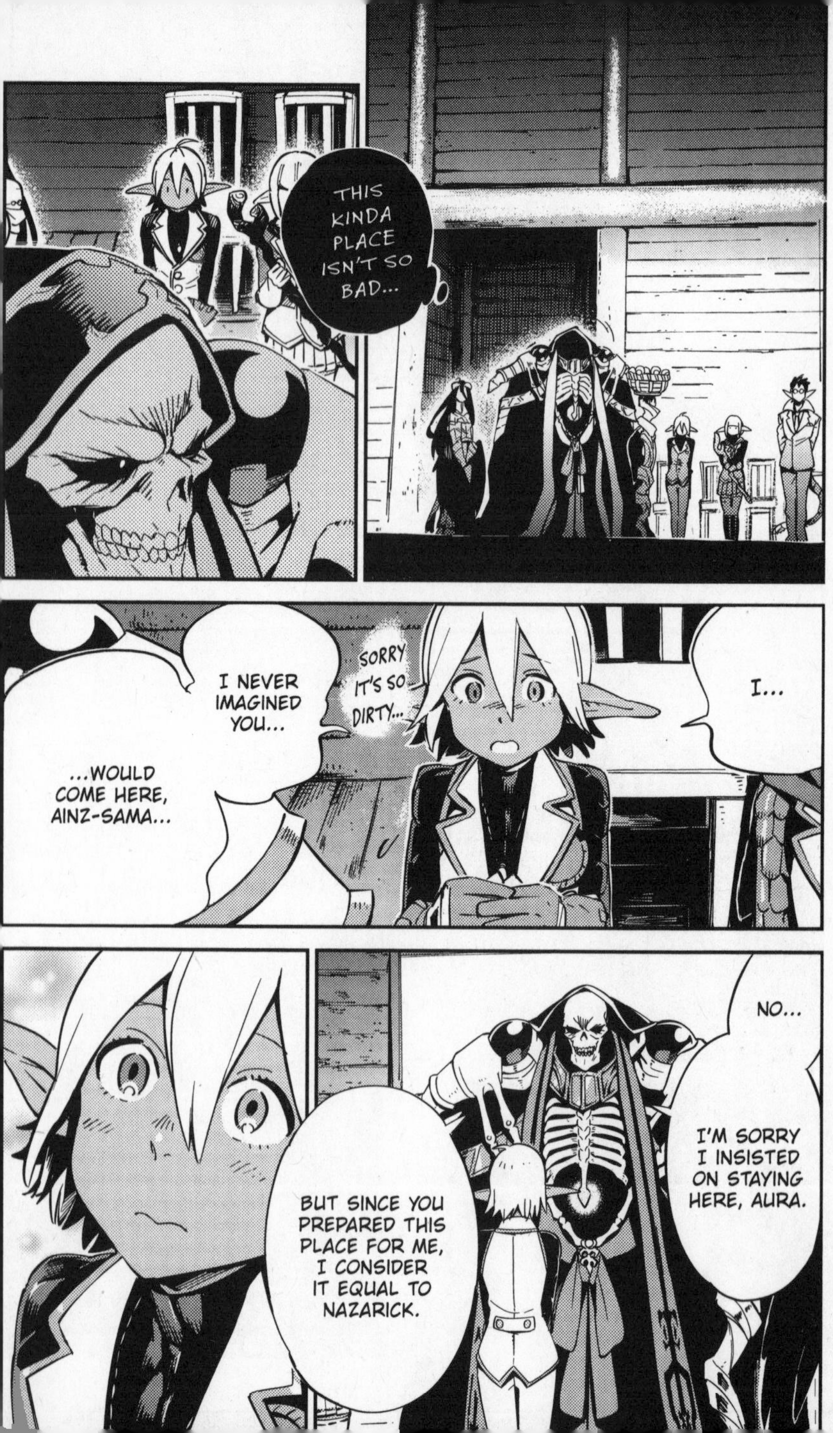
THIS KINDA PLACE ISN'T SO BAD...
I...
SORRY IT'S SO DIRTY...
I NEVER IMAGINED YOU...
...WOULD COME HERE, AINZ-SAMA...
NO...
I'M SORRY I INSISTED ON STAYING HERE, AURA.
BUT SINCE YOU PREPARED THIS PLACE FOR ME, I CONSIDER IT EQUAL TO NAZARICK.

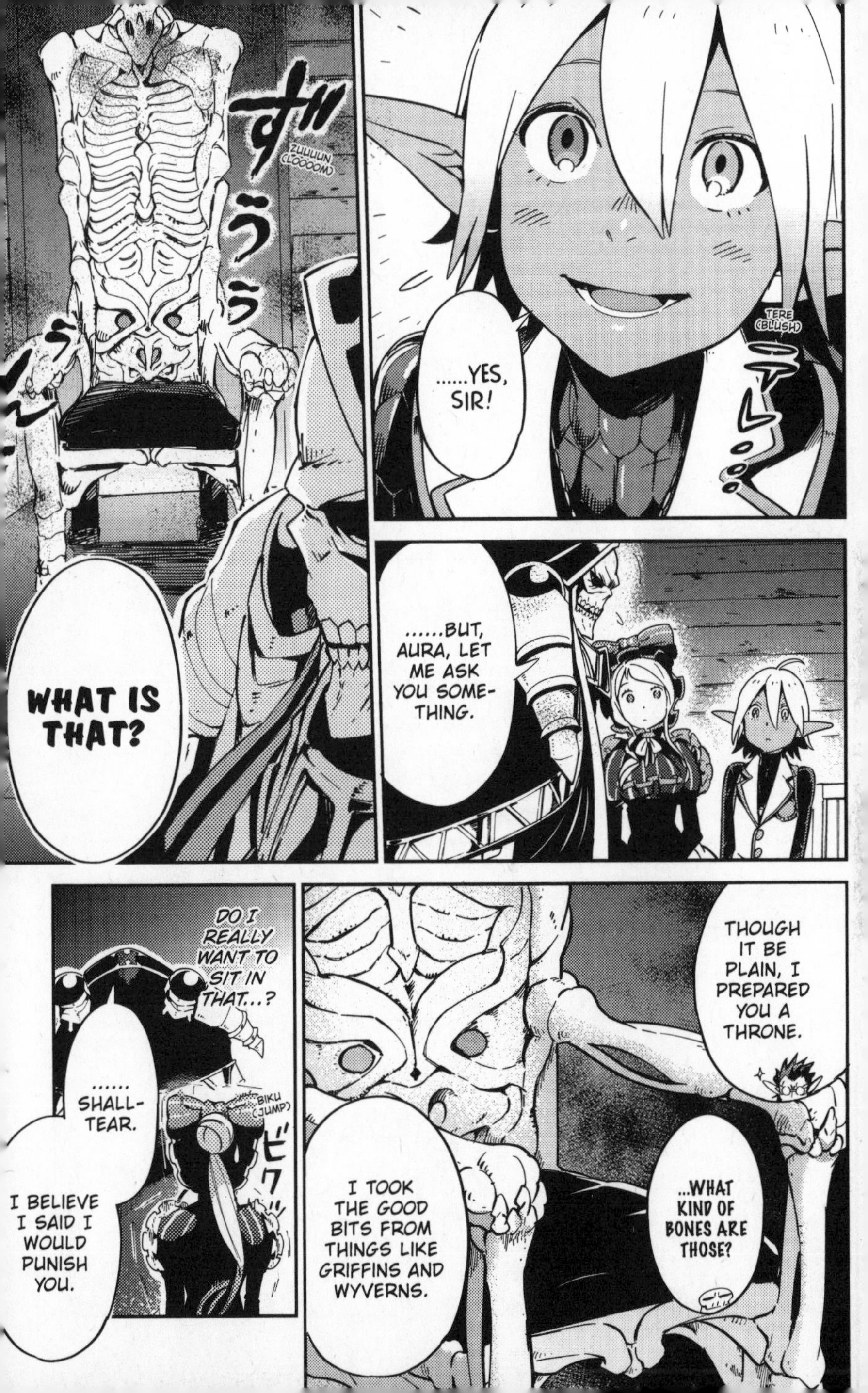
TERE (BLUSH)
......YES, SIR!
......BUT, AURA, LET ME ASK YOU SOMETHING.
ZUUUUN (LOOOOM)
WHAT IS THAT?
THOUGH IT BE PLAIN, I PREPARED YOU A THRONE.
...WHAT KIND OF BONES ARE THOSE?
I TOOK THE GOOD BITS FROM THINGS LIKE GRIFFINS AND WYVERNS.
DO I REALLY WANT TO SIT IN THAT...?
...... SHALL-TEAR.
BIKU (JUMP)
I BELIEVE I SAID I WOULD PUNISH YOU.

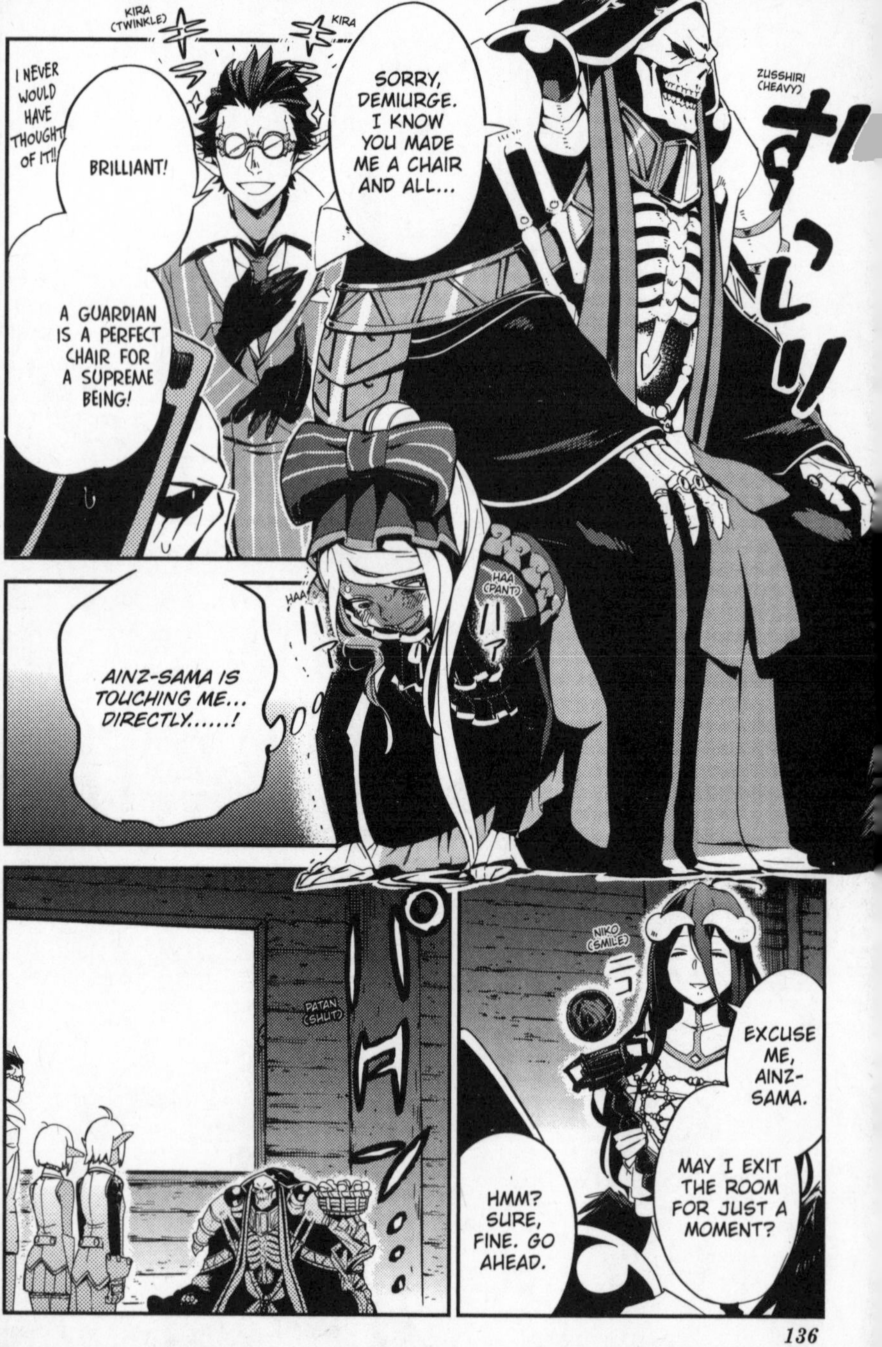
ZUSSHIRI (HEAVY)
SORRY, DEMIURGE. I KNOW YOU MADE ME A CHAIR AND ALL...
KIRA
KIRA (TWINKLE)
BRILLIANT!
I NEVER WOULD HAVE THOUGHT OF IT!!
A GUARDIAN IS A PERFECT CHAIR FOR A SUPREME BEING!
HAA (PANT)
HAA
AINZ-SAMA IS TOUCHING ME... DIRECTLY......!
NIKO (SMILE)
EXCUSE ME, AINZ-SAMA.
MAY I EXIT THE ROOM FOR JUST A MOMENT?
HMM? SURE, FINE. GO AHEAD.
PATAN (SHUT)

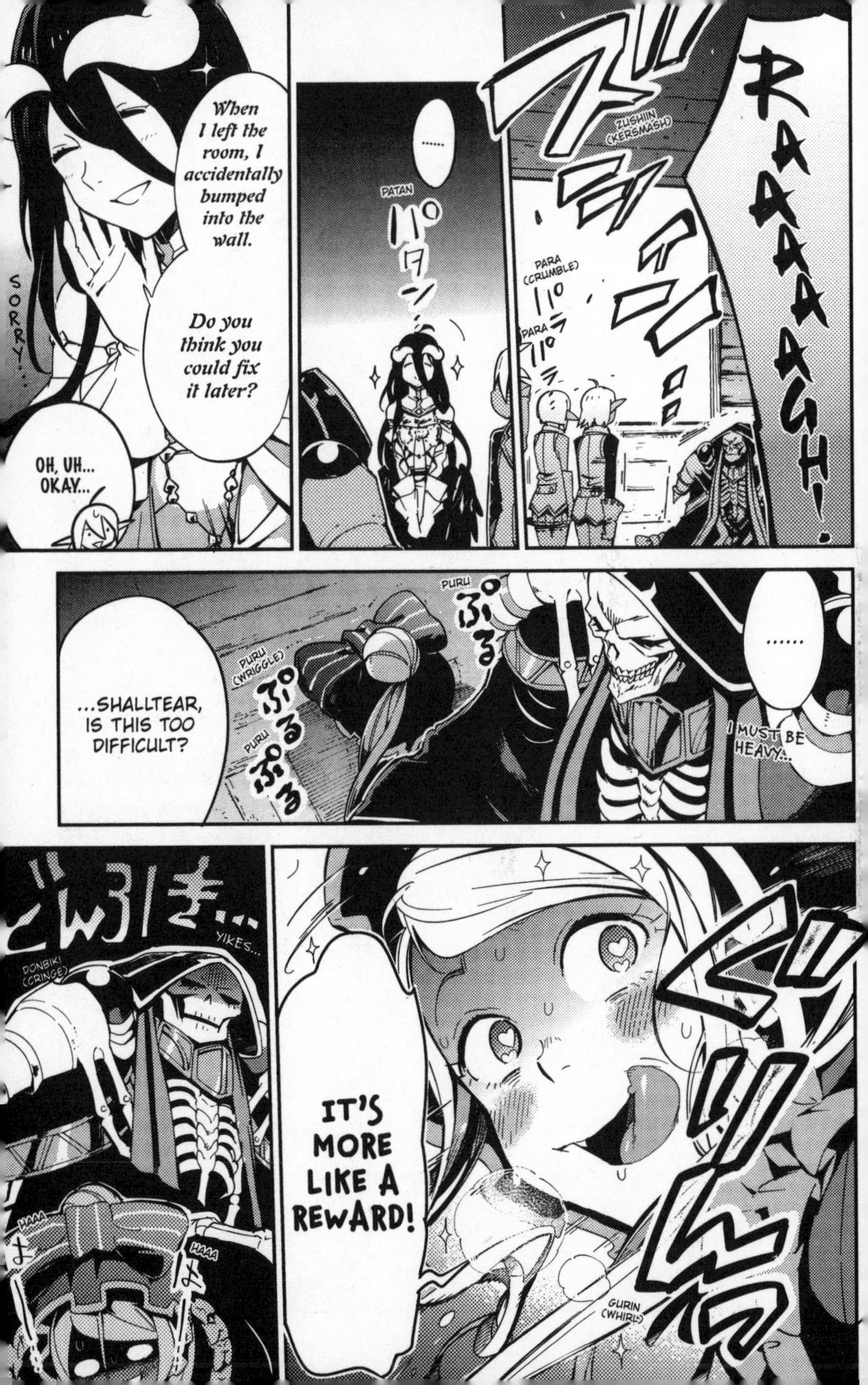
RAAAAAAGH!
ZUSHIIN (KERSMASH)
PARA (CRUMBLE)
PARA
......
PATAN
When I left the room, I accidentally bumped into the wall.
SORRY...
Do you think you could fix it later?
OH, UH... OKAY...
......
I MUST BE HEAVY...
PURU
PURU (WRIGGLE)
PURU
...SHALLTEAR, IS THIS TOO DIFFICULT?
IT'S MORE LIKE A REWARD!
GURIN (WHIRL)
YIKES...
DONBIKI (CRINGE)
HAAA
HAAA

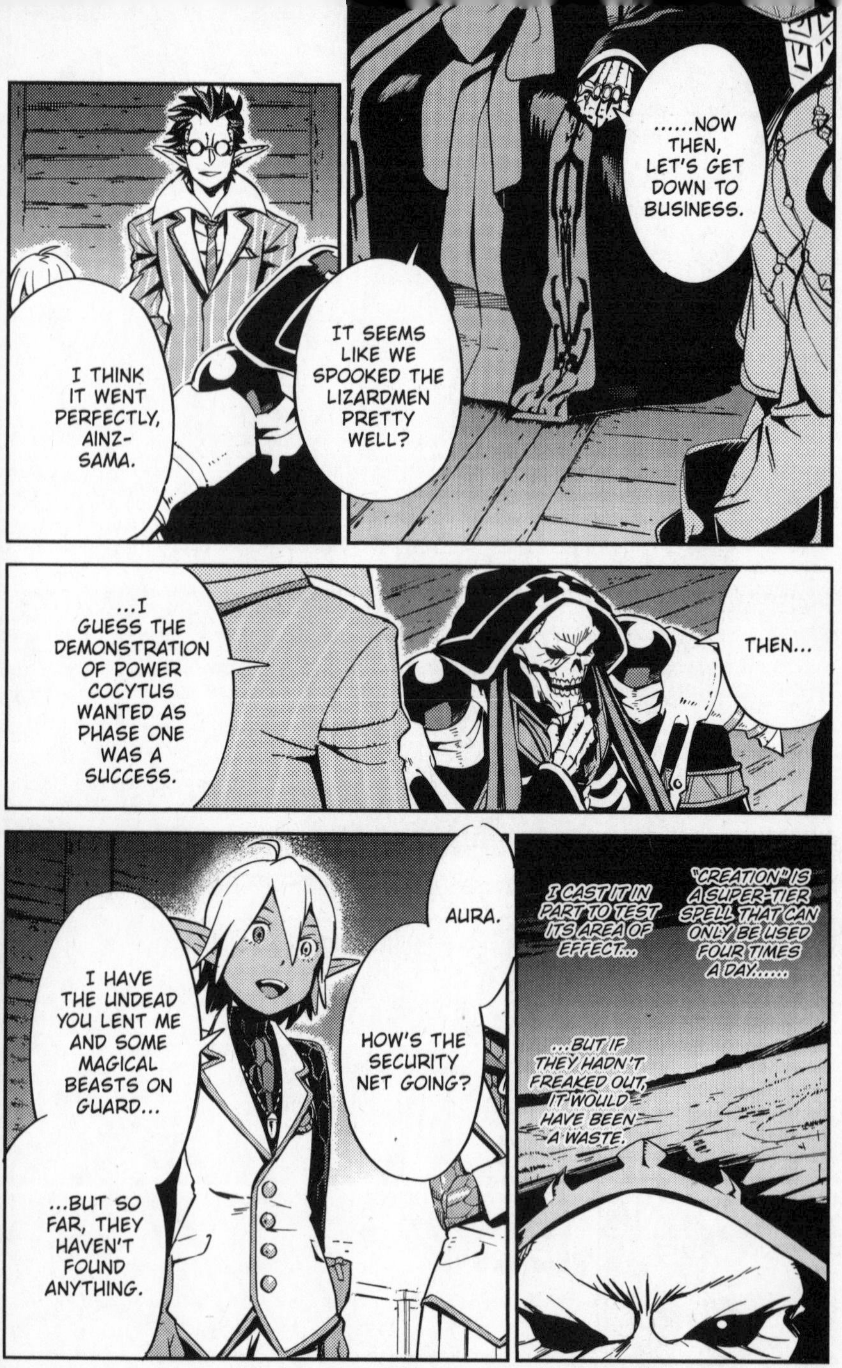
......NOW THEN, LET'S GET DOWN TO BUSINESS.
IT SEEMS LIKE WE SPOOKED THE LIZARDMEN PRETTY WELL?
I THINK IT WENT PERFECTLY, AINZ-SAMA.
THEN...
...I GUESS THE DEMONSTRATION OF POWER COCYTUS WANTED AS PHASE ONE WAS A SUCCESS.
"CREATION" IS A SUPER-TIER SPELL THAT CAN ONLY BE USED FOUR TIMES A DAY......
I CAST IT IN PART TO TEST ITS AREA OF EFFECT...
...BUT IF THEY HADN'T FREAKED OUT, IT WOULD HAVE BEEN A WASTE.
AURA.
HOW'S THE SECURITY NET GOING?
I HAVE THE UNDEAD YOU LENT ME AND SOME MAGICAL BEASTS ON GUARD...
...BUT SO FAR, THEY HAVEN'T FOUND ANYTHING.

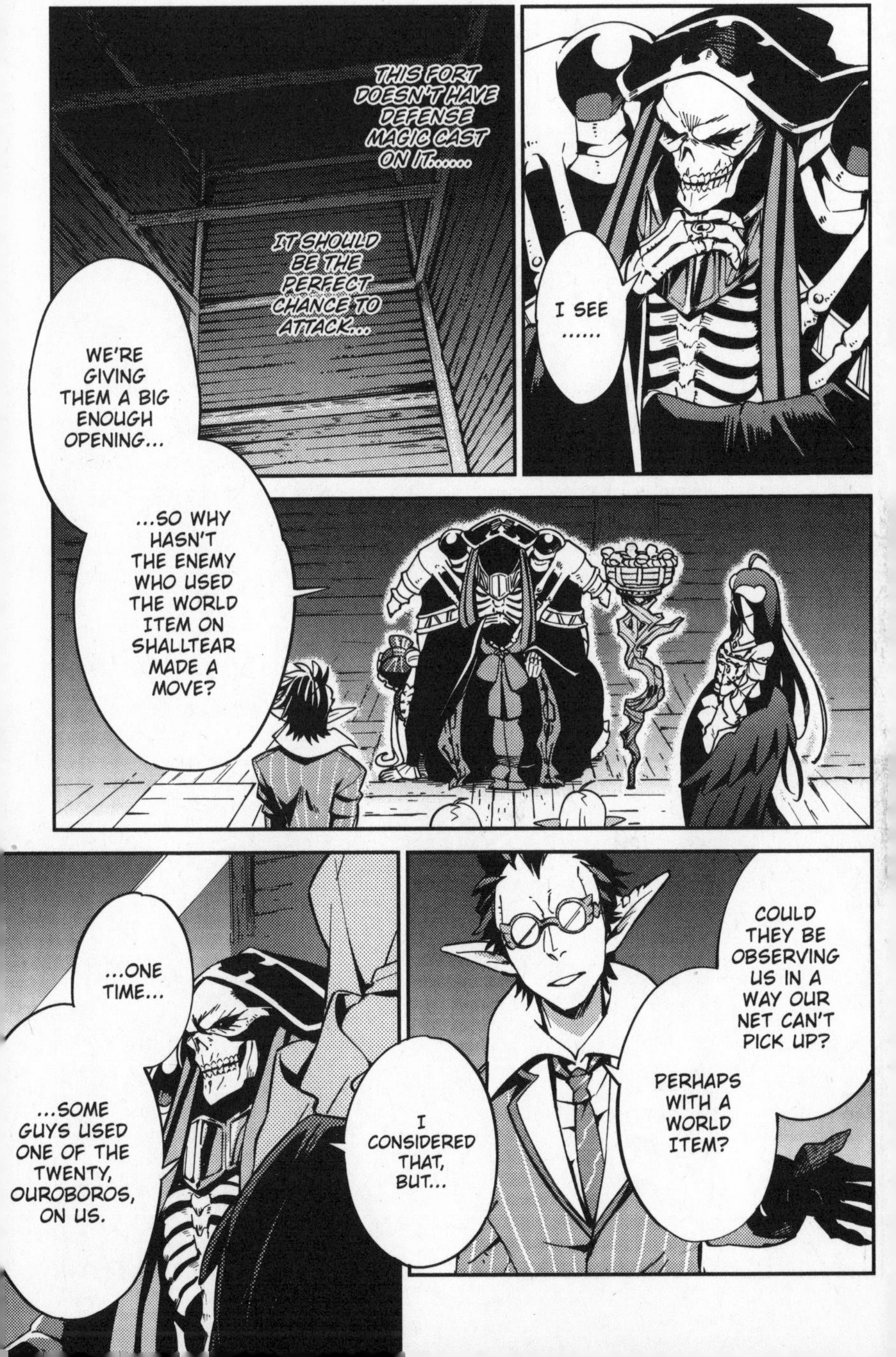
I SEE ......
THIS FORT DOESN'T HAVE DEFENSE MAGIC CAST ON IT......
IT SHOULD BE THE PERFECT CHANCE TO ATTACK...
WE'RE GIVING THEM A BIG ENOUGH OPENING...
...SO WHY HASN'T THE ENEMY WHO USED THE WORLD ITEM ON SHALLTEAR MADE A MOVE?
COULD THEY BE OBSERVING US IN A WAY OUR NET CAN'T PICK UP?
PERHAPS WITH A WORLD ITEM?
I CONSIDERED THAT, BUT...
...ONE TIME...
...SOME GUYS USED ONE OF THE TWENTY, OUROBOROS, ON US.

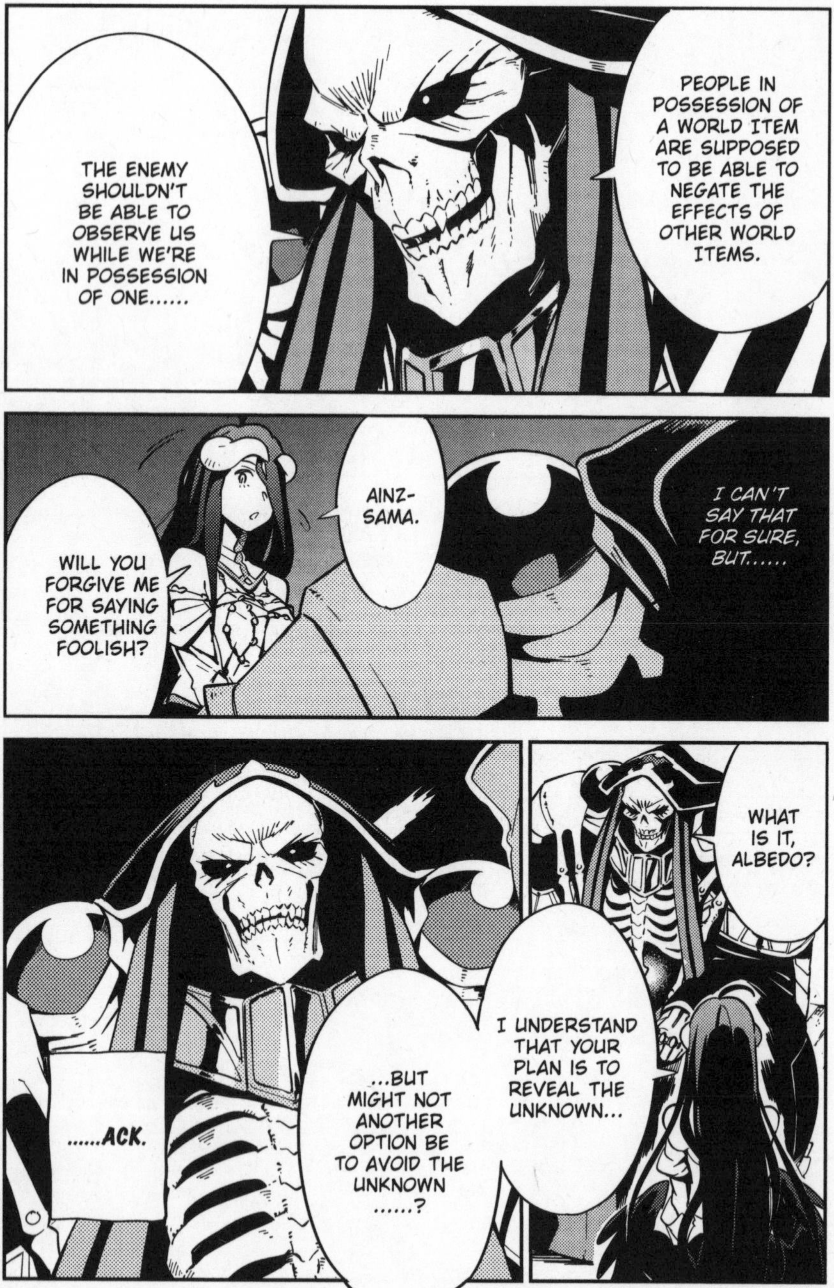
PEOPLE IN POSSESSION OF A WORLD ITEM ARE SUPPOSED TO BE ABLE TO NEGATE THE EFFECTS OF OTHER WORLD ITEMS.
THE ENEMY SHOULDN'T BE ABLE TO OBSERVE US WHILE WE'RE IN POSSESSION OF ONE......
I CAN'T SAY THAT FOR SURE, BUT......
AINZ-SAMA.
WILL YOU FORGIVE ME FOR SAYING SOMETHING FOOLISH?
WHAT IS IT, ALBEDO?
I UNDERSTAND THAT YOUR PLAN IS TO REVEAL THE UNKNOWN...
...BUT MIGHT NOT ANOTHER OPTION BE TO AVOID THE UNKNOWN ......?
......ACK.

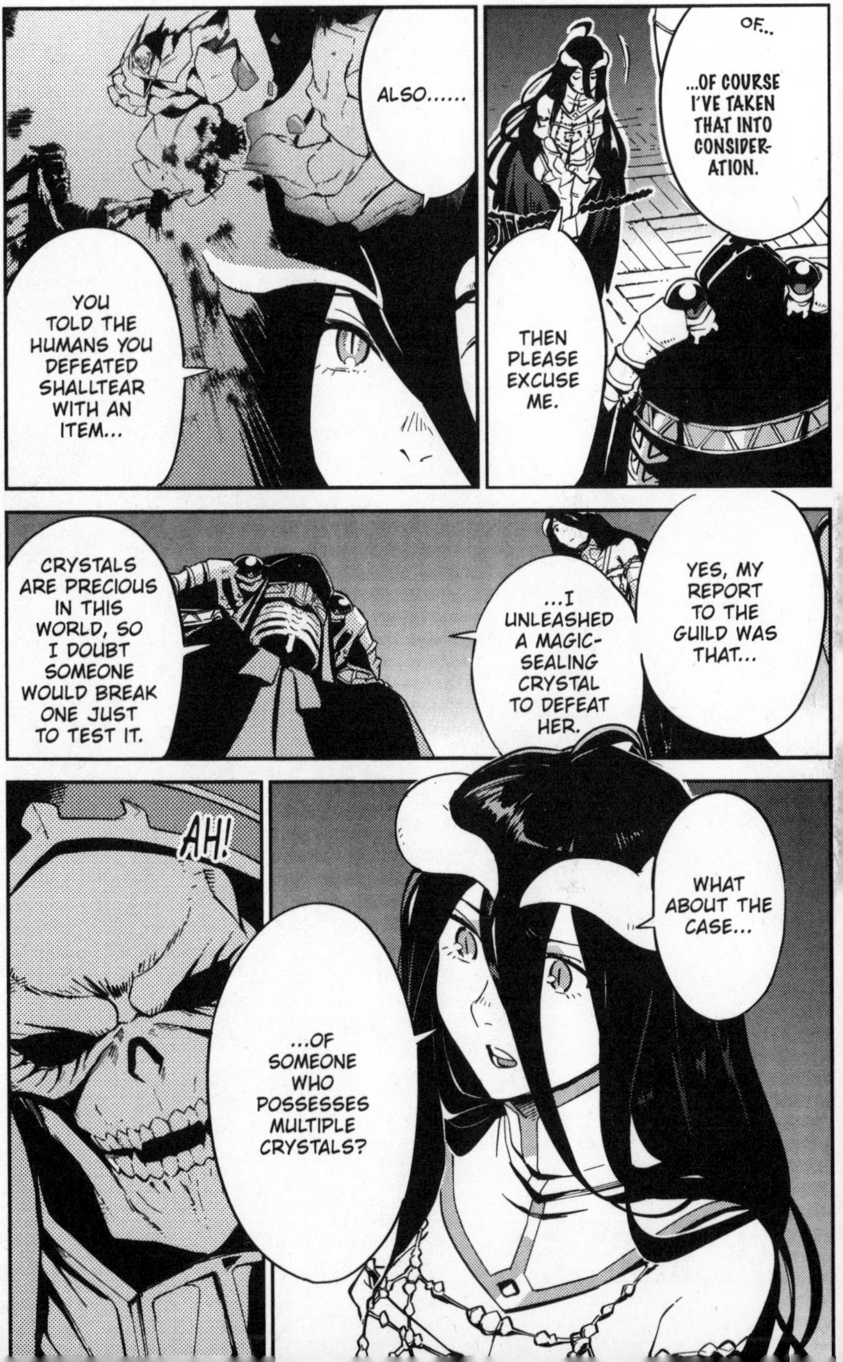
OF...
...OF COURSE I'VE TAKEN THAT INTO CONSIDER-ATION.
THEN PLEASE EXCUSE ME.
ALSO......
YOU TOLD THE HUMANS YOU DEFEATED SHALLTEAR WITH AN ITEM...
YES, MY REPORT TO THE GUILD WAS THAT...
...I UNLEASHED A MAGIC-SEALING CRYSTAL TO DEFEAT HER.
CRYSTALS ARE PRECIOUS IN THIS WORLD, SO I DOUBT SOMEONE WOULD BREAK ONE JUST TO TEST IT.
WHAT ABOUT THE CASE...
...OF SOMEONE WHO POSSESSES MULTIPLE CRYSTALS?
AH!

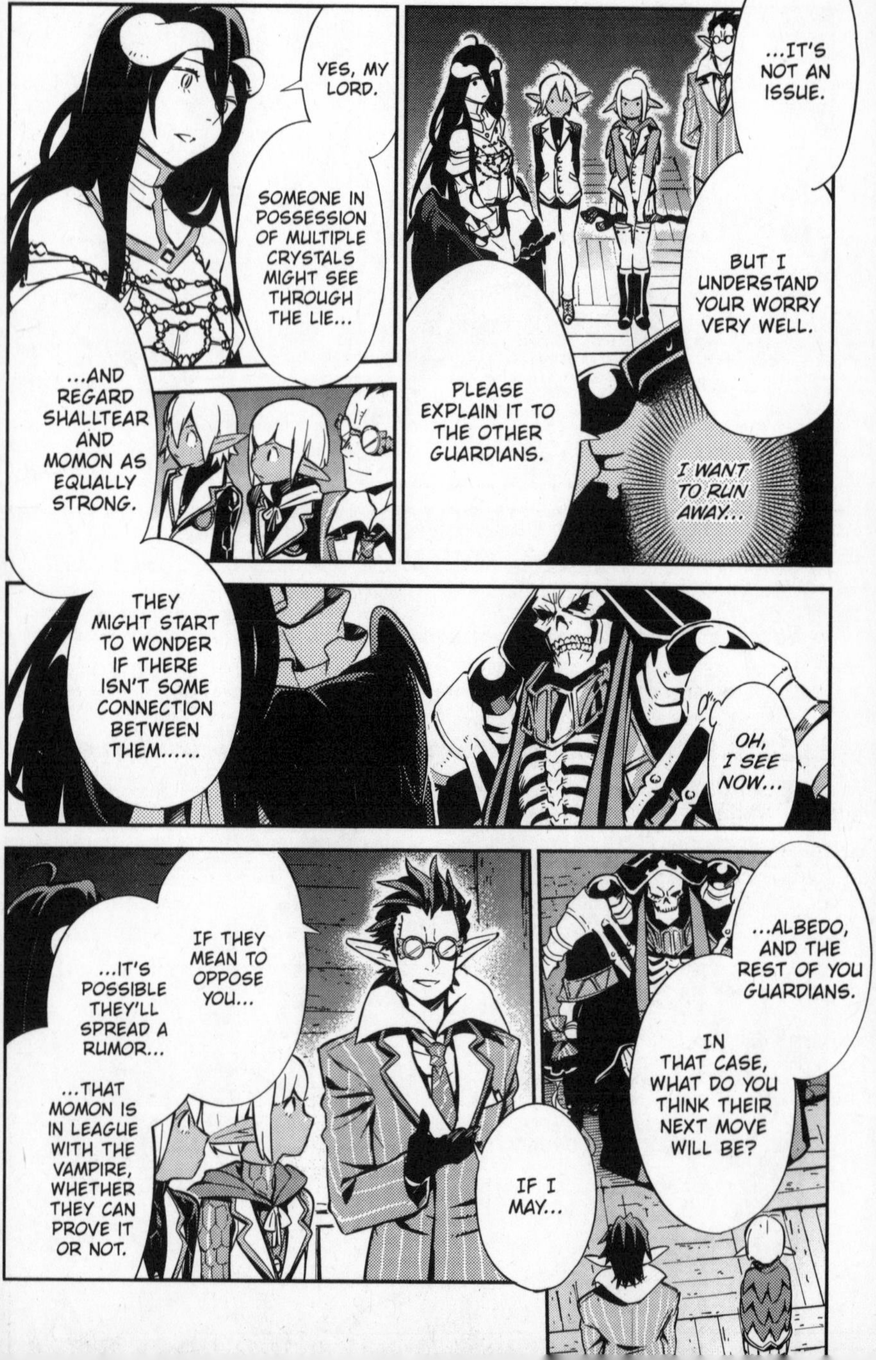
...IT'S NOT AN ISSUE.
BUT I UNDERSTAND YOUR WORRY VERY WELL.
PLEASE EXPLAIN IT TO THE OTHER GUARDIANS.
I WANT TO RUN AWAY...
YES, MY LORD.
SOMEONE IN POSSESSION OF MULTIPLE CRYSTALS MIGHT SEE THROUGH THE LIE...
...AND REGARD SHALLTEAR AND MOMON AS EQUALLY STRONG.
THEY MIGHT START TO WONDER IF THERE ISN'T SOME CONNECTION BETWEEN THEM......
OH, I SEE NOW...
...ALBEDO, AND THE REST OF YOU GUARDIANS.
IN THAT CASE, WHAT DO YOU THINK THEIR NEXT MOVE WILL BE?
IF I MAY...
IF THEY MEAN TO OPPOSE YOU...
...IT'S POSSIBLE THEY'LL SPREAD A RUMOR...
...THAT MOMON IS IN LEAGUE WITH THE VAMPIRE, WHETHER THEY CAN PROVE IT OR NOT.

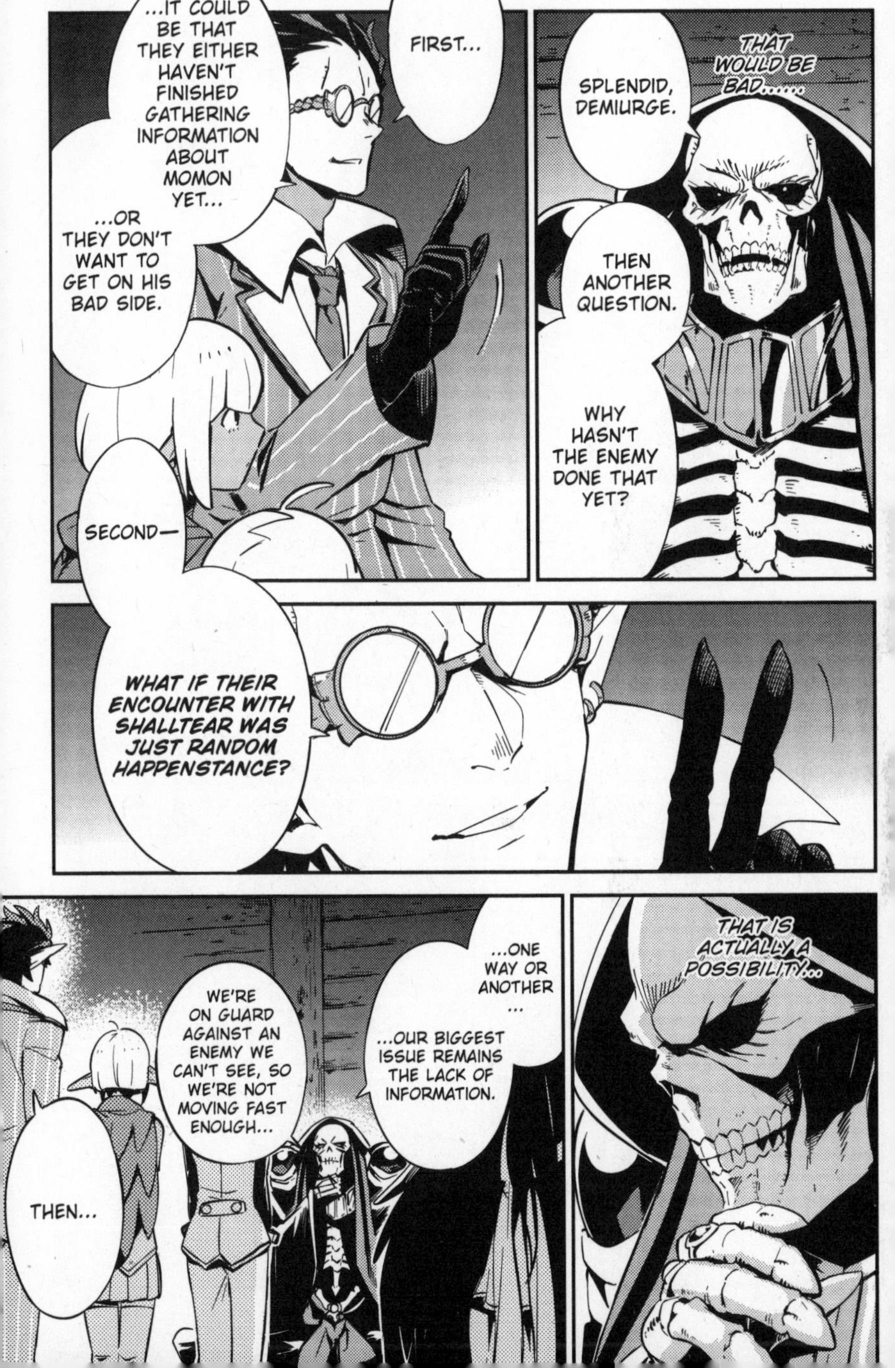
THAT WOULD BE BAD......
SPLENDID, DEMIURGE.
THEN ANOTHER QUESTION.
WHY HASN'T THE ENEMY DONE THAT YET?
FIRST...
...IT COULD BE THAT THEY EITHER HAVEN'T FINISHED GATHERING INFORMATION ABOUT MOMON YET...
...OR THEY DON'T WANT TO GET ON HIS BAD SIDE.
SECOND—
WHAT IF THEIR ENCOUNTER WITH SHALLTEAR WAS JUST RANDOM HAPPENSTANCE?
THAT IS ACTUALLY A POSSIBILITY...
...ONE WAY OR ANOTHER ...
...OUR BIGGEST ISSUE REMAINS THE LACK OF INFORMATION.
WE'RE ON GUARD AGAINST AN ENEMY WE CAN'T SEE, SO WE'RE NOT MOVING FAST ENOUGH...
THEN...

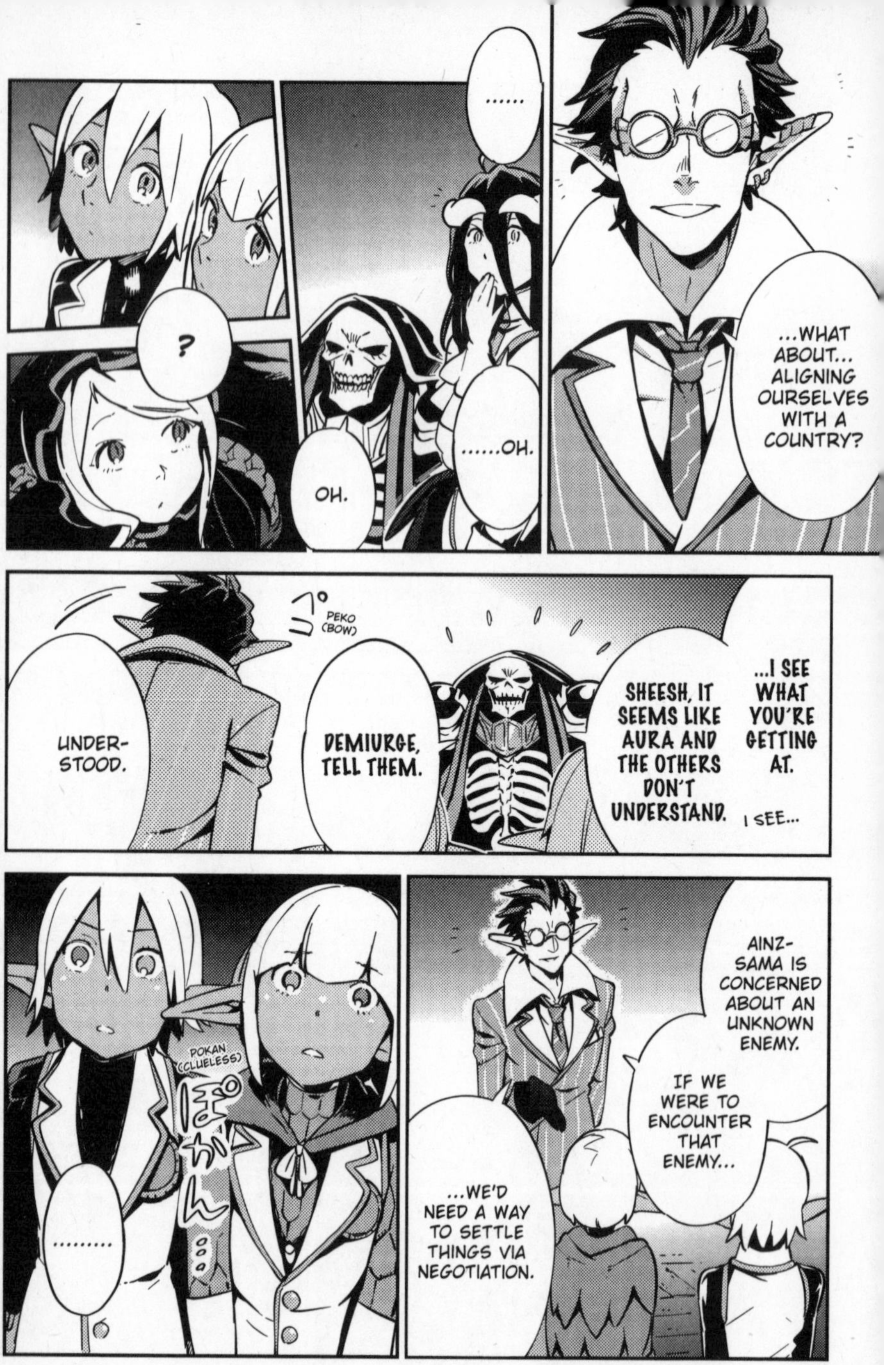
...WHAT ABOUT... ALIGNING OURSELVES WITH A COUNTRY?
......
......OH.
OH.
?
...I SEE WHAT YOU'RE GETTING AT.
I SEE...
SHEESH, IT SEEMS LIKE AURA AND THE OTHERS DON'T UNDERSTAND.
DEMIURGE, TELL THEM.
PEKO (BOW)
UNDER-STOOD.
AINZ-SAMA IS CONCERNED ABOUT AN UNKNOWN ENEMY.
IF WE WERE TO ENCOUNTER THAT ENEMY...
...WE'D NEED A WAY TO SETTLE THINGS VIA NEGOTIATION.
POKAN (CLUELESS)
ぽかん
....

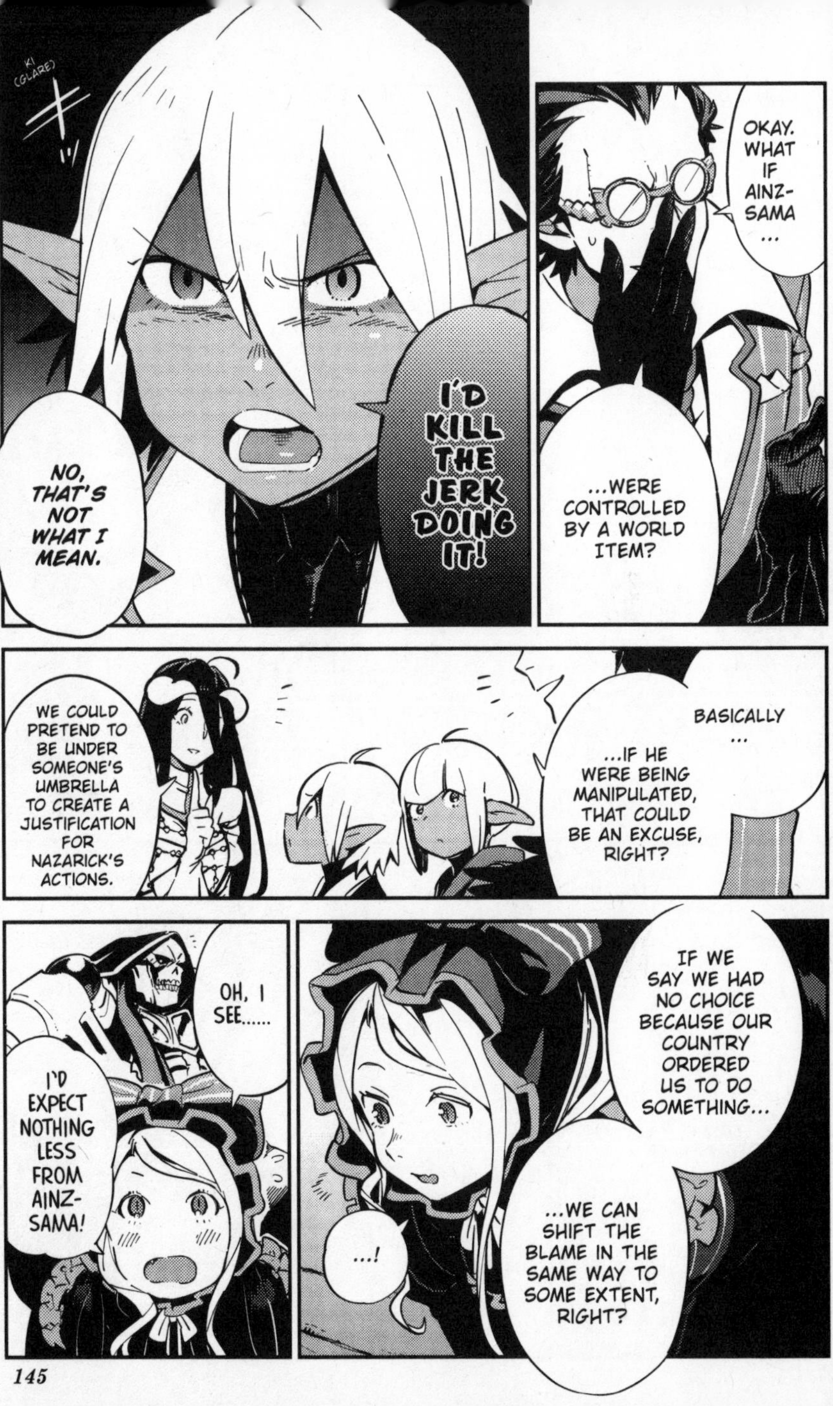
OKAY. WHAT IF AINZ-SAMA ...
...WERE CONTROLLED BY A WORLD ITEM?
KI (GLARE)
I'D KILL THE JERK DOING IT!
NO, THAT'S NOT WHAT I MEAN.
BASICALLY ...
...IF HE WERE BEING MANIPULATED, THAT COULD BE AN EXCUSE, RIGHT?
WE COULD PRETEND TO BE UNDER SOMEONE'S UMBRELLA TO CREATE A JUSTIFICATION FOR NAZARICK'S ACTIONS.
IF WE SAY WE HAD NO CHOICE BECAUSE OUR COUNTRY ORDERED US TO DO SOMETHING...
...WE CAN SHIFT THE BLAME IN THE SAME WAY TO SOME EXTENT, RIGHT?
...!
OH, I SEE......
I'D EXPECT NOTHING LESS FROM AINZ-SAMA!

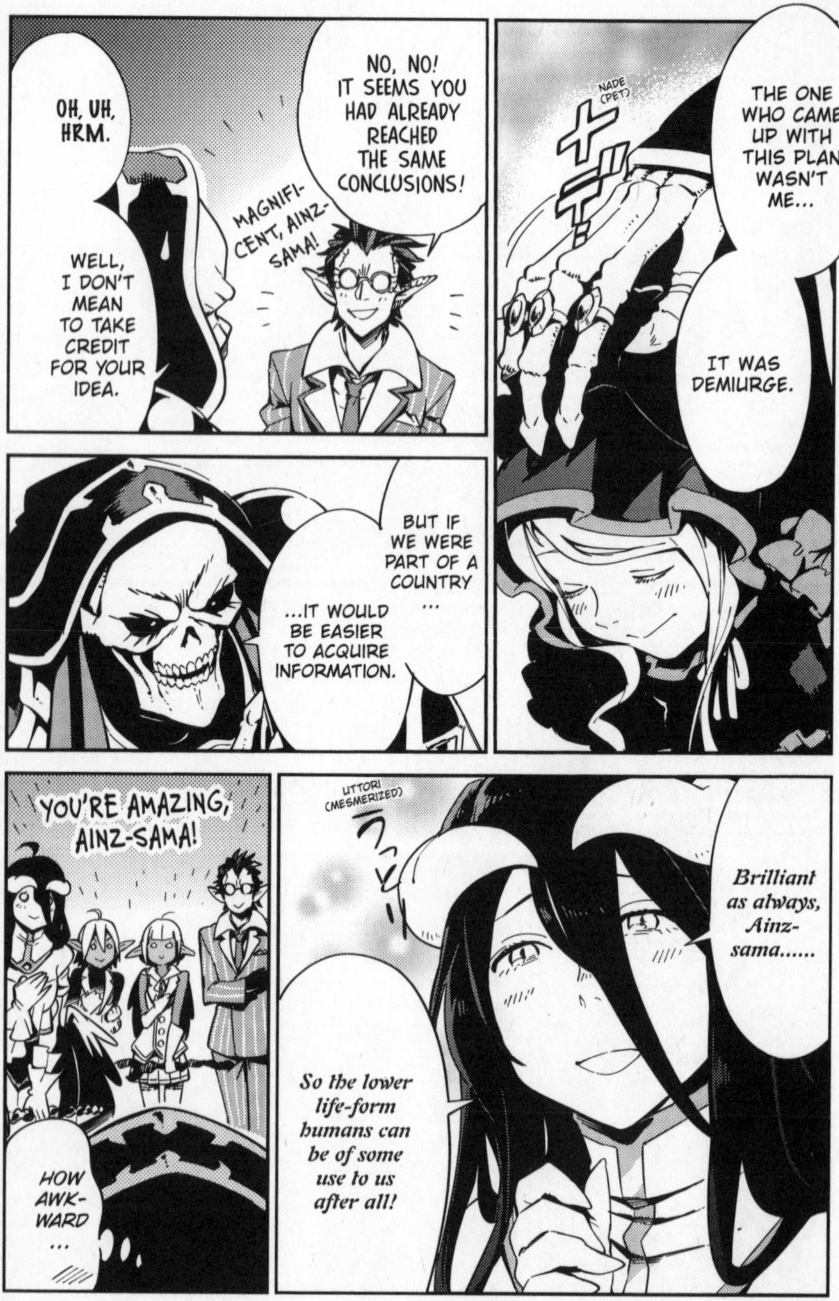
NADE (PET)
THE ONE WHO CAME UP WITH THIS PLAN WASN'T ME...
IT WAS DEMIURGE.
NO, NO! IT SEEMS YOU HAD ALREADY REACHED THE SAME CONCLUSIONS!
MAGNIFICENT, AINZ-SAMA!
OH, UH, HRM.
WELL, I DON'T MEAN TO TAKE CREDIT FOR YOUR IDEA.
BUT IF WE WERE PART OF A COUNTRY ...
...IT WOULD BE EASIER TO ACQUIRE INFORMATION.
UTTORI (MESMERIZED)
Brilliant as always, Ainz-sama......
So the lower life-form humans can be of some use to us after all!
YOU'RE AMAZING, AINZ-SAMA!
HOW AWK-WARD ...

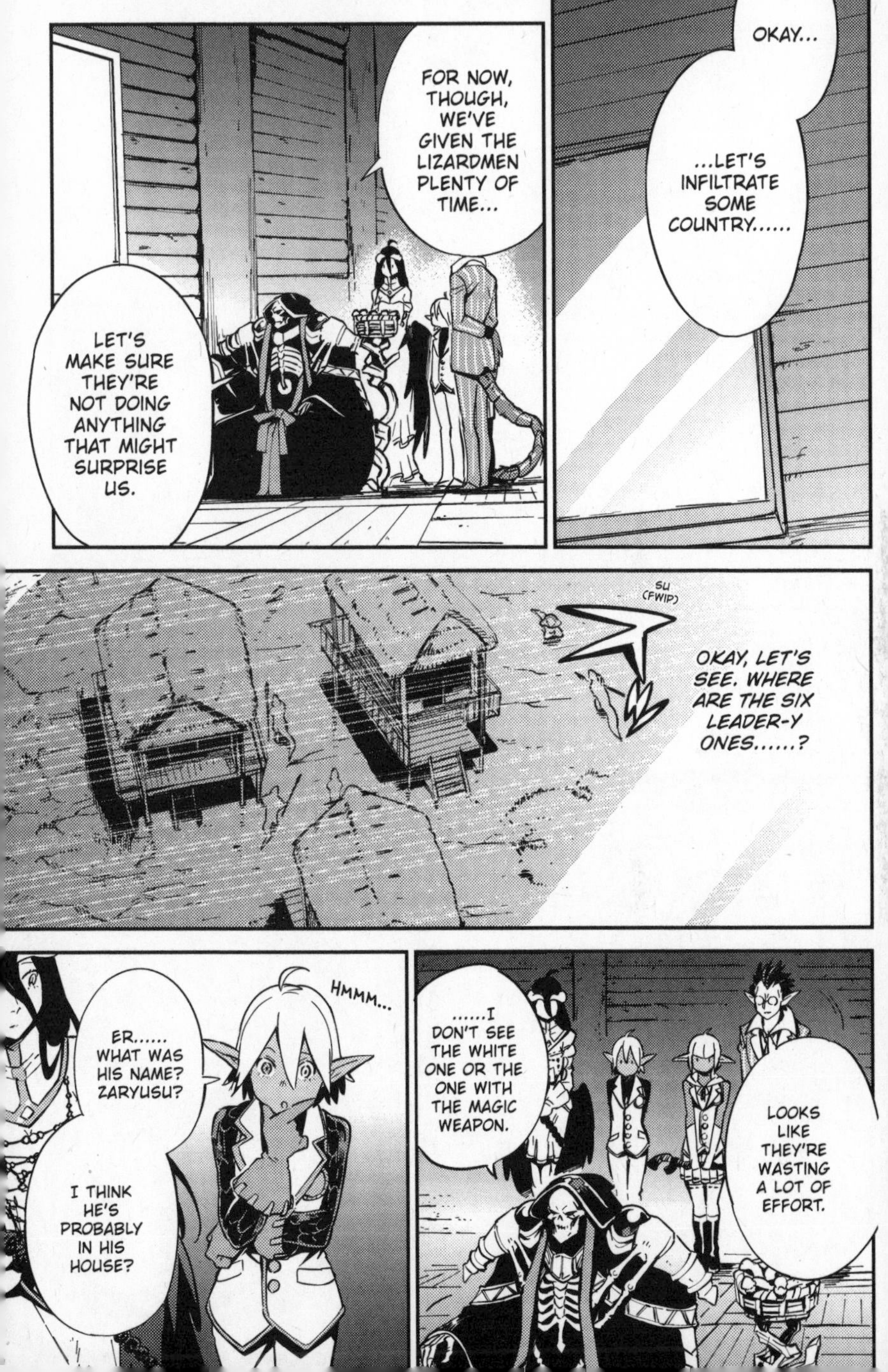
OKAY...
...LET'S INFILTRATE SOME COUNTRY......
FOR NOW, THOUGH, WE'VE GIVEN THE LIZARDMEN PLENTY OF TIME...
LET'S MAKE SURE THEY'RE NOT DOING ANYTHING THAT MIGHT SURPRISE US.
SU (FWIP)
OKAY, LET'S SEE. WHERE ARE THE SIX LEADER-Y ONES......?
......I DON'T SEE THE WHITE ONE OR THE ONE WITH THE MAGIC WEAPON.
LOOKS LIKE THEY'RE WASTING A LOT OF EFFORT.
HMMM...
ER...... WHAT WAS HIS NAME? ZARYUSU?
I THINK HE'S PROBABLY IN HIS HOUSE?

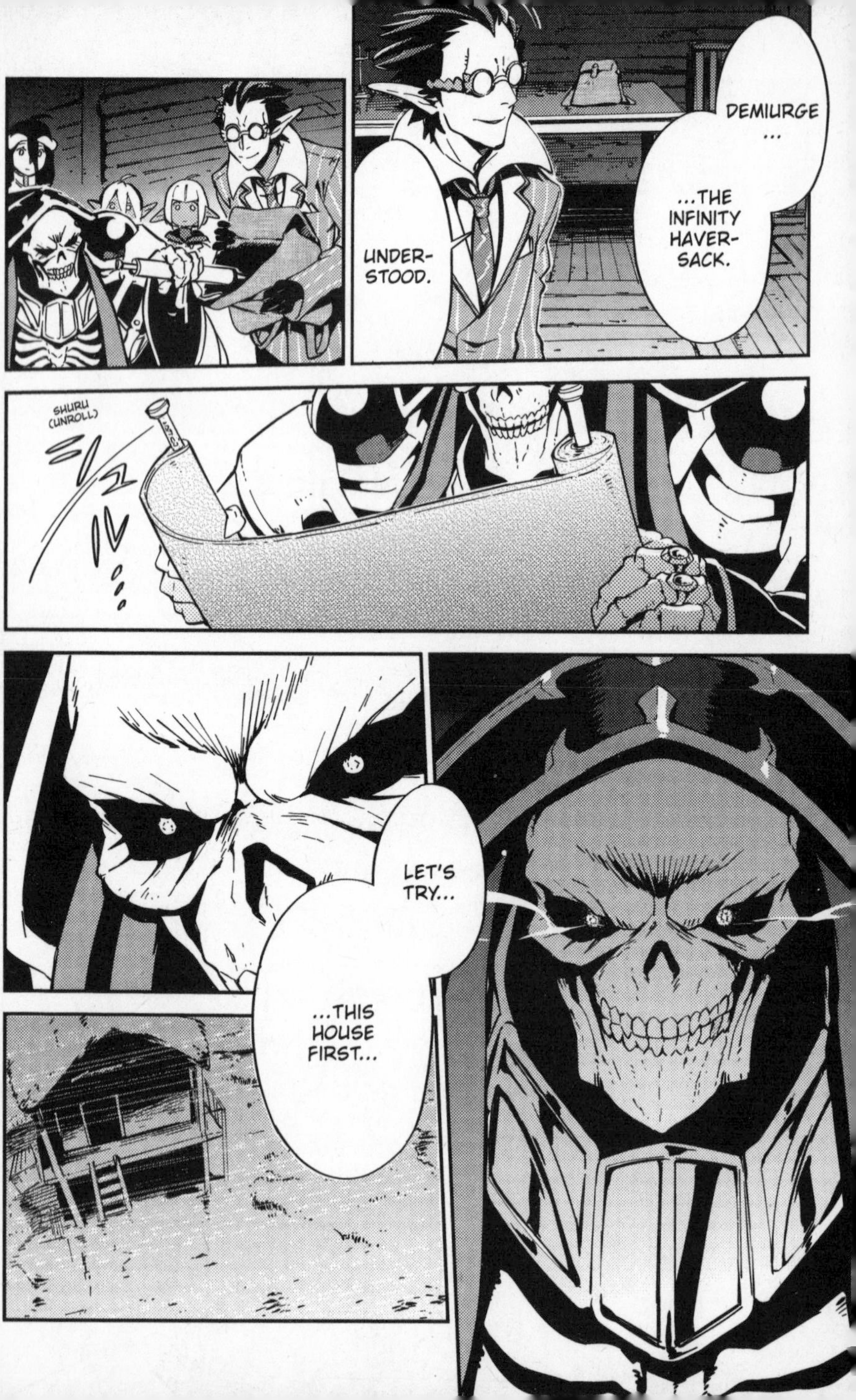
DEMIURGE ...
...THE INFINITY HAVER-SACK.
UNDER-STOOD.
SHURU (UNROLL)
LET'S TRY...
...THIS HOUSE FIRST...

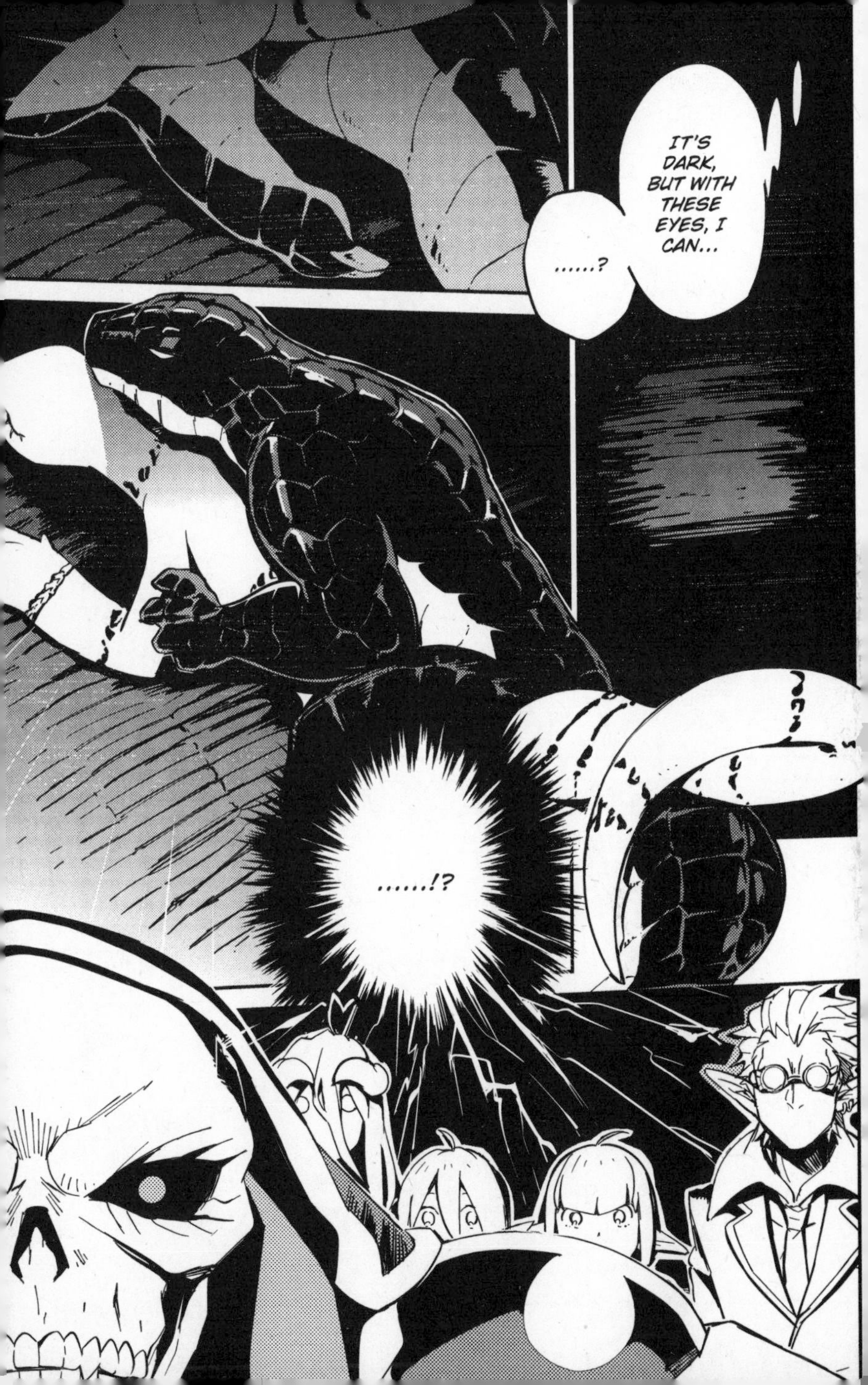
IT'S DARK, BUT WITH THESE EYES, I CAN...
......?
......!?

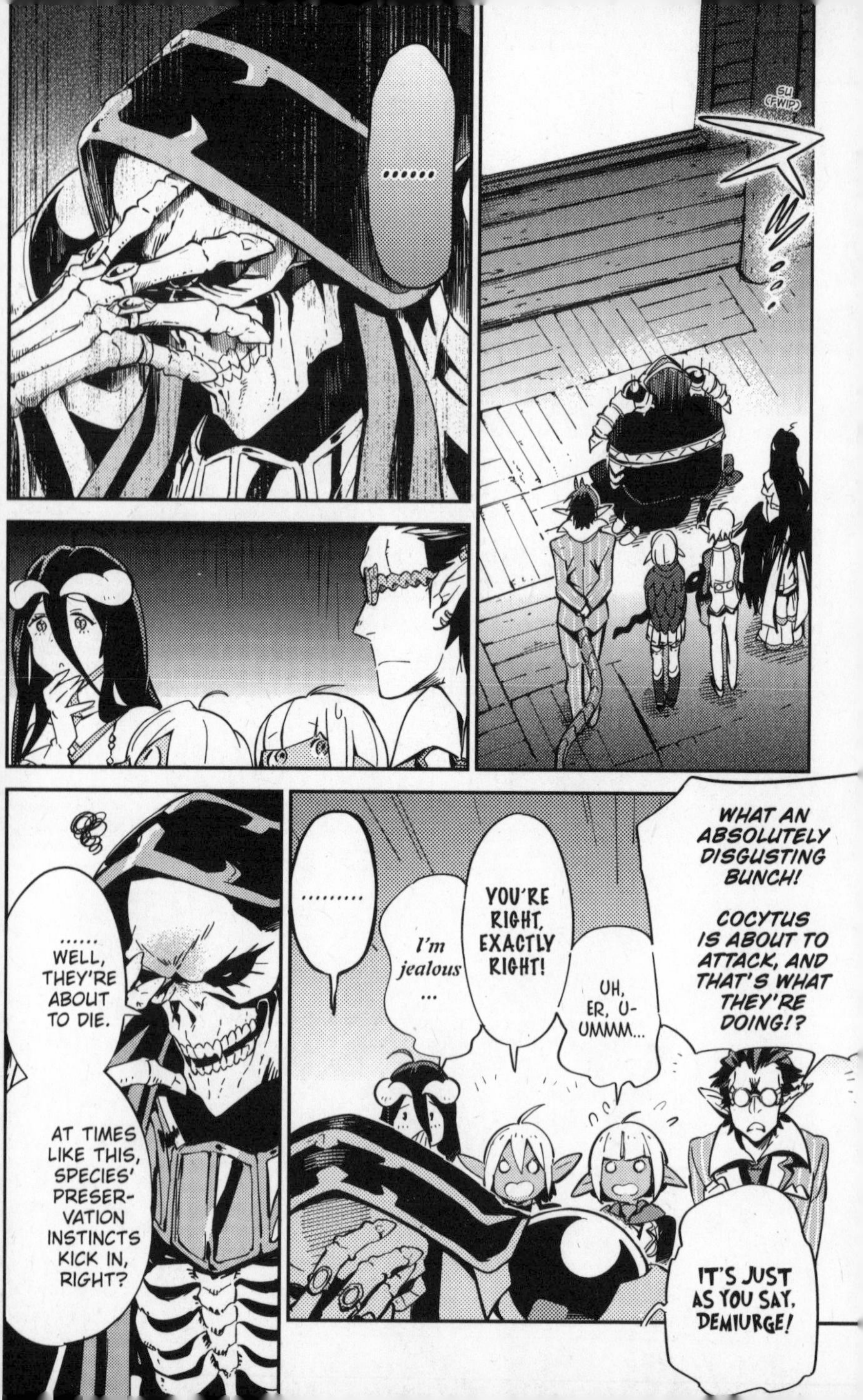
SU (FWIP)
......
WHAT AN ABSOLUTELY DISGUSTING BUNCH!
COCYTUS IS ABOUT TO ATTACK, AND THAT'S WHAT THEY'RE DOING!?
UH, ER, U-UMMM...
YOU'RE RIGHT, EXACTLY RIGHT!
I'm jealous ...
....
IT'S JUST AS YOU SAY, DEMIURGE!
...... WELL, THEY'RE ABOUT TO DIE.
AT TIMES LIKE THIS, SPECIES' PRESERVATION INSTINCTS KICK IN, RIGHT?

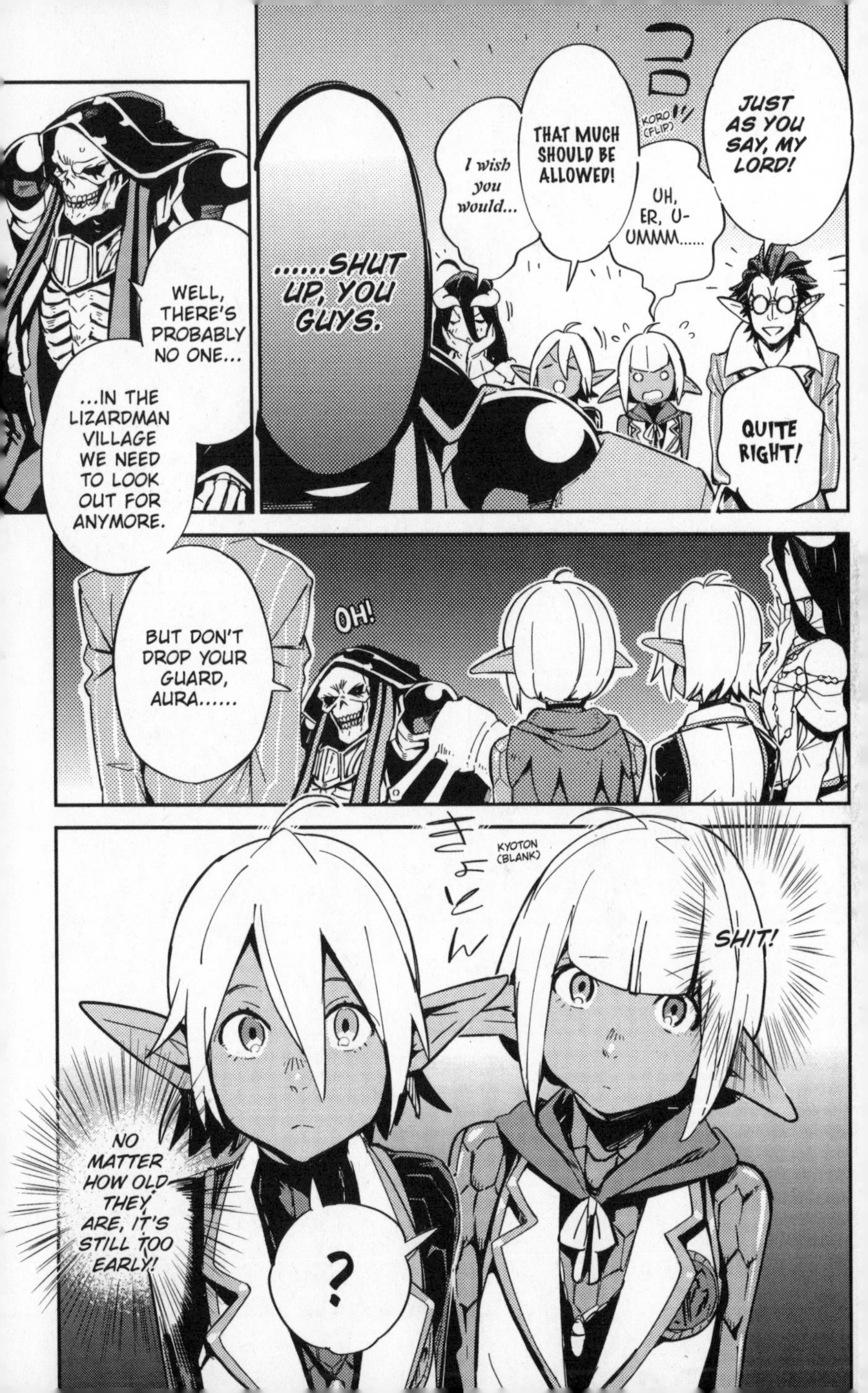
JUST AS YOU SAY, MY LORD!
KORO (FLIP)
THAT MUCH SHOULD BE ALLOWED!
UH, ER, U-UMMM......
I wish you would...
QUITE RIGHT!
......SHUT UP, YOU GUYS.
WELL, THERE'S PROBABLY NO ONE...
...IN THE LIZARDMAN VILLAGE WE NEED TO LOOK OUT FOR ANYMORE.
BUT DON'T DROP YOUR GUARD, AURA......
OH!
KYOTON (BLANK)
SHIT!
NO MATTER HOW OLD THEY ARE, IT'S STILL TOO EARLY!
?

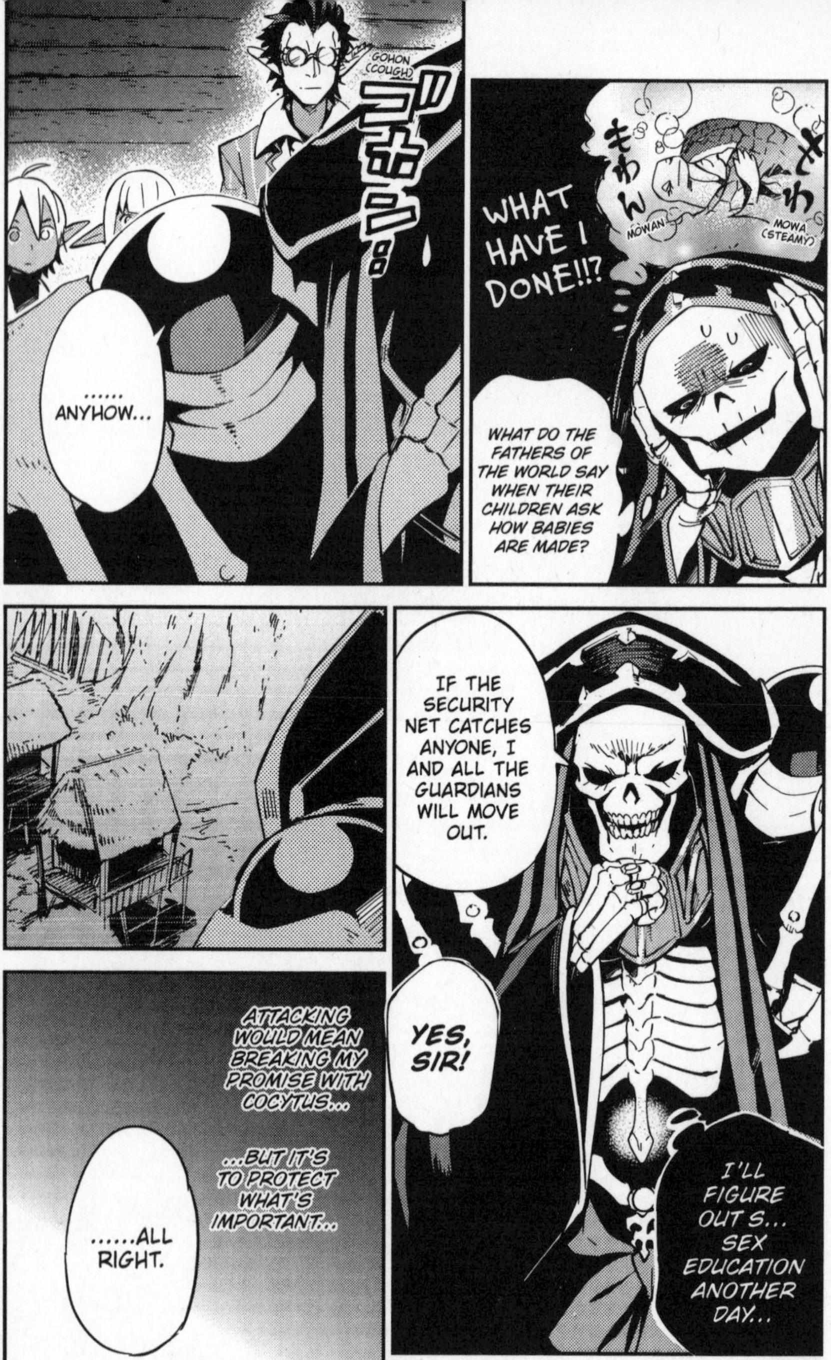
もわ
MOWA (STEAMY)
もわん
MOWAN
WHAT HAVE I DONE!!?
WHAT DO THE FATHERS OF THE WORLD SAY WHEN THEIR CHILDREN ASK HOW BABIES ARE MADE?
ゴホン
GOHON (COUGH)
...... ANYHOW...
IF THE SECURITY NET CATCHES ANYONE, I AND ALL THE GUARDIANS WILL MOVE OUT.
YES, SIR!
I'LL FIGURE OUT S... SEX EDUCATION ANOTHER DAY...
ATTACKING WOULD MEAN BREAKING MY PROMISE WITH COCYTUS...
...BUT IT'S TO PROTECT WHAT'S IMPORTANT...
......ALL RIGHT.

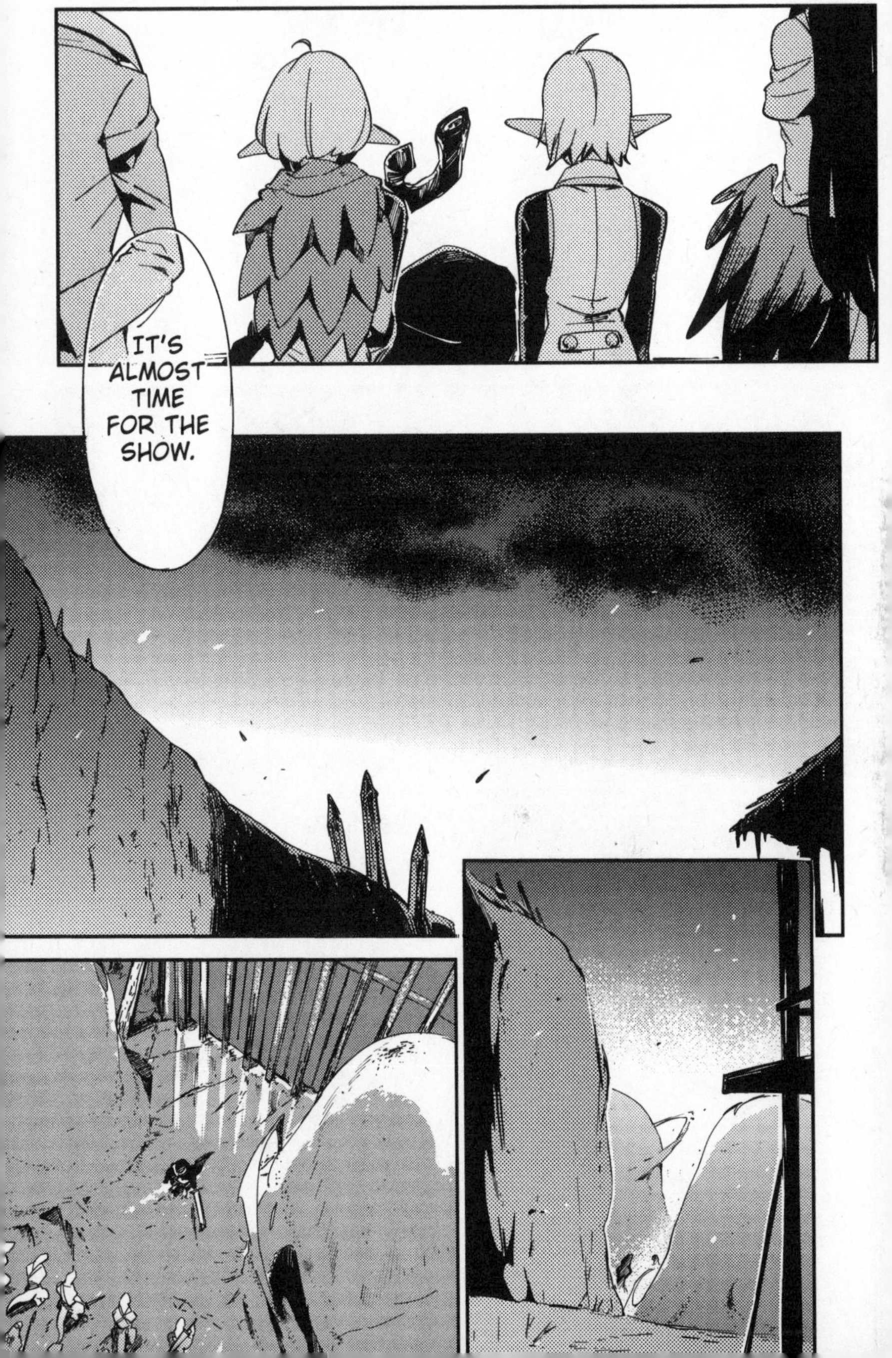
IT'S ALMOST TIME FOR THE SHOW.

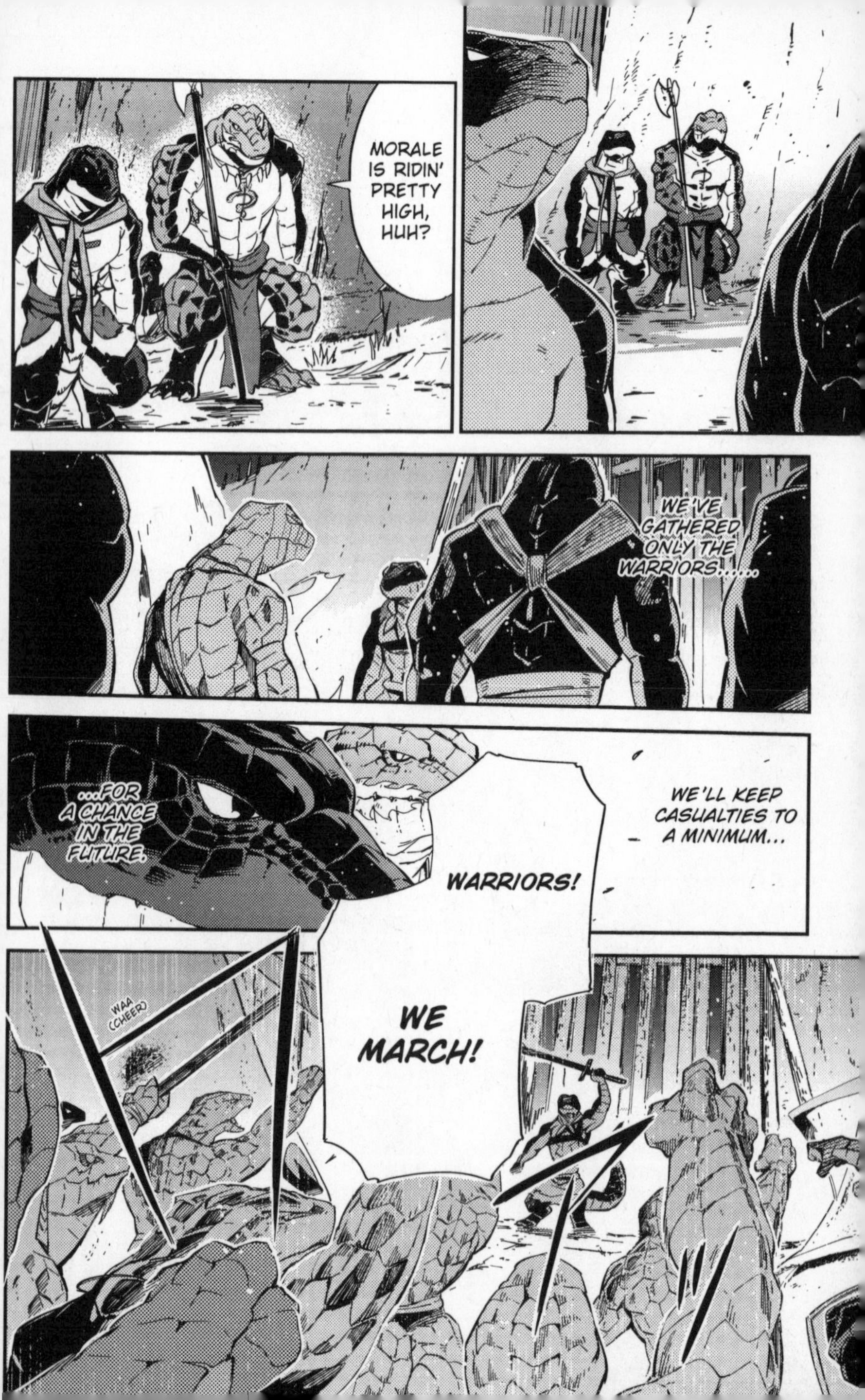
MORALE IS RIDIN' PRETTY HIGH, HUH?
WE'VE GATHERED ONLY THE WARRIORS......
WE'LL KEEP CASUALTIES TO A MINIMUM...
...FOR A CHANCE IN THE FUTURE.
WARRIORS!
WE MARCH!
WAA (CHEER)

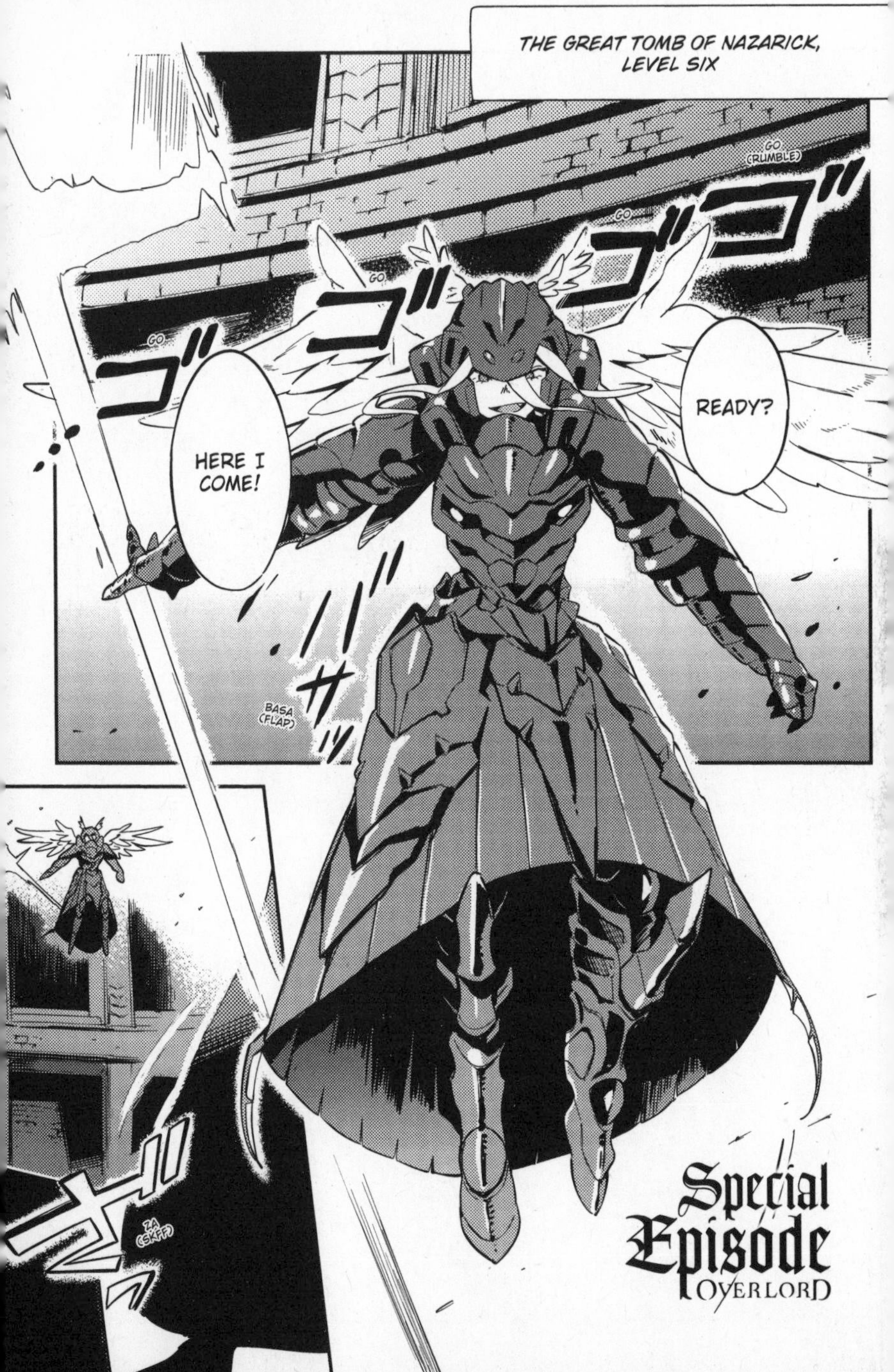
THE GREAT TOMB OF NAZARICK, LEVEL SIX
GO (RUMBLE)
GO
GO
GO
READY?
HERE I COME!
BASA (FLAP)
ZA (SKFF)
Special Episode
OVERLORD

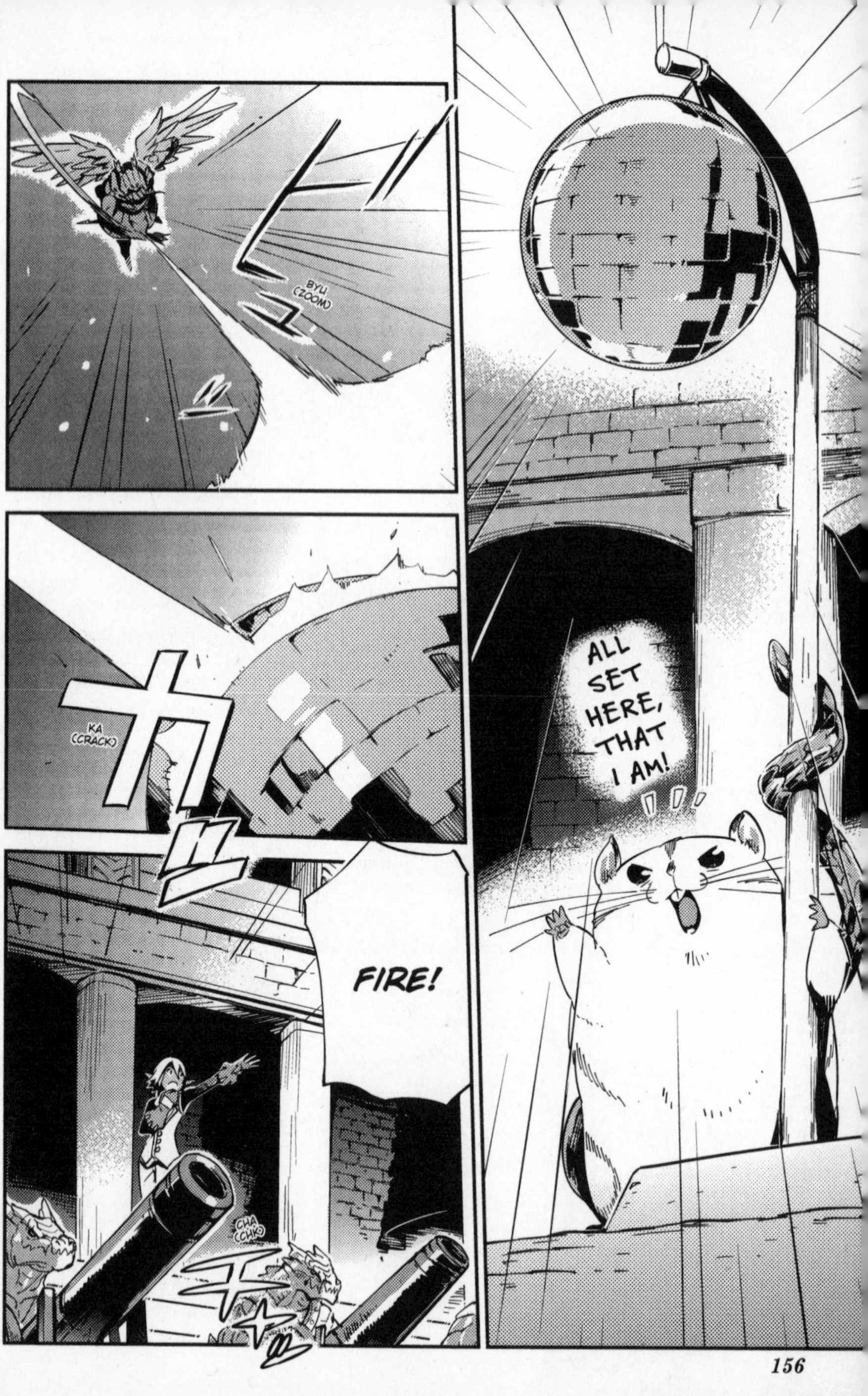
ALL SET HERE, THAT I AM!
BYU (ZOOM)
KA (CRACK)
FIRE!
CHA (CHK)

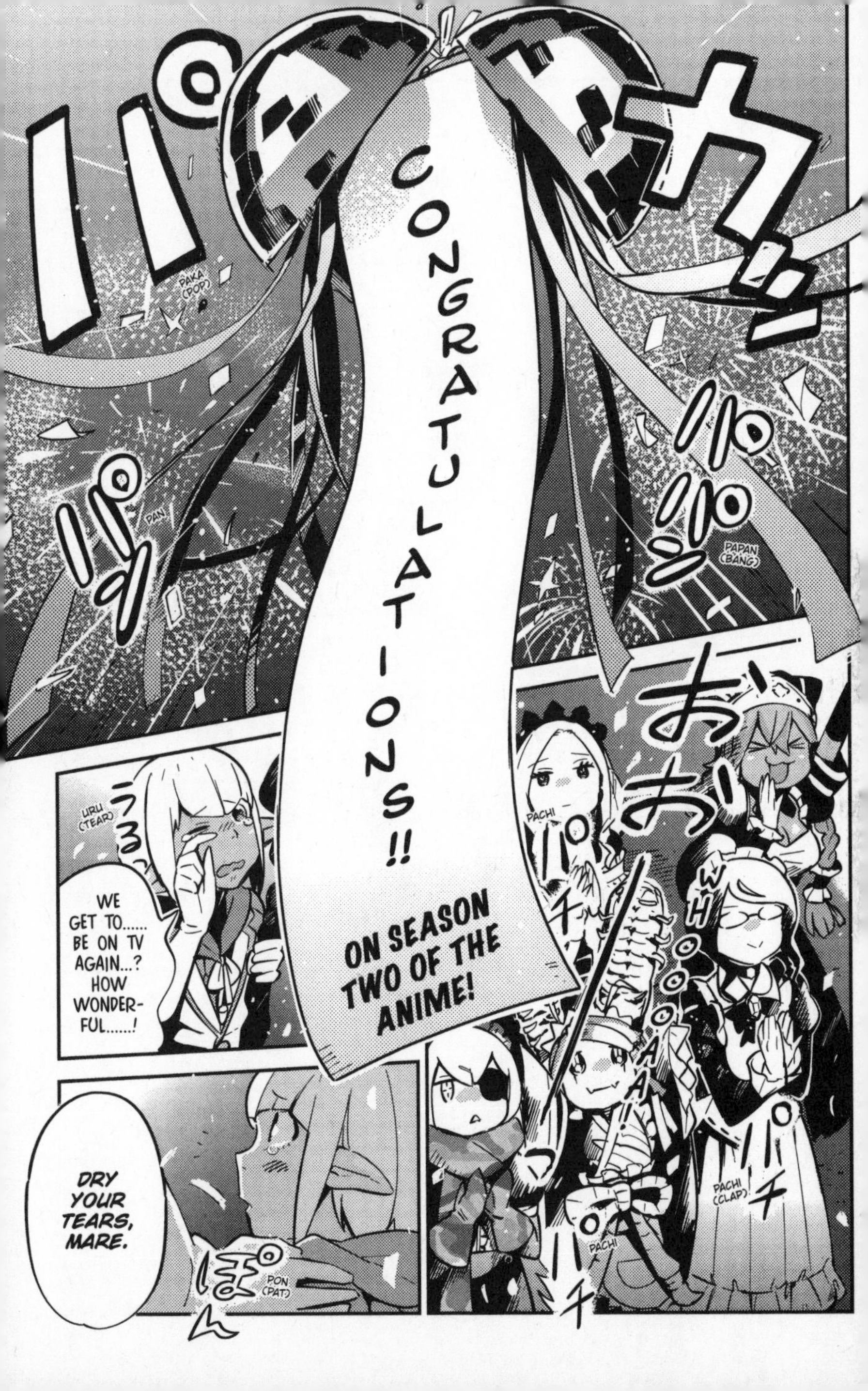

PAKA (POP)
PAPAN (BANG)
PAN
CONGRATULATIONS!!
ON SEASON TWO OF THE ANIME!
PACHI
WHOOOOAA!!
URU (TEAR)
WE GET TO...... BE ON TV AGAIN...? HOW WONDERFUL......!
PACHI (CLAP)
PACHI
DRY YOUR TEARS, MARE.
PON (PAT)

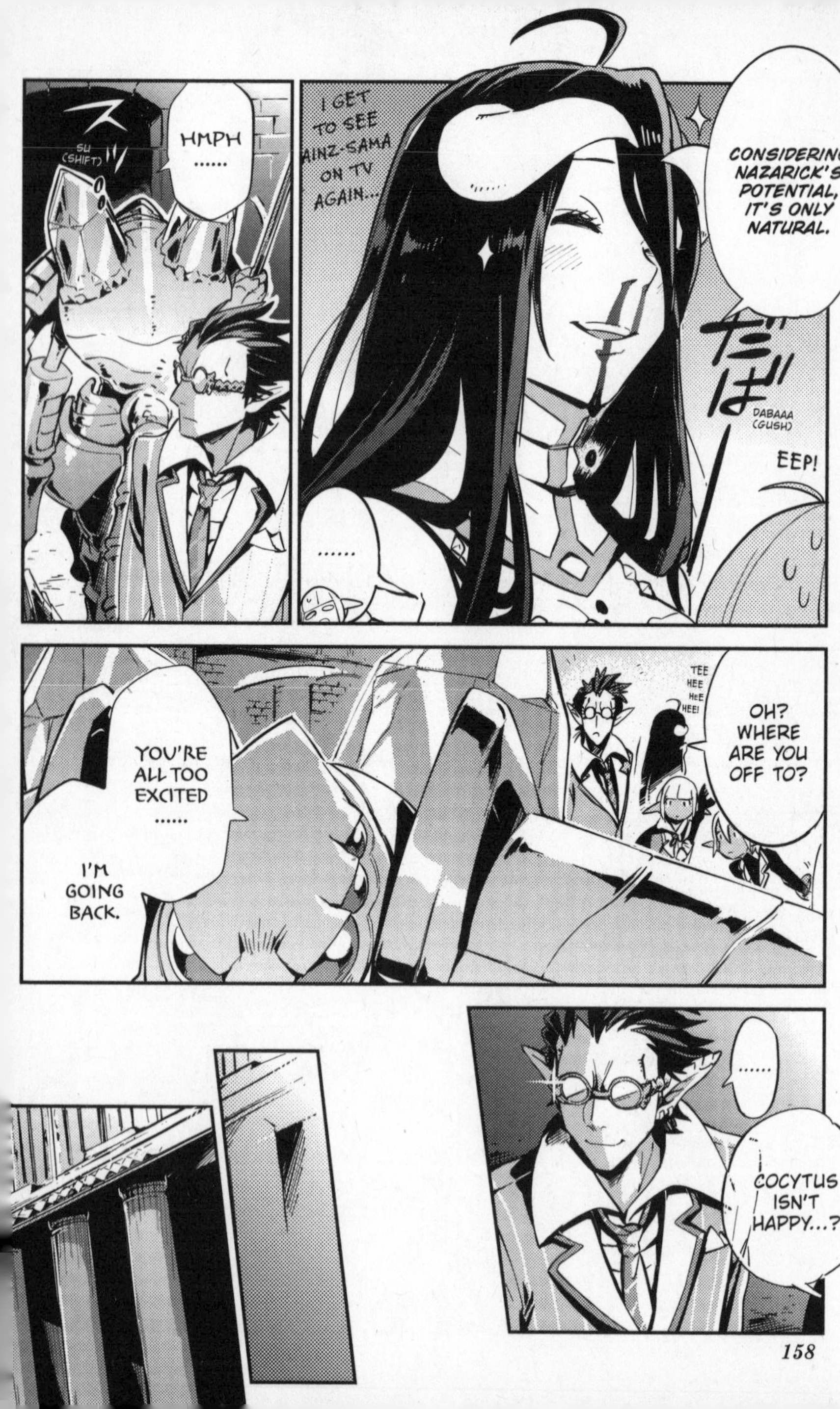
CONSIDERING NAZARICK'S POTENTIAL, IT'S ONLY NATURAL.
I GET TO SEE AINZ-SAMA ON TV AGAIN...
だば
DABAAA (GUSH)
EEP!
......
HMPH ......
SU (SHIFT)
OH? WHERE ARE YOU OFF TO?
TEE HEE HEE HEE!
YOU'RE ALL TOO EXCITED ......
I'M GOING BACK.
......
COCYTUS ISN'T HAPPY...?

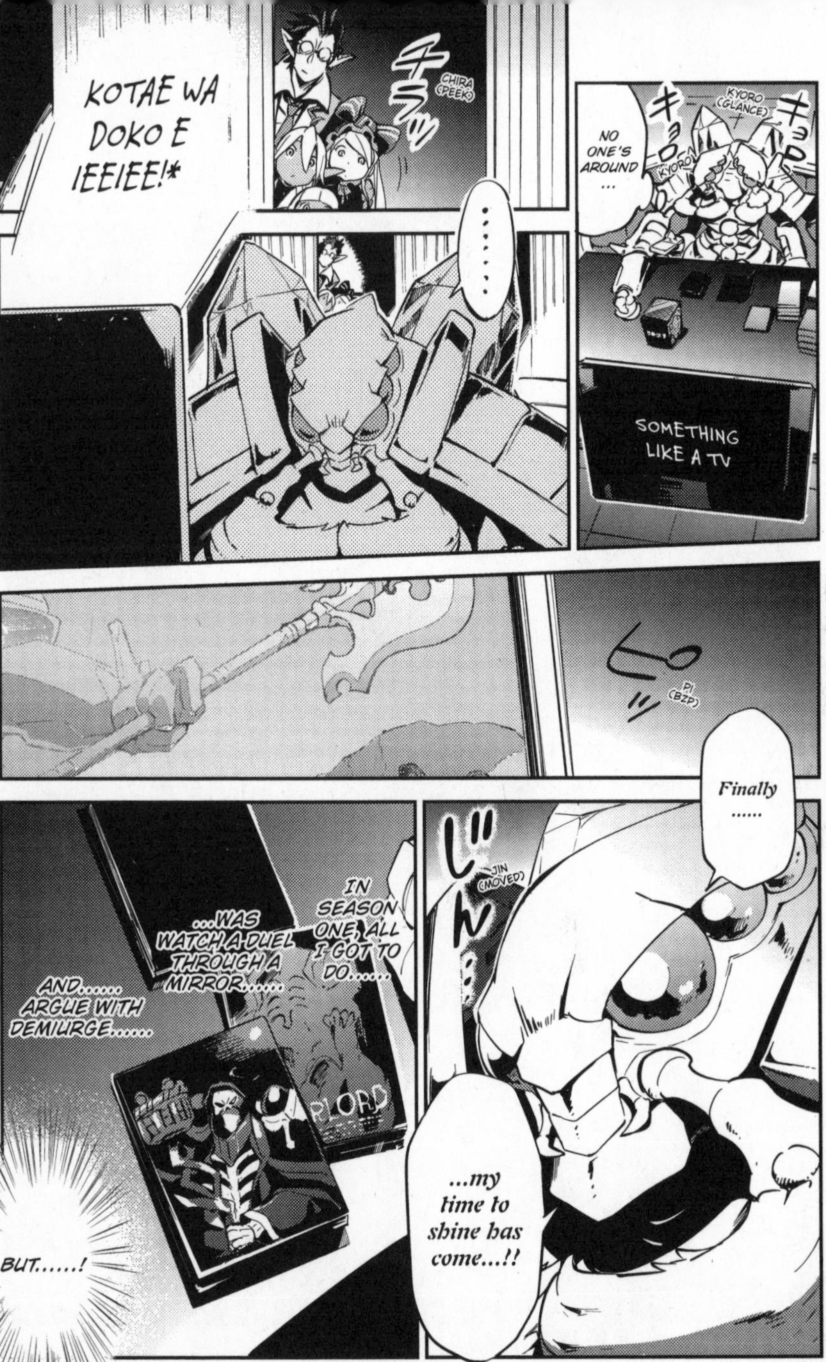

NO ONE'S AROUND...
KYORO (GLANCE)
KYORO
SOMETHING LIKE A TV
KOTAE WA DOKO E IEEEIEE!*
CHIRA (PEEK)
......
PI (BZP)
Finally......
JIN (MOVED)
...my time to shine has come...!!
IN SEASON ONE, ALL I GOT TO DO......
...WAS WATCH A DUEL THROUGH A MIRROR......
AND...... ARGUE WITH DEMIURGE......
BUT......!

* THIS IS THE BEGINNING OF THE OPENING THEME TO THE ANIME.

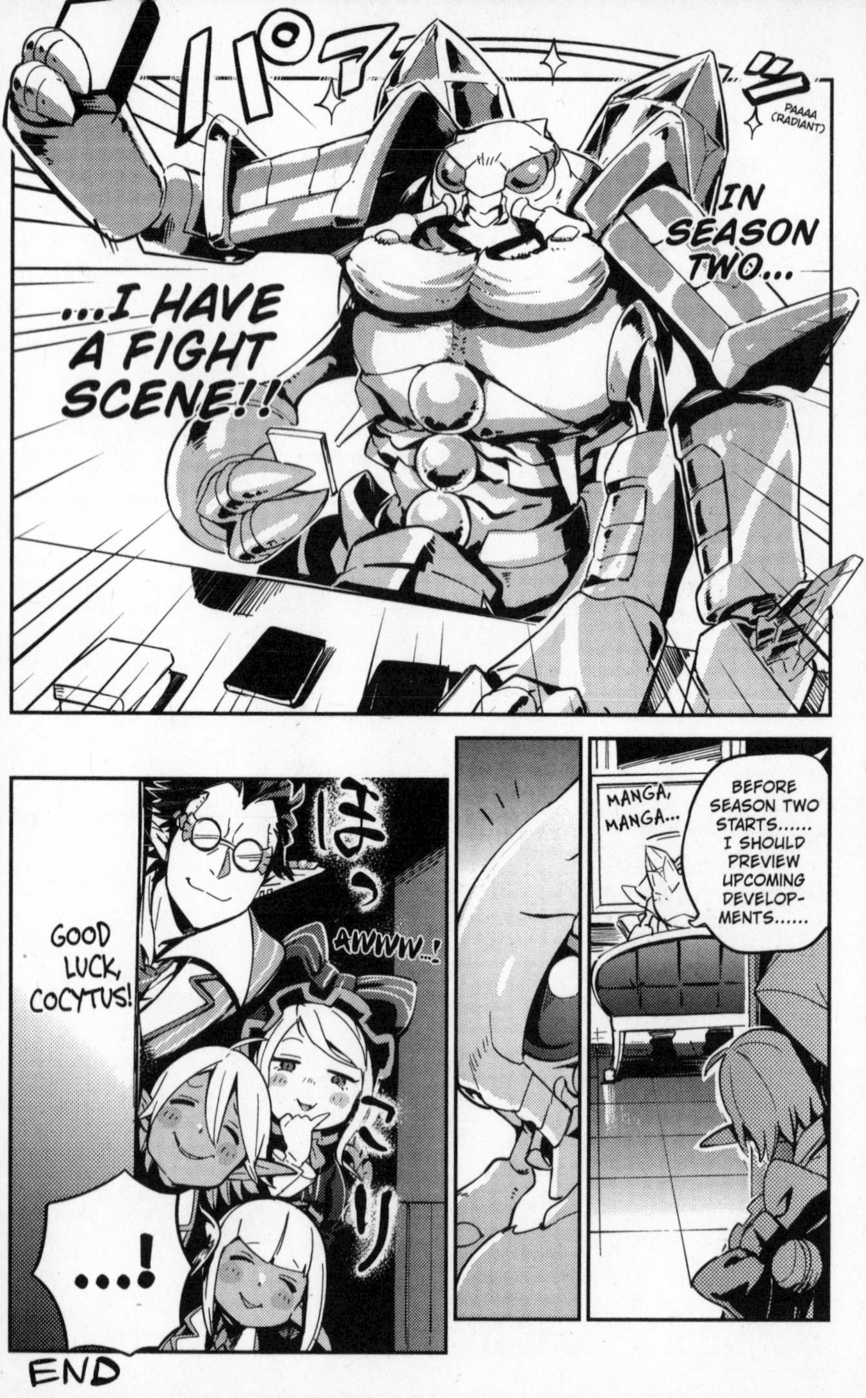

PAAAA (RADIANT)
IN SEASON TWO...
...I HAVE A FIGHT SCENE!!
BEFORE SEASON TWO STARTS...... I SHOULD PREVIEW UPCOMING DEVELOP-MENTS......
MANGA, MANGA...
AWWW...!
GOOD LUCK, COCYTUS!
...!

END

Cocytus

Guardian of the fifth level, also known as "Sovereign of the Frozen River." He is one of Nazarick's three level-100 warrior NPCs. When armed, he is said to have Nazarick's most powerful attack.

Body
Sturdily built, eight feet tall, with four arms and a tail. He can equip a weapon in each hand.

Icicle-like spikes jut out from his insectan exoskeleton, and his back and shoulders are like hulking glaciers. As befitting the Sovereign of the Frozen River, his body continuously gives off a chill aura. Anyone without resistance who approaches receives damage and finds their movement obstructed.

Races & Classes
Race Levels: Insect Fighter 10, Vermin Lord 10, etc.

Class Levels: Saber Sage 10, Asura 5, Knight of Niflheim 5, etc.

Equipment
Imperial Sword Zanshin
An *ōdachi* with a blade over six feet long. The keenest weapon of the twenty-one in Cocytus's possession. Used to belong to Cocytus's Creator, the Warrior Takemikazuchi.

Decapitation Fang
Cocytus's favorite weapon, a halberd with a silver gleam.

Outer Skin Armor
Due to his race, Cocytus is unable to equip protective gear. Instead, his outer skin is as tough as armor, and its hardness and resistance increase as he levels up. Normally, when equipment breaks, it needs to be repaired, but if his outer skin armor gets damaged, it can be fixed with healing magic. Plus, even if he dies, it can't be looted by his enemies. Though it has those benefits, even at level 100, it doesn't perform as well as god-tier gear, so it's inferior to the gear of other players at the same level. For that reason, if he wants higher defense, he has to use bodily armament-strengthening skills.

Personality
Widely regarded as a samurai, his character is stoic. He will treat anyone who possesses a warrior spirit with respect, even someone of a lower rank.

Also, while most members of Nazarick are set with karma points leaning toward evil, he is a rare neutral NPC.

Subordinates
He commands a crack squad of insectile beings like himself. Besides that, the personal guard for his residence Snowball Earth is a level-80 ice monster called a frost virgin.

In the
next volume,
the Lizardman
arc comes
to a close.
Our story
continues with
the Kingdom
arc...

Overlord Vol. 8 Coming November 2018!

OVERLORD ❼

Art: Hugin Miyama
Original Story: Kugane Maruyama
Character Design: so-bin
Scenario: Satoshi Oshio

Translation: Emily Balistrieri • **Lettering: Brndn Blakeslee**

OVERLORD Volume 7
© Hugin MIYAMA 2017
© Satoshi OSHIO 2017
© 2012 Kugane Maruyama
First published in Japan in 2017 by KADOKAWA CORPORATION, Tokyo
English translation rights arranged with KADOKAWA CORPORATION, Tokyo
through Tuttle-Mori Agency, Inc.

English translation © 2018 by Yen Press, LLC

Yen Press
1290 Avenue of the Americas
New York, NY 10104

Visit us at yenpress.com
facebook.com/yenpress
twitter.com/yenpress
yenpress.tumblr.com
instagram.com/yenpress

First Yen Press Edition: July 2018

Yen Press is an imprint of Yen Press, LLC.
The Yen Press name and logo are trademarks of Yen Press, LLC.

Library of Congress Control Number: 2016932688

ISBNs: 978-1-9753-5335-3 (paperback)
       978-1-9753-5382-7 (ebook)

10 9 8 7 6 5 4 3 2 1

WOR

Printed in the United States of America